ADDITIONAL
THE HIDDEN GIFTS OF T.

"Simply written yet embedded with gems, this book will help parents understand introverts and facilitate their full development. Now we need one for extroverts."
—ELIZABETH MURPHY, ED.D., author of *The Developing Child,* co-creator of Murphy-Meisgeier Indicator for Children

"Insightful and full of specific suggestions for understanding and working with introverted children, *The Hidden Gifts of the Introverted Child* should be required reading for parents, educators, and anyone who works with children."
—JAMES W. DAVIS, co-founder, Institute for Educational Advancement

"Dr. Laney has organized extraordinarily complicated concepts in a way that is easy to understand and a pleasure to read. Anyone interested in helping themselves or others enhance their life skills should pay very careful attention to this marvelous new contribution."
—BARRY MUNITZ, president and chief executive officer, the J. Paul Getty Trust

"Dr. Laney's valuable research is a breath of fresh air. Misunderstood introverts will now finally be accepted and appreciated. This book offers parents practical guidance about how to develop their children's gifts. A must read!"
—DR. CONNIE LILLIAS, director, Center for Mental Health Training Foundation; and Fellow, Zero to Three Foundation

"Using Dr. Laney's compassionate and wise advice, we can help youth use and develop their assets. A great resource . . ."
—VALERIE HUNTER, M.A., M.F.T., O.T.R., deputy director, National Program Office, Developing Leadership in Reducing Substance Abuse, Robert Wood Johnson Foundation

The Hidden Gifts of the Introverted Child

Helping Your Child Thrive in an Extroverted World

Marti Olsen Laney, Psy.D.

Author of *The Introvert Advantage*

WORKMAN PUBLISHING • NEW YORK

Illustration by Harry Bates
Cover photograph by Andersen Ross / Getty Images

Library of Congress Cataloging-in-Publication Data
Laney, Marti Olsen.
The hidden gifts of the introverted child / Marti Olsen Laney.
p. cm.
Includes index.
ISBN-13: 978-0-7611-3987-4; ISBN-10: 0-7611-3987-7 (hc : alk. paper)
ISBN-13: 978-0-7611-3524-1; ISBN-10: 0-7611-3524-3 (pbk. : alk. paper)
1. Introversion in children. 2. Child rearing. I. Title
BF723.I68L36 2005
155.4'18232—dc22   2005043684

Workman books are available at special discount when purchased in
bulk for premiums and sales promotions as well as for fund-raising or
educational use. Special editions or book excerpts can also be created
to specification. For details, contact the Special Sales Director at the
address below.

Workman Publishing Company, Inc.
708 Broadway
New York, NY 10003-9555
www.workman.com

Design by Paul Gamarello

Printed in the United States of America
First printing: December 2005

10 9 8 7 6 5 4 3 2 1

Dedication

This book is dedicated to
introverted children everywhere,
and to the adults who pause
to listen to their voices.

Acknowledgments

"All you do is sit staring at a blank sheet of paper
until the drops of blood form on your forehead."
—Gene Fowler

Any creative endeavor is challenging. Cooking a special dish, making a film, writing a book, or raising an innie or outie child takes time and dedication. And nothing creative happens without collaboration. Contrary to the old saying, "A watched pot never boils," preparing a book requires months or even years of caring attention from a gaggle of chefs. So I wish to thank all of the cooks in the Workman Publishing family, as well as my own family, friends, and clients who have contributed to the ingredients in this bubbly brew.

I especially want to thank all of the researchers (many of whom are innies) who watch lots of scientific pots. I respect and appreciate their capacity to cook up new questions to study. Their investigations of the brain have given us valuable insights into the hardwiring that shapes the introvert/extrovert continuum. I hope that these understandings will help change the dismal stereotypes introverted children often face.

And last, I want to thank all of the parents, teachers, counselors, ministers, and others who are willing to see introverted children in a new light.

Contents

Embarking

The Introverted Child: Marching to a More Hesitant Drummer

"I'm a bagel on a plate of onion rolls."—Barbra Streisand as Fanny Brice in Funny Girl

L et me introduce you to a child who shares many characteristics with the introverted children I have met and worked with.

Even at a very young age, she was easily drained by activities, such as birthday parties, that energize many children. A social visit would hardly be underway before she'd start tugging at her mother's sleeve, urging her to take her home. At preschool, she liked to watch other children play, but it took a while before she decided to join in. In photographs, she looks slightly dazed, or even as if she's about to cry or hide behind a nearby door or shrub.

School meant leaving her comfortable home and entering what seemed like a vast, deafening space filled with apprehension and confusion: a veritable three-ring circus of a classroom. She could hardly hear the teacher—or even think. She knew the times tables at home, but when asked to recite them before the group, the numbers flew right out of her head. She hated large groups of all kinds. She dreaded being called on. By second grade, she devised a technique to reduce classroom anxiety. When the teacher scanned the room for a student to answer her question, the girl would execute the "drop and cover": This involved "accidentally" dropping a pencil and then diving under her desk to hunt for the elusive yellow No. 2. As soon as one of her quick-thinking classmates furnished the answer, she would miraculously find the pencil and sit upright again.

Though quiet at school, at home she could talk her mother's ear off. She wondered why she could sometimes chat away like a magpie and then other times find absolutely nothing to say. She felt like Ariel in the animated Disney film *The Little Mermaid*, after Ursula the sea witch stole her voice.

How do I know so much about this little girl? Because I'm describing my childhood self.

Like most introverted children, I was very much in tune with my own internal rhythms but often fatigued and overwhelmed by interacting with the larger social world. The way I experienced the world led me to several conclusions about myself. Because I was tentative about joining in games, I concluded that I was an oddball. Because, even when I knew the material, I couldn't trust myself to retrieve answers on the spot, I concluded that something was wrong with my memory or that I was not very smart. Because I was so quiet around others, I concluded that I had little to offer.

Many children who tend toward introversion draw similar conclusions about themselves. And this is where I want to help. I know from my own experience and from my twenty-plus years of clinical practice that an introverted child does not have anything wrong with her intelligence or memory. She need not be relegated to the social and academic sidelines. Indeed, she has a great deal to offer. But introverted children *do* need support from their parents and others to help them blossom. Face it: We live in a fast-paced, in-your-face, sound-bite world that's geared toward extroverts. Yet, by understanding the nature of introversion, parents, teachers, and family members can help introverted children take full advantage of their considerable brainpower and other personal strengths.

Back to my childhood for a moment. Despite my less-than-spellbinding student persona, a strange but wonderful thing happened: Many teachers befriended me. We had conversations about current events, classroom dynamics, and topics we were studying in class. I asked them questions about their life experiences and listened to what they had to say. One teacher took me to see *West Side Story*. Another introduced me to opera; I was deeply touched when he gave me my first opera record—a copy of *Aida*. Looking back, I suspect that these teachers were introverts who had recognized one of their own species. But more important was the conclusion I drew from these affirming relationships: that the world held lots of exciting possibilities when I met people one-on-one.

This capacity for depth, self-awareness, and close relationships with others is the flipside of the introvert's way. An introvert has the ability to focus. The propensity to listen. The inclination to get to know people well. Those times in my childhood when I felt forced to play by an extrovert's rules, I found myself lacking. But under circumstances where I could accept those aspects of myself on my own terms, I thrived. For parents, adjusting a child's environment from one to the other is just a small shift. But for the child, it can mean the difference between struggling to find a voice and accepting, even reveling, in who he is.

Supporting Your Innie

Many readers of my first book, *The Introvert Advantage*, have told me that it resonated deeply with them. Often they've said, "I wish this information had been available to me when I was a child.

It would have saved me years of thinking that something was wrong with me." It frustrates and pains me to hear so many stories about how misunderstood and overlooked most introverted people felt when they were growing up. The adult introverts I talk to wish that their families, teachers, counselors, and clergy had understood their introverted nature and been able to help them. The alienation and loneliness they felt is tragic because it was unnecessary.

Caring parents of introverted children continually ask me how they can support their "innie" child's growth. The desire is there; those in a position to help simply don't know what these children need or how they can provide it. I also hear from introverted parents about how they struggle with parenting extroverted children. My goal is to close the gap between innies and "outies," or extroverts, and to teach the language of introverts to parents and other caretakers who need to speak it. I watch people's reactions to my introverted grandchildren, and I hear from introverted children and their parents in my psychotherapy practice. And I certainly remember my own struggles as an introverted child trying to find my way.

The number-one concern I hear from parents and other adults working with introverted children is, "Will they succeed in the extroverted world as adults if they stay as they are? Shouldn't they be pushed to be more extroverted?" And my answer is a loud—loud, at least, for an introvert—and resounding NO. Trying to impose a new personality onto an introvert will only lower his self-esteem, increase his guilt and shame about who he is, and perhaps add crippling shyness to his introverted temperament. Introverted children really are small wonders. Accept them as they are. By supporting their natural resources you will allow their gifts to grow. Being an introvert and being self-assured are not mutually exclusive. Confident introverted children will forge adult lives of meaning, value, and creativity.

Often, however, innies are late bloomers. This is because the brain functions that govern their mental orientation are the latest to mature. (Don't worry—I explain all of this in Chapter 2.) These "introverted brains" are hardwired to support careers in the arts and professions that require years of training. Introverts predominate in fields such as science, architecture, education, computer science, solo sports, psychology, the visual, literary, and dramatic arts, and—believe it or not—the military. This is due to their excellent ability to focus and their willingness to explore topics in depth. Contrary to common assumptions, introverts are also CEOs, salespeople, actors, television hosts, celebrities, famous athletes, and politicians. Introverts are achievers. But they would not have to contend with so many painful or confused childhood years if more adults could help them identify their strengths and encourage them to cherish these abilities. Everyone benefits when introverts get the help they need in order to grow into their gifts. It makes the world a richer place.

How I Researched This Book

"Because of your true self, you are you and nobody else."—Dario Nardi

After my first book was published, I met and talked to introverts from all over the United States and Canada. I also received thousands of e-mails from introverts throughout the world, telling me their thoughts. I have also interviewed parents, teachers, and, most important, introverted children about their unique experiences.

Meanwhile, I pored over the latest academic studies. Researchers have found that of all the personality traits studied, where someone stands on the introvert/extrovert continuum is the most predictable trait over time. The reliability of this personality dimension raised the question: What are the physiological underpinnings of introversion and extroversion? This launched literally thousands of research experiments attempting to determine the underlying processes that make someone an introvert or an extrovert. Once, all we had were theories and personality tests like the Myers-Briggs Type Indicator (MBTI) as a means of identifying temperament. Now we have precise scientific tools such as magnetic resonance imaging (MRI), positron emission tomography (PET) scans, data from brain-damaged stroke patients, and long-term twin studies to help us understand, probe, and map the inner workings of the brain and body.

Studies that shed light on the nature and origins of introversion are fascinating to me. They demonstrate that there are physiological reasons why introverts are the way they are and confirm my view that attempting to change an innie into an outie is not merely dam-

Twelve People You'd Be Surprised to Learn Are (or Were) Introverts

"Lots of people with big ears are famous." —from the film Dumbo

One might think that actors, celebrities, presidents, and others who capture the public eye would be extroverts. However, lots of those whose names dominate the marquee or the front page are temperamentally introverts. Here are just twelve of the many:

- JOHNNY CARSON. According to *The Oregonian*, "Carson was an introvert, a Midwesterner with sharp comic timing."

- DIANE SAWYER, who said, "People assume you can't be an introvert and be on television. They're wrong."

- WARREN BUFFETT, INVESTOR AND CEO OF BERKSHIRE HATHAWAY, INC. "Warren Buffett is an inspector-type introvert." (*The Warren Buffett Way,* by Robert Hagstrom)

- JULIA ROBERTS, who naps through most of her lunch breaks. "It makes me a much nicer person," she says.

- JOHNNY DEPP. Asked why he moved to France, Depp replied, "Simplicity, really. There I wasn't thrown into the spotlight."

aging but futile. Many innies feel ashamed that types of interactions that others find so easy are challenging for them. The scientific basis for introversion can assure introverted children and their parents that there is nothing wrong with them and that their difficulties are not for lack of skill or trying.

Most of the tens of thousands of physiological and psychological studies don't reach the general public (unless of course they are sensational enough to catch the eye of the media). I have done my best to include findings relevant to introverts in numerous fields, including physiology, anatomy, neuroscience, education, stress reduction, personality, creativity, early childhood development, psychoanalysis,

- MICHAEL DELL, former CEO of Dell Computer Corporation, who *BusinessWeek* says describes himself as an "off-the-chart introvert."

- JACQUELINE KENNEDY. "She would get on the same track with you, and listen, making you feel that what you had to say was the most important thing in the world." (*What Jackie Taught Us*, by Tina Flaherty)

- BILL GATES. When he was in sixth grade, his extroverted mother thought Gates needed counseling. She didn't understand why her son stayed in his basement room so much. When she asked him what he was doing, he responded with some irritation, "Thinking." (*In Search of the Real Bill Gates*, by Walter Isaacson)

- STEVE MARTIN. "Martin is now an art connoisseur and is known to sequester himself alone in a room of paintings for hours on end to refresh his mind and spirit. He's a very private and introspective man." (*Steve Martin: The Magic Years*, by longtime friend Morris Walker)

- KEANU REEVES. "He's Hollywood's ultimate introvert," says *Entertainment Magazine.*

- AUDREY HEPBURN. "I'm an introvert," she told interviewer Rex Reed.

- JOAN ALLEN, who says, "My career is not a skyrocket kind of thing. It has worked well for my temperament." Her company is named "Little by Little."

genetics, cognitive science, evolutionary psychology, addiction, and sociology. I have also interviewed parents, teachers, and introverted children themselves about their experiences.

Although each introverted child is unique, they do have many common characteristics. Introverted children have rich inner lives, and understanding them is like embarking on an incredible journey. It is not difficult to learn to speak "innie," and the rewards are great. Your experience as a parent will be enriched as your child develops strengths, concludes for herself that it is *better than okay* to be an innie, and learns to flourish in the extroverted world.

The most common pitfalls for introverted children are getting lost in their interior world and being overlooked by the outside world. When parents make it a point to talk to and truly listen to their innie children, those children learn to move with ease between their inner thoughts and the social world. If innie children grow up feeling accepted and comfortable in their family interactions, they will believe in themselves and have solid self-esteem. They will be able to move easily between their lush inner realm and the exterior world. They will know how to keep their "energy tanks" full and how to manage the stimulation of their surroundings. Read on to find out *why* introverted children behave as they do and *how* you can help them reach their potential.

PART I

Appreciating Different Designs

"You never really understand a person until you consider things from their point of view."

—Harper Lee

CHAPTER 1

Was an Introverted Child Dropped Down Your Chimney?

What Introversion Is— And What It Isn't

"One is always in the dark about one's own personality. One needs others to get to know oneself."

—Carl Jung

Ten-year-old Matthew can seem like two different kids. He loves his home and his dogs and is interested in tons of things, particularly when it comes to nature and animals. When he's in a familiar setting, Matthew can be quite energetic and chatty; he'll be happy to tell any visitor about how birds attract their mates or about the three-day-old foal he got to pet. In other settings, however, he is usually quiet. He holds his body and his face still. He watches and observes before joining into activities. Although Matthew likes to play with his friend Sam after school, he complains if he has to stay too late because the kids all do their homework together in the crowded, noisy gym. "I can't concentrate," he laments.

Matthew falls on the introverted end of the temperament continuum. His natural energy, perceptions, and decisions flow inward toward his private world of thoughts, feelings, and ideas. He enjoys mulling things over because it's stimulating and energizing to him. He's happy to share what he's thinking and experiencing. But too many external activities deplete his energy.

With Austin, also ten, what you see is what you get. As soon as his mom picks him up after school, he's chatting away about his day. On the ride home he yells out the car window to his friends. He is talkative and expressive and takes little convincing when it comes to trying out new experiences. Austin wants to know what's on the agenda after he and his mom get home. Can his friend Aaron come over? It's too nice a day to simply sit at home! He likes to do his homework at the kitchen table so he doesn't miss out on anything.

Austin is on the extroverted end of the temperament continuum. His energy flows out toward the external world of activities, things, and people. He scans the environment for stimuli. He is drawn toward hustle and bustle, which invigorates him. Being alone for too long saps his energy.

Many people think of introverts and extroverts like this: You're at a party and the introvert is hovering in the shadows, clinging to the wall and growing petals and leaves. The extrovert is wearing a brightly colored lampshade as a hat and pushing into the center of every conversation. But introverts and extroverts aren't necessarily defined by their behavior. Rather, these terms reflect a person's *source of energy* and *orientation* to the world. Matthew and Austin are both bright, engaging children. Each of them may be lively or quiet, chipper or moody, depending on the situation or setting.

Introversion is actually an inborn temperament based on your child's genetic makeup. Temperament is not personality per se; it is a constellation of traits that governs one's lifelong pattern of reacting and behaving to certain situations. Introverts generally prefer stimulation in small, manageable doses, whereas extroverts seek lots of action and excitement. An introvert may pursue topics in depth, while an extrovert would be more oriented toward breadth—trying many different things. An introvert often needs time to "process" his emotions before responding; an extrovert is more likely to react in the moment. A person's temperament cannot be changed at will. Understanding your child's temperament, however, can help you nurture his strengths and minimize his discomfort.

In our society, extroverts outnumber introverts by about three to one. However, it's not always a matter of being all one or the other; most people possess both introverted and extroverted tendencies. It's useful to think of a continuum, with "pure" introverts on one side and "pure" extroverts on the other. Most people fall somewhere in the middle of the continuum. For example, I like to think of introversion/extroversion as resembling right-handedness or left-handedness. A right-handed person can still use her left hand, but the right hand is dominant. Granted, this analogy only takes us so far. As I mentioned, introverts and extroverts fall on a continuum. Some innies are very introverted, some less so; likewise with extroverts. And because energy ebbs and flows, some introverts may seem more or less introverted from one day to the next. Nonetheless, I like the analogy because we can all imagine what it's like to have to use our "wrong" hand for extended periods. That's similar to what introverts experience when they try to meet the expectations of an extroverted world.

A Matter of Energy

The main difference between the introverted child and her extroverted counterpart is in how she derives, spends, and conserves energy. Each of us finds certain situations energizing and others enervating. The introverted child draws energy from within. She needs to have access to her thoughts, feelings, and perceptions in order to have a sense of vitality and equilibrium. Too much external stimulation—activity, noise, chatter—is depleting to her and leaves her feeling drained. By contrast, the extroverted child is energized by the outside world. She's happiest when she's surrounded by lots of people and plenty of action. The extrovert is wearied by too much quiet or solitude.

I think of introverts as energy *conservers*, like rechargeable batteries that need "down time" to restore their reserves. Extroverts are energy *spenders*. Their motto is "Go, go, go." Both introverted and extroverted children need to balance their natural tendencies. An innie needs to engage with the outside world so as not to lose confidence or lose himself in his own head. Without some periods of relaxation and contemplation, an outie can find himself spinning his wheels.

All people possess the neurological systems to function in both introverted and extroverted ways. If your child didn't have this capacity, she wouldn't be able to know what was happening inside of her or be able to stay tuned to the outside world. Systems in the body are like teeter-totters: If one side is up, the other is down. All systems in the body have an "on" switch to give us some get-up-and-go. They also have an "off" switch, to put on the brakes. One side revs up a child for action. The other calms her down for restoration. A thoughtful parent can help children 1) learn how to renew their energy, and 2) achieve some balance of internal and external stimulation.

Where Did the Idea of Introversion Come From?

"To plant a seed is a hopeful deed."—Anonymous

Throughout time, people have attempted to explain the puzzle of temperament. The Greeks in the age of Hippocrates noticed that behavior tended to fall into clusters or patterns. They concluded that this was due to the presence or absence of certain fluids in the body and the brain. They settled on four yucky, but visceral, substances called *humors*: blood, phlegm, yellow bile, and black bile. They linked these with the four elements (fire, water, air, and earth, respectively) and determined that temperament and illness were related to how well balanced these four humors/elements were in the body. Early observers of human nature noted that some people are externally focused, impulsive, and fast-paced, while others are internally focused, persistent, and slower-paced. This difference in temperament is illustrated in the Greek writer Aesop's classic fable *The Tortoise and the Hare*. As you probably remember, the hare and the tortoise decide to have a race. Hare is speedy and overconfident about his prospects. He knows he can win easily, so he goofs off and takes a rest. Tortoise just keeps plodding along and, to everybody's surprise, wins the race. This universal tale reflects temperament differences that people noticed in ancient times.

The development of psychological testing in the mid-twentieth century confirmed that personality traits and tendencies are consistent and enduring—that, in short, they are part of who we are. Other aspects of temperament that are studied include: being open-minded vs. closed-minded; feeling vs. thinking; neurotic vs. mentally healthy; irritable vs. easygoing; and aggressive vs. cooperative. Such tests as the Minnesota Multiphasic Personality Inventory (MMPI), the California Psychological Inventory (CPI), and the Myers-Briggs Type Indicator (MBTI) are administered by the millions in schools, businesses, and clinical settings. However, recognizing that temperament exists is one thing, but understanding where it comes from is another.

Today we know that the Greeks were on the right track in connecting the brain and the body when it comes to temperament. Genes influence the way our brains are organized. And the way our brains are organized—the chemicals, circuitry, and the parts that dominate—influences the way our bodies react and respond. The results are the various temperaments that manifest themselves in children's behavior.

The different hardwiring for introverted and extroverted children result in vital differences in:

• **How they process information.** Innies use a longer brain pathway that integrates unconscious and complex information. As a result, processing information requires more time than it does for extroverts. But innies are also able to incorporate more emotional and intellectual content relevant to the new data.

• **How their bodies function.** It is harder for introverts to get their bodies moving since they predominate on the side of the nervous system that requires conscious thought. In other words, they have to make a conscious decision: "Move body!"

• **The memory system they use.** Innies more often use their long-term memory than their short-term memory. This affords them a wealth of material, but it takes time to retrieve and reconstruct bits of memory from storage banks located all around the brain.

• **How they behave.** Innies tend to be hesitant in unfamiliar situations. They may freeze or shut down in emergency situations.

• **How they communicate.** Innies speak after collecting, processing, and drawing conclusions about their thoughts and feelings.

• **Where they focus their attention.** Introverts are highly observant and tend to delve deep into what interests them.

• **How their energy is restored.** Innies need a low-stimulation environment in order to recharge.

What Introversion Isn't

Introverts have been misunderstood for as long as the term has existed. In a sense, the concept of introversion itself was "switched at birth." In the early 1900s, Carl Jung, Alfred Adler, and Sigmund Freud, all noted psychoanalysts and original thinkers, were working together. Jung came up with his theory about personality types and coined the terms *introvert* and *extravert* based on observing Freud's and Adler's opposing views of their patients' symptoms. To Jung, Adler focused on the internal world of the patient while Freud stressed the external world and its effects. Jung called Adler's inward focus *introverted* and Freud's outward orientation *extraverted* (now often spelled with an o). Jung thought both points of reference were appropriate and that each orientation reflected healthy, inborn temperaments.

Then the three men had a falling-out. Freud, the most prominent, was angry with Jung and Adler for disputing his ideas. Knowing both men were introverts, he began to write about introversion in a negative light, altering its definition to mean "being too preoccupied with the self," "avoiding the world," and "narcissistic." Since Freud was so widely read and studied, this negative connotation and misconception of the term *introvert* became accepted. Unfortunately, this misunderstanding of the term persists today. (Adler, by the way, later conceived the breakthrough theory of the "inferiority complex," which was similarly discounted by Freud.)

In this age of burgeoning brain research, there is a lot of confusion and disagreement about such terms as *shyness, social anxiety, high sensitivity, autism and Asperger's syndrome, sensory integration dysfunction, dyslexia,* and disorders such as ADD (attention deficit disorder) and ADHD (attention-deficit/hyperactivity disorder), along with other problems that affect children's lives. Introversion may be mentioned in connection with some of these conditions, many of which are not well understood. What we do know is that they are by no means limited to introverts. Some researchers wonder if these conditions should even be looked at as syndromes or types of dysfunction as opposed to merely the far side of the normal brain continuum. Perhaps this focus on children's brain function is a result of the expectations we place on children today. Perhaps they simply reflect different ways brains take in and give out information. What these conditions seem to share is a lack of integration and excessive over- or under-functioning of a brain or body system.

The disorders I've mentioned involve the major processing systems in the body. These include the attentional system, arousal system, sensory input pathways, autonomic nervous system, motivational systems, and the emotions. The genetic disposition toward introversion or extroversion affects many of these systems, which may be why introversion is often conflated or confused with these particular conditions in children. However, it is important to recognize introversion for what it is—and *only* for what it is—so as not to pathologize the introverted child.

To clarify what introversion is—and what it is not—let's correct some myths about introverts.

Myth: Introverted children are shy.

Fact: Introversion is frequently confused with shyness. The misunderstanding here stems from thinking about introversion only in terms of socializing. Being an introvert affects a child's overall temperament and thus affects all areas of his life. These traits may determine how an introvert *prefers* to socialize. However, while an innie's social behavior may look like shyness, it is not the same.

Unlike introversion, shyness is not related to energy needs or enjoying different forms of socializing. A shy person can be just as uncomfortable with one person as in a large group. One key difference between shyness and introversion is how information is processed in social situations. Shy kids feel anticipatory anxiety. They check out the other children and anticipate negative reactions. An introvert may anticipate a negative *experience*—because she doesn't want to socialize—but not necessarily a negative response. Shy people *want* to be more social, but they are anxious in social situations and may think others don't like them. Both introverts and extroverts can be shy.

Shyness is a nearly universal experience; at one time or another, almost all of us have felt shy. Still, clearly some people are shyer than others. There may be a genetic component, but it is usually greatly influenced by environment and experience. Shy children have a

Some May Confuse Introversion with Other Childhood Problems

Over the years, I have found that introversion can be confused with certain other childhood disorders in the public eye. In most cases, however, innies are no more vulnerable to these problems than are outies. These problems include:

- *Sensory integration dysfunction*
- *High sensitivity*
- *ADD and ADHD spectrum*
- *Autism and Asperger's syndrome*
- *Social anxiety and other anxiety disorders*

For more about these issues and how they differ from introversion, see Appendix: Syndromes and Disorders That Are Sometimes Confused with Introversion on page 279.

debilitating fear of humiliation, embarrassment, and criticism. They may also be inhibited, wary of strangers, and timid in situations where there is a risk of failure. Teachers, family members, and peers may react poorly to shy children. Often they are rejected, teased, picked on, or neglected. Unfortunately, such negative experiences can reinforce their fears and their belief that others don't like them.

Leading shyness expert Bernardo Carducci distinguishes between introversion and shyness in his book, *The Shyness Breakthrough: A No-Stress Plan to Help Your Child Warm Up, Open Up, and Join the Fun:* "Introverts are not necessarily shy. They have social skills and self-esteem necessary for interacting successfully with others but simply require privacy to recharge their batteries and they actually enjoy solitude. Shy people want to be noticed, liked, and accepted but they lack the skills and the thoughts, feelings, and attitudes that could help them manage social interaction."

An introverted child can't change her basic hardwiring. However, tendencies toward shyness can be significantly reduced through increasing self-esteem, learning social skills, and minimizing fear and anxiety. If your innie is leaning toward shyness, you can help her manage and reduce it. Explain to your shy child the difference between shyness and introversion. Let her know you will try to help her learn to feel more comfortable in social situations. Do your best to model relaxed, friendly behavior toward people you are meeting for the first time. After your innie watches you, she may feel more confident interacting with her own peers.

Myth: Introverted children are not friendly.

Fact: Introverts may be quite friendly. They just may not be in an ideal position to express it in every situation. For instance, Matthew, our prototypical ten-year-old innie who opened this chapter, is extremely friendly. He loves to talk to people—once he knows them. In the school gym where he is overwhelmed by the noise and the crowd, he is not likely to seem very forthcoming. But if you catch him at home or if you express an interest in animals he will be quite gregarious.

Parents can help create bridges for their innie by helping other people understand his or her way of being friendly, and by creating scenarios that allow their child to express that friendliness.

Myth: Introverted children are not interested in other people.

Fact: Introverted children are *very* interested in other people. They simply can't take in too much all at once. Introverts most enjoy being with other people when they can learn a lot about them, one-on-one. That was the ticket for me when I was young. I had trouble socializing in a group, but I came alive when people, particularly my attentive teachers, spoke to me one-on-one. I was captivated by their stories and experiences, and it showed. Introverts are excellent listeners—largely because they're genuinely interested in what other people have to say and thus really listen.

Myth: Introverted children are self-absorbed.

Fact: While it's true that introverts are focused on their own thoughts and feelings, they are also extremely interested in learning about *other people's* thoughts and feelings. And they are very tolerant of those who are different. It's ironic that introverts are thought of as self-absorbed. Studies show that innies work more cooperatively in groups than do extroverts. Extroverts are often thought of as "people persons" because they like to be around others. But this is often because they need to be around people to feel good—not necessarily because they like or are interested in them.

Detecting Introversion Early On

"Every adult needs a child to teach;
it's the way adults learn."—Frank A. Clark

Temperament tends to show up early in children. Studies show that most children remain true to the temperament pattern they first exhibit beginning around four months of age.

Think about what your child was like as an infant and see where you would place her on the "Hundred Acre Wood" scale. The characters from *Winnie-the-Pooh* are enduring icons in part because they represent familiar human behavior patterns. Was your child bouncy like Tigger? Nervous like Piglet? Focused on food like Pooh? Calm like Christopher Robin? Or was he a quiet observer like Owl?

Who'd Have Thunk It?

Researchers (who have lots of time on their hands, I suppose) have found that when a drop of lemon juice is placed on their tongue, introverted children release more saliva than extroverted children do.

How to Spot an Innie or an Outie

Does your child . . .

• Speak softly, and occasionally pause to hunt for words?

• Act quiet in many situations, but may be chatty in comfortable surroundings?

• Feel tired after social outings and need time to recharge in quiet?

• Look and sound hesitant at times?

• Stand a bit away from the action and observe?

• Enter new situations slowly?

• Have one or two good friends and regard others as acquaintances?

• Look disinterested, glazed over, or overwhelmed at times?

• Stop talking if interrupted?

• Hold her body still when out in public and have an expression that doesn't reveal emotion?

• Look away when speaking but make good eye contact when listening?

• Clam up if tired, overwhelmed, or uncomfortable?

If so, your child may be more introverted.

Let's peek in on little baby Oliver. He watches and seems to be studying his family and his surroundings with intense, dark eyes. He appears to take in everything; you can almost see the little wheels turning in his brain. He doesn't move his arms and legs as much as some babies do, especially when he's in an unfamiliar environment. Sometimes he is hard to read. What does he need? He is usually calm, but may explode into tears without warning and can be hard to soothe. He likes a routine and can be upset by too many changes. When he is given too many toys or exposed to lots of strange, new faces, he may appear withdrawn, fall asleep, cry, or become clingy.

Does your child . . .

- Talk with a snappy patter and loud voice—even more so if nervous?
- Like to switch subjects often?
- Have the capacity to sound like he knows more than he does about a subject?
- Stand close to the person he's talking to?
- Interrupt conversations?
- Look away when listening?
- Use a lot of facial expressions and body language?
- Glaze over when you talk in long sentences or about a subject in depth?
- Walk away if a conversation goes on for too long?
- Think of most people as friends?
- Jump into new situations easily?
- Feel charged up after stimulating activities?
- Complain or feel drained if he spends too much time alone?

If so, your child is more extroverted.

When things are noisy or everyone is rushing around, he may startle at noises. He is cautious; he may not reach for a new toy right away.

At other ages, an introverted temperament can reveal itself in different ways. For example, a toddler may be slow to warm up to a new situation. In preschool, she may be slow to talk to people that she's not particularly relaxed around. In elementary school, an innie may not speak up in class unless she knows the subject well. A middle school innie might like to work and play alone more than other kids do. An introvert in high school might start dating later and might choose to do other things, such as driving, later as well.

Realizing how your introverted child has been contending with extroverted expectations since babyhood can help you appreciate what he's been up against. The chances are you've been adjusting your behavior to accommodate your innie since day one. But you may also have been pushing him in certain ways, because that's what you thought he needed. Identifying your child's temperament increases understanding and reduces power struggles and frustration on all sides. Temperament determines so much—from what excites you to how you communicate to how you handle conflicts. And it starts so early.

Is Your Child Introverted? A Quiz

Where does your child fall on the introvert/extrovert spectrum? (And where do you?) Answer True or False to the following statements (True if it generally applies, False if it generally doesn't), then add up your True answers to find out.

My child:

1. Is energized by time alone in her room or favorite place.

2. Concentrates deeply if a book or project interests him.

3. Dislikes being interrupted when speaking or involved in a project; rarely interrupts others.

4. Prefers to observe for a while before joining in games.

5. Becomes irritable in crowded places or if she shares a space with others for long periods of time, particularly if she is tired.

6. Listens attentively with good eye contact, but his glance tends to drift away when speaking.

7. Keeps her face and body still or shows little expression, especially if tired or in a large group of children.

8. Sometimes has delayed, hesitant, or low-key responses.

9. Needs time to think before answering a question and may need to rehearse before speaking out.

10. Listens more than he talks, unless the topic is of personal interest. In this case, he may talk up a storm, especially if he's in a comfortable setting.

11. Doesn't boast about her knowledge or achievements; she may understand more than she lets on.

12. Feels overwhelmed, rather than energized, by an activity-filled schedule.

13. Sometimes has word-retrieval problems and often speaks in a quiet voice, marked by pauses.

14. Is highly tuned into her own perceptions, ideas, thoughts, feelings, and reactions.

15. Doesn't like to be the center of attention.

16. Can seem unpredictable: chatty at home or in other comfortable settings and subdued elsewhere; energized one day, low energy the next.

17. May be regarded by classmates as quiet, calm, withdrawn, reserved, or aloof.

18. Is observant and sometimes picks up on details others—even adults—don't see.

19. Likes consistency, and does best when given ample transition time.

20. Feels anxious when presented with deadlines for a project or a test.

21. May "zone out" if too much is going on, or when watching TV or a video.

22. Has one or two close friends, but may know lots of kids.

23. Has an affinity for creative expression and quiet, imaginative play.

24. Feels drained after parties or group activities, even when she enjoyed them.

Add up the True answers. If you tally between:

17–24 Trues: Your child is introverted. It is extremely important to understand how to help keep his energy flowing. He will need to conserve energy and spend it wisely in the outside world, and likely will need your help learning to do this. It's also important to show that you understand and accept his temperament.

9–16 Trues: Your child falls in the middle range. Like being able to use her right and left hand, your child is both introverted and extroverted. She may feel torn between needing to be alone and wanting to be out and about. Try to assess when she feels energized by outside activities and when she needs quiet time by herself to recharge, so that you can help her develop a schedule that is best for her.

1–8 Trues: Your child is extroverted. He is energized by people, activities, and things. Try to keep him busy, but also help teach him to value downtime and reflection.

If you're still not sure if the child (or any person) you are thinking about is an innie or an outie, ask yourself: Does he need to reduce stimulation by creating time alone (or with a special person) or to reflect in quiet in order to feel refreshed *most of the time*? If so, he is more introverted. It's not that innies don't enjoy being with people; it's just that they need time alone. Likewise, if a person tends to withdraw under stress, he is probably more introverted. If your child is generally peppy and craves outside activity with or without people most of the time, she is probably more extroverted.

The Heart of the Matter

- *Introversion and extroversion are both normal temperaments.*
- *Innies and outies often respond in different ways to the same situation.*
- *Parenting becomes easier when you understand your own temperament and your child's.*

CHAPTER 2

Innies and Outies Are Hardwired

Brain Physiology Creates Introverted and Extroverted Temperaments

"All the world's a laboratory

to the inquiring mind."

—Martin Fisher

Four-year-old twins Joshua and Rachel return home with their mother after being picked up at preschool. "He-llo!" Joshua calls out as Mom opens the front door. "Daddy, Daddy, we're here!" Rachel yells. The children are excited because Dad's home for lunch. They dash into the living room, only to stop dead in their tracks at the sight of a tall man they don't know standing before them. Smiling, their father tells them he has an unexpected guest— one of his old school chums is in town. Joshua stands still, looking down at his shoes. He backs up a bit as Rachel rushes forward and asks, "What's your name?" Joshua begins circling the edge of the room, taking peeks at the stranger. He watches Dad, Mom, and Rachel talking with the friendly man. After a moment, Joshua ventures over to perch on his father's knee. Soon they're all laughing.

Why the different reactions? In researching my first book, *The Introvert Advantage*, I pored over thousands of studies in psychology, physiology, and neuroscience, and interviewed hundreds of innies. The conclusion I came to as to why two people respond so differently to the same situation is that their brains and bodies are "wired" differently. Specifically, introverts' and extroverts' hard-wiring differs in two important ways: 1) the first wiring "fork" in the brain sends innies and outies down two separate *neurotransmitter pathways;* and 2) introverts and extroverts use two different *sides of the nervous system*. Since then, exciting new research in neuroscience not only validates my original notion, but is expanding our understanding of the physiology of introverts and extroverts.

Elements of Temperament Design

> *"Ages coil within / The minute Circumference*
> *Of a single Brain. . . ."—Emily Dickinson*

Children show distinct temperamental tendencies from day one, but whether these tendencies are truly innate or are mainly a product of upbringing has long been a matter of debate. Now neuroscience has given us an answer to the age-old question of "nature vs. nurture," and that answer is yes . . . and yes. Yes, children are born with an innate temperament. And yes, parents are vitally important to how that temperament is nurtured.

Numerous scientific studies have shown that some traits, such as the degree to which one is extroverted or introverted, are highly influenced by genetic history. Furthermore, introversion and extroversion are among the most stable and heritable of the personality traits studied. In other words, Aesop was right all those centuries ago: Some children are speedy and impulsive like the hare, and others are slower and steadier like the tortoise.

But just how do genes create an innie child? Let's find out.

Jolt Juices

Jerome Kagan, a Harvard researcher and coauthor of *The Long Shadow of Temperament,* says that brain biochemistry plays a big role in temperament. Everyone has brain chemicals and over sixty neurotransmitters—at least that's how many have been identified so far—but each child's genes will determine his or her own special blend of neurotransmitters.

A child's genes encode the formulas that make up his or her brain chemicals and neurotransmitters. These formulas are biologically 99.9 percent the same in all humans—that's why humans have common clusters of traits that produce certain patterns of behavior. But it's that 0.1 percent difference in our inherited genetic chemical recipes that accounts for our individual differences, from height to hair color to who becomes a concert pianist.

So the first piece of this puzzle is that your genes, with millions of years of DNA coiled within (as Emily Dickinson presciently wrote in her poem), determine which neurotransmitters will govern your child's brain.

Brain cells, or neurons, must communicate with one another to make the mind and body work. Picture the ceiling of the Sistine Chapel, where God is reaching out to Adam. Their fingers a-l-m-o-s-t touch. Brain cells are like that: They almost touch. It's in that slight space between the cells, called *synapses,* where all the action takes place. This is where messages can be shuttled from one cell to inform another cell.

These synapses, or "gaps of possibilities," are the second piece of the puzzle. They allow neurotransmitters to travel over literally billions of routes to link cells together. But neurons have locks that admit only one neurotransmitter key. The key fits the cell's lock and signals the cell to either "fire" or "stop firing." If the cell fires, then that area of the brain goes to work and the child shows certain behaviors. If it doesn't fire, it stays dormant and the behavior isn't activated.

Brain Routes

The third piece of the puzzle is that each child's brain creates different pathways as her or his main neurotransmitters consistently switch on or off specific cells. Neurons that fire together are wired together into chains of cells that become well-traveled pathways, forming networks in the brain. Scientists have been able to map these neurotransmitter pathways and networks and have determined what functions they affect. Traveling certain pathways more often than others, linking cells according to their own unique design, creates a child's temperament.

Innies' and Outies' Favorite Neurotransmitters

"The ultimate medical definition of life is brain activity. . . .It's the first step toward achieving a more abundant life."—Eric Braverman, M.D.

J. Allan Hobson, a professor of psychiatry at Harvard, has written at length about the next piece of the puzzle: the influence of two specific neurotransmitters, *acetylcholine* and *dopamine*. According to Hobson, these two main chemical "jolt juices" significantly influence vital brain functions and therefore have a huge impact on behavior. They are two major circuits connecting all levels of the brain. Acetylcholine governs vital functions in the brain, including concentrating, consciousness, alert states, shifts between waking and sleeping, voluntary movement, and memory storage. The dopamine pathways represent the most powerful reward systems in the brain. They turn off certain types of complex brain functions and turn on involuntary movement, so they prompt children to act now and think later.

Bridging Mind and Body

The next puzzle piece is explained by leading brain researchers Stephen Kosslyn and Oliver Koenig in their book *Wet Mind*. They agree that acetylcholine and dopamine trigger the nervous system; indeed, they say these are the main links between the brain and the body. However, they note that they function on opposite sides of the autonomic nervous system: Dopamine activates in the *sympathetic* nervous system and acetylcholine operates in the *parasympathetic* nervous system. The sympathetic nervous system is the "fight, fright, or flight" system; the parasympathetic nervous system is the "rest and digest" system. Sure enough, studies show that introverts are dominant on the parasympathetic side of the nervous system, which uses acetylcholine as its main neurotransmitter. I have termed this the "Put on the Brakes" system. Extroverts are dominant on the sympathetic side of the nervous system, which uses dopamine as its main neurotransmitter. I call this the "Give It the Gas" system. I'll get back to these two systems shortly.

Balancing Act

The final piece of the temperament puzzle are your child's innate "set points." Our genes create set points in our bodies to keep us alive. Set points are analogous to a home's heating and cooling system with its built-in thermostat. You set it at the optimal point for you—say, sixty-eight degrees. When it dips too far below that temperature, your heater kicks in and warms up the house. If the house gets too hot, the air conditioning brings it back to the set point. Your child's body is the same; it maintains homeostasis by staying within certain ranges. There are set points for vital bodily functions such as temperature, blood pressure, glucose, heart rate, and many others. Set points signal when they are getting out of range so that the body can take action to maintain

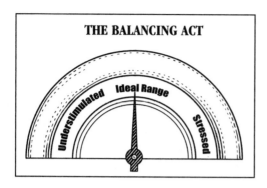

THE BALANCING ACT

Understimulated   Ideal Range   Stressed

Innies and outies maintain balance when they are functioning around their "set point." They can function outside their natural range for a short time. But they will be stressed if they have to stay out of range for too long.

balance. For example, when your child's temperature shoots up, her body attempts to cool her off by sweating, becoming less active, giving her the urge to throw off the covers, and sending blood to the skin to cool her interior.

Brain researcher Allan Schore believes that temperament is molded by where a child's set point lies along the natural introvert-extrovert continuum. This genetically determined set point is where this person's brain and body function best with the least effort. The continuum is like a teeter-totter. A child can make small adjustments around his set-point range without losing too much energy or becoming too stressed. It is stressful and takes extra energy to function outside one's range for any length of time.

Whether a child is an introvert or an extrovert is determined by where her set point falls on the systems that manage energy. Energy can be confusing because it's constantly in flux. An innie might be well rested and lively one day and, then, if she hasn't had sufficient recharging time, dragging her wagon the next. This lack of consistency can be really confusing to outies, who are almost always energetic. Introverts are conservers, and they recharge their energy in peace and quiet or by reducing external stimulation. Extroverts are energy spenders; they restore their energy by being out and about, being active, and being around other people.

This energy disparity has a tremendous impact on innies. Everything an innie does in the outside world requires an expenditure of energy. Everything an outie does in the outside world *gives* him energy. This one detail makes a gigantic difference in how innies experience going out into the world. It also has a huge impact on how others perceive them.

Introversion and extroversion are not black and white. No one is completely one way or another—we all must function at times on either side of the continuum. But we do have dominant sides established by set points, so, just as all children are either right- or left-handed, right- or left-brained, and right- or left-eyed, we are all introverted or extroverted.

Try the following exercise to make this concept more tangible. Write a paragraph with your nondominant hand. Notice the energy it takes to write this, compared to writing with your dominant hand. Using your dominant hand is effortless; you don't even have to consciously think about doing it. It's where you function best and feel the most comfortable. But when you write with your nondominant hand, your penmanship deteriorates. It may even be harder to think. Likewise, using your nondominant foot won't give you your most accurate kick on the soccer field.

Innie and Outie Reward Routes

"To find for each person his true character, to differentiate him from all others, means to know him."—Hermann Hesse

Let's take a closer look at acetylcholine, the neurotransmitter that dominates for introverts. Acetylcholine triggers the brain's ability to focus and concentrate deeply for long periods. It slows down the body when it is awake so the brain can concentrate. It can also signal the voluntary muscles to get up and go. Paradoxically, acetylcholine also paralyzes the body when you are asleep and fires up the brain during rapid eye movement (REM) dream sleep. During REM sleep, the brain is even more active than during the day.

(continued on page 28)

"Jolt" and "No Jolt" Juices

Lots of neurotransmitters and other chemicals flow like a river of Jamba Juice through the brain. Each variety of neurotransmitter has a dedicated mission, resulting in different behaviors, thoughts, and emotions.

Neurotransmitters either excite or inhibit a brain cell. When they excite a chain of brain cells, it looks like a row of tumbling dominoes. When they inhibit, they tell the dominoes not to tumble.

These are the most important neurotransmitters and their main assignments:

Acetylcholine says, "Let's think about it." This is the superstar of thought, concentration, and voluntary movement. It controls vital activities that govern arousal, attention, awareness, perceptual learning, sleep, and waking. It's the main neurotransmitter used by innies' "Put on the Brakes" nervous system. A deficiency of acetylcholine disrupts learning and cognitive function and causes memory loss. Acetylcholine neurons are the first to degenerate in Alzheimer's disease.

Dopamine says, "If it feels good, do it." This is one of our most rewarding neurotransmitters. Dopamine regulates movement, pleasure, and action. It is essential for alert awareness, especially the feeling of excitement about something *new*. It's the main neurotransmitter for outies, built by the building blocks released by the "Give It the Gas" nervous system. It is also the most addictive of all neurotransmitters.

Enkephalins and endorphins say, "I'm feeling no pain." Like pain medication, they dull pain, reduce stress, and promote a floaty, tranquil calm. They are activated to counteract stress. They, too, can be addicting. They are released during pain, relaxation practices, vigorous exercise, and eating red hot chili peppers.

Serotonin says, "Not too much and not too little." This "juice" helps to trigger sleep and affects mood, peace, and tranquillity. Yet it's a puzzling neurotransmitter. You can't be awake or concentrate without it, but too much and you feel tired and unfocused and may nod off. It's the master impulse modulator. It inhibits aggression, depression, anxiety, and impulsivity while promoting calm. It is one of the main neurotransmitters used in antidepressants.

GABA says, "Chill out." This is the most widespread inhibitory neurotransmitter in the brain. Low GABA (gamma-aminobutyric acid) and low serotonin are related to high aggression and violence. Levels of GABA drop when watching violence. It suppresses emotion and is often used to treat anxiety.

Glutamate says, "Let's party." Glutamate is the brain's major "jolt juice." Quick and clear thinking are impossible without it. If too much is constantly released, it causes the brain to burn itself out, as we see in users of methamphetamine or cocaine. It is vital for forging links between neurons for learning and long-term memory.

Norepinephrine says, "Better safe than sorry!" It's the alarm bell. It recognizes danger and organizes the brain to respond to it by releasing adrenaline. Adrenaline is related to tension, excitement, and energy. It is released by the "Give It the Gas" nervous system. It increases physical and mental arousal, heightens mood and vigilance, and enhances readiness to act.

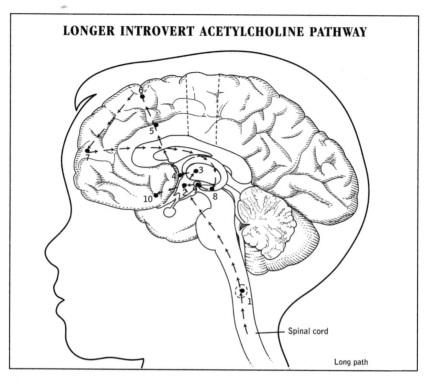

LONGER INTROVERT ACETYLCHOLINE PATHWAY

1. **Reticular Activating System**—Activator: Acetylcholine activates the Front Attention System; signals "Something is interesting."
2. **Hypothalamus**—Master Regulator: Regulates basic body functions and turns on the braking side of the nervous system.
3. **Front Thalamus**—Relay Station: Receives external stimuli, reduces it, and shuttles it to the front of the brain.
4. **Right Front Insular**—Integrator: Combines emotional skills such as empathy and self-reflection; assigns emotional meaning, notices errors and makes decisions. Integrates slower "what" or "why" visual and auditory pathways.
5. **Left-Mid Cingulate**—Social Secretary: Prioritizes, grants entry into CEO area; attends to the internal world. Emotions trigger the autonomic nervous system.
6. **Broca's Area**—Left Lobe: Plans speech and activates self-talk.
7. **Right and Left Front Lobes**—CEO Processors: Acetylcholine creates beta waves and "hap hits" during high brain activity. Selects, plans, and chooses ideas or actions. Develops expectations. Evaluates outcomes.
8. **Left Hippocampus**—Consolidator: Acetylcholine collects, stamps as personal, stores long-term memories.
9. **Amygdala**—Threat System: Attends to threats with fear, anxiety, and anger. Signals social panic and triggers storage of negative experiences.
10. **Right Front Temporal Lobe**—Processor: Integrates short-term memory, emotions, sensory input, and learning. Triggers voluntary muscles.

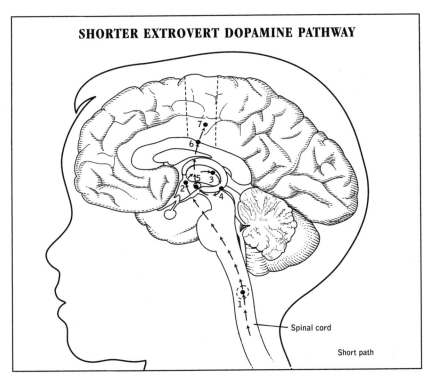

SHORTER EXTROVERT DOPAMINE PATHWAY

Spinal cord

Short path

1. **Reticular Activating System**—Activator: Dopamine activates alert alpha brain waves, "hap hits," and triggers the Back Attention System which notices any movement.
2. **Hypothalamus**—Master Regulator: Regulates basic body functions and triggers the "Give It the Gas" system.
3. **Right and Left Back Thalamus**—Relay Station: Increases and relays external sensory input to higher association areas.
4. **Right Back Insular**—Integrator: Integrates several regions of the brain including the "where" and "when" visual, and the faster auditory pathway.
5. **Left Amygdala**—Threat System: Triggers fear, anxiety, and anger if a real or perceived threat. Dopamine initiates acting without thought.
6. **Right and Left Front Cingulate Gyrus**—Social Secretary: Party central; stops or starts speaking, triggers interest in others, shifts attention quickly for good cocktail party skills. Focuses on the outside world, pleasure, and what's new and exciting. Based on emotional signals, the automatic nervous system and speaking are started or stopped.
7. **Right and Left Temporal Lobes**—Processor: Processes and integrates emotions, external sensory input, and learning. Working memory operates here. Sends messages up to the motor area to move muscles.

A little understood but highly important fact is that acetylcholine activates another reward system. It's subtle, but very powerful. The acetylcholine pathway travels from the brain stem, stimulating aspects of hearing and seeing linked to learning, all the way up to the executive brain functions in the frontal lobes. It travels a feedback loop between the brain and the body's "Put on the Brakes" system. Researchers found that rats will give up food and sex in order to be stimulated on the acetylcholine pathway. When human brains are stimulated by acetylcholine they feel alert, enjoy what they're doing, and are more relaxed. When we're using our noodles, acetylcholine releases potent but delicate "hap hits" (a term happiness researchers use for feelings of satisfaction and enjoyment). This explains why some introverts derive profound satisfaction from studying, say, a single type of beetle for their entire life. For extroverts this mild reward is hardly noticeable.

Dopamine is most commonly known as the major reward pathway in the brain, influencing a number of powerful dopamine reward routes. Extroverts primarily travel on one of the dopamine pathways that releases extremely gratifying "hap hits." These rewards promote novelty-seeking behavior, quick actions, and the urge to move quickly in order to get more of them. Dopamine pathways can promote addiction, because they release quick, intense zaps of elation. For introverts, however, a jolt of dopamine can cause anxiety and overstimulation.

Innie and Outie Pathways

Debra L. Johnson and her colleagues conducted a brain-imaging study using positron emission tomography (PET) on the brain activity of people with established introverted and extroverted temperaments. Their findings, which were published in the *American Journal of Psychiatry,* showed that extroverts and introverts had different amounts of blood flowing to different regions of the brain. Extroverts had lower blood flow in the behavioral inhibition system in the frontal lobes, but more activity in the *back* of the brain, in areas that underlie an intense thirst for sensory and emotional stimuli. Introverts had higher blood flow in the *frontal lobes*—home to the system that inhibits behavior and promotes planning and thinking before acting.

Dr. Johnson and other researchers provide us with a detailed map of the acetylcholine and dopamine pathways involved. (*Note:* The illustrations and descriptions depicting these on page 28–29 are highly simplified.)

Put on the Brakes or Give It the Gas

"Every body *has a story."*
—*From the TV show,* Dr. G: Medical Examiner

The brain is a ball of electrical activity. As children grow, their brains harness and organize all the electrical activity by creating pathways and networks that stop and start thoughts, feelings, and behavior. Remember how your infant waved his hand around and finally was able to grasp a sippy cup? As pathways are developed, they increase the child's ability to focus energy so he can gain physical, intellectual, and psychological control.

As children grow, they gather sensory input from their bodies and the environment, evaluate it, and generate more sophisticated and appropriate responses. An appropriate response could be taking external action like running, walking, or speaking; an appropriate internal action would be to have an idea, thought, or feeling. The brain and body are always attempting to balance the need for responses to be fast or accurate. Responses are carried out with the help of the three branches of the nervous system. The Central Nervous System consists of the brain and the spinal cord. The Peripheral Nervous System is a group of nerves looping messages from the body to the brain and back again. And the last branch is the Autonomic Nervous System which controls out-of-awareness body functions. The brain processes enormous amounts of information,

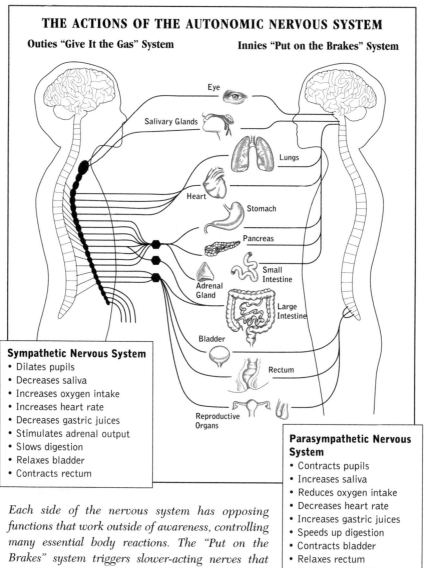

THE ACTIONS OF THE AUTONOMIC NERVOUS SYSTEM

Outies "Give It the Gas" System

Innies "Put on the Brakes" System

Eye

Salivary Glands

Lungs

Heart

Stomach

Pancreas

Small Intestine

Adrenal Gland

Large Intestine

Bladder

Rectum

Reproductive Organs

Sympathetic Nervous System
- Dilates pupils
- Decreases saliva
- Increases oxygen intake
- Increases heart rate
- Decreases gastric juices
- Stimulates adrenal output
- Slows digestion
- Relaxes bladder
- Contracts rectum

Parasympathetic Nervous System
- Contracts pupils
- Increases saliva
- Reduces oxygen intake
- Decreases heart rate
- Increases gastric juices
- Speeds up digestion
- Contracts bladder
- Relaxes rectum
- Activates sexual functions

Each side of the nervous system has opposing functions that work outside of awareness, controlling many essential body reactions. The "Put on the Brakes" system triggers slower-acting nerves that target specific organs. Muscles relax, norepinephrine and energy are stored, food is metabolized, waste excreted, and mating can occur. Acetylcholine increases blood flow and activity and alertness in the front of the brain.

Fast-acting nerves signal the "Give It the Gas" system. The torso and limbs spring into action for fight, flight, or fright. Oxygen increases, glucose energizes muscles, norepinephrine and adrenaline are released for fuel. Thinking areas are turned off, but dopamine increases alertness in the back of the brain.

and based on its evaluation of the need for speed and/or accuracy, it zips instructions to the body about how to respond via the spinal cord to the two branches of the antonomic nervous system.

The *autonomic* (meaning "self-governing") *nervous system* coordinates the body's self-regulating functions such as heartbeat, digestion, and breathing. This frees the brain to manage sight, speech, hearing, thinking, emotion, and voluntary movement.

There are two branches of the autonomic nervous system: the *parasympathetic* and the *sympathetic*. The parasympathetic nervous system is our restoration side; it's your child's "Put on the Brakes" system. The "fight, fright, or flight" sympathetic nervous system is our action side. It is your child's "Give It the Gas" system. The two sides work in opposition to each other, and when one is turned on the other is usually turned off.

Outies are more comfortable on the "Give It the Gas" side, and innies are more at home on the "Put on the Brakes" side of the nervous system. You can observe the difference when you correct your kids by saying no. When an innie is extroverting, she is excited. Let's say your daughter grabs her sister's ball and you respond with a firm, "No, give it back." Her emotional gearshift applies the brakes; she slows down and gives back the ball. The sensation of slowing down is familiar to her. If you say no too harshly or too often, however, it may shut her down too much. After such rebukes, an innie would be neither motivated nor willing to waste her energy to shift up to the more stimulating (and uncomfortable) "Give It the Gas" side of the nervous system.

If an outie is excited and you say no when he grabs a ball, he may have more resistance to stopping. He doesn't like the feeling of the "Put on the Brakes" system. However, if you don't set limits, he won't develop a well-functioning emotional gearshift. He won't be able to calm himself when he overdoes it, or when he needs to adjust to others, or needs to rest. If he has to be limited quite often, it's important to redirect his energy, lest it turn into anger and rebellion. Physical activities like shooting hoops, jumping on a trampoline, or throwing a ball are good outlets.

The Innie Brain and Body Tract

> *"The chief function of the body is to*
> *carry the brain."—Thomas Edison*

Innies' brains are very active. They have more blood flow and higher activity in the frontal lobes, and they are using faster beta brain waves. The acetylcholine pathway is long, and it requires overnight processing to store and retrieve information. This pathway arrives at the emotional center (the amygdala) last, so innies usually have delayed emotional responses. It turns on the "Put on the Brakes" system so that the body isn't using as much energy, allowing the innie to conserve energy since his brain is burning up fuel fast.

Innies have busy brains, so they tend to:
- Reduce eye contact when speaking
- Increase eye contact when listening
- Surprise others with their depth of knowledge
- Shy away from external attention or stimuli
- Appear glazed or zoned out when tired or stressed
- Have trouble turning off their brains to sleep

Innies travel the l-o-n-g acetylcholine pathway, so they are likely to:
- Start talking in the middle of a thought
- Have active internal voices
- Use the preplanning and planning functions of the brain
- Use the more time-consuming emotional and decision-making areas of the brain
- Enjoy the familiar
- Learn best in context
- Have a good sense of humor, although only close people may see it
- Look to internal rewards
- Have vivid dreams and talk about them

- Turn off outside world when concentrating
- Have to hunt for words, especially if they are tired
- Have good memories if they learn to retrieve the information
- Seem to forget what they know
- Converse with people in their heads, perhaps thinking they said something out loud when they didn't
- Be clearer about their perceptions, thoughts, and feelings after sleeping on it
- Experience some things as personal
- Get "hap hits" when concentrating on something of interest
- Write or talk to a trusted person to become conscious of all of their thoughts and feelings

The activation of the "Put on the Brakes" system means that innies:

- May be hard to get going in the morning
- May freeze under stress
- May walk, talk, and eat slowly
- May have a soft voice
- Need time to ease into new situations
- Hesitate and can say no to themselves
- May need to regulate body temperature and protein intake since they are almost always metabolizing food and blood flows to their core organs and away from their extremities
- Must have breaks in less stimulating environment to restore energy
- May have cooler hands and feet (may need to wear socks to stay asleep at night)
- Usually keep their body still to conserve energy for deep concentration
- May notice pain more because they are more aware of their internal body sensations
- Appear relaxed, calm, but alert
- Can be territorial—people physically close to them drain their energy
- Enjoy social events but feel drained by them
- Are alert and observant

The Outie Brain and Body Tract

The brain of an extrovert has less internal stimuli than that of an introvert. Therefore outies are constantly scanning the outside world to gather new stimuli. They need lots of input to fuel their quick reward system—they tire of the familiar easily. Their chemistry triggers the "Give It the Gas" system, and they're off to the races.

Outies are constantly seeking new input, so they tend to:

• Dislike too much downtime—need action
• Increase their eye contact when speaking and lessen it when listening
• Be drawn to movement, which catches their attention
• Enjoy attention, talking, and activities

Short dopamine pathway means outies:

• Shoot from the lip
• Are motivated to get what they want *now*
• Have good short-term memory that allows quick thinking
• Can also forget what they learn quickly
• Do well on timed tests and may enjoy pressure
• Feel invigorated by activities, discussion, novelty, and parties
• Are more vulnerable to addictions
• Want lots of positive feedback

The Boot and the Bonnet

"The brain is a factory with many products."
—*Rita Carter*

Stimulus flows through the brain in a revolution. Input in—input out. The brain takes in outside stimuli and interweaves it with memories and associations and creates perceptions. They spin around

- Need rewards
- Learn by doing and talking
- May recall names and faces better than innies do
- Tell personal info
- Are easy to get to know

The activating of the "Give It the Gas" system means that outies:

- Jump out of bed in the morning
- Become anxious and antsy under stress
- May walk, talk, and eat quickly
- May speak in a loud voice
- Need activity and interaction with other children to gain energy
- May talk about pain more
- Need to shut out stimuli to sleep
- Are uncomfortable with nothing to do
- May experience physical problems if they don't slow down
- Appear active and outgoing
- Enjoy movement and exercising
- Have a high energy level—don't need to eat as often
- May have attention problems

the brain, collecting more complexity until they develop into a thought or action.

Most of us are aware of a division between the left and right hemispheres of the brain. However, the brain is *also* separated by a fissure between the front and the back. This is often described as the brain's demarcation line between *doing* and *being*. It's also the line that divides introverted and extroverted functioning. Innies' brains are more active in the front or *bonnet* (what the British call the hood of a car) of the brain, which governs doing. Outies are more active in the back or *boot* (trunk, to the British) of the brain, which governs being. Counterintuitive, isn't it? It would seem that introverts should be the "be-ers," not the "do-ers." But perceiving the outside world and taking *involuntary* action are in the being part of the brain. Contemplation and deciding on *voluntary* action are in the doing areas. In terms of the brain, "action" has a broad meaning. Movement means thinking, feeling, or dreaming and the involuntary or voluntary movement of muscles.

How They Differ

The extroverted boot brain collects sensory data that flows in from the outside world. Its main function is to transform this data into perceptions by selecting, encoding, and comparing the new data to old feelings and memories. Actions are taken based on these perceptions. These actions are involuntary automatic reactions, based on quickly developed perceptions initiated from the back of the brain.

The boot brain kicks the new perception up to the introverted bonnet brain, the most evolved part of the brain and the most complex area of brain functioning. The bonnet brain—sometimes referred to by brain researchers as the executive or CEO of the brain—reflects and plans. Patterns are created, reflected on, balanced, and verified before, during, and after action. This affords the ability to anticipate, or project oneself into the future, and reflect on what has already happened. Innies often mentally try out what they could do and what they *might* have done, without actually doing it.

Complex emotions and self-awareness are functions in the executive part of the brain in the right frontal area. The executive left frontal area is where complex decisions are made. This is the last part of the brain to develop—in our mid-twenties—*which is probably why innies are often late bloomers*. The frontal lobes primarily serve to guide planning. This is where we talk to ourselves, monitor appropriate behavior, and select or inhibit actions; this is where alternatives are considered and goals are set. The planning area selects one or two choices and develops them into internal thoughts or ideas. If external action is needed, then instructions for voluntary movements are initiated.

Problems arise if the communication loop from the bonnet or the boot is ignored or gets stuck. If children aren't helped to move out of their comfort zone, they can spin their wheels in their automatic way of functioning. A stuck outie takes lots of impulsive action but doesn't pause to reflect and plan for more complex choices. Stuck for an innie means they cogitate forever instead of trying out ideas and actions in the outside world.

Here's an example of the complementary strengths of the boot and the bonnet brain: "I'm packing," I say to my husband, Mike. It's a few days before we're due to go on vacation. He looks skeptical. I picture my closet and visually select the clothes I want to take. The day before the trip, I set my blue suitcase on the bed. As I pass the closet, I pluck out a few items and toss them in the bag. Later in the day I fold and arrange my pre-chosen clothes in my suitcase. I'm done and ready long before I need to leave. The bonnet has served me well.

Now for the boot. It's V-Day, the day we leave for vacation. I'm picturing palm trees swaying near a sparkling ocean. Mike isn't packed, and it's an hour before we have to leave for the airport. He flings his suitcase on the bed and tosses in some clothes from the closet. He sits on top of the suitcase to smash it closed, barely able to fasten the locks. He's ready to leave for the airport. The boot can take quick, decisive action at a moment's notice. Good for any emergency, too.

Innies and Outies in the Forest and the Trees

"A woodland full of color is awesome as a forest fire; and a single tree is like a dancing tongue of flame to warm the heart."   *—Hal Borland*

Humans have four major areas of the brain that impact how they cope with life. These regions are specialized and built to work both independently and together as partners. So far we've addressed the front of the brain, where innies function most, and the back of the brain, where an outie's functioning is strongest. Now we'll consider the two other areas: the right and left hemispheres. From the outside, the two hemispheres look almost identical. However, they have fundamentally different processing functions.

Every child will be dominant in one of the hemispheres. If your innie is more left-brained she may be logical and serious; she may find words easily, have more energy, be more judgmental, and she may not have as many social skills. A right-brained innie may be more playful, have better developed social skills and artistic talent, but may have more trouble speaking confidently, and often have the experience of feeling flooded and overwhelmed.

Each side of the brain processes information from a different point of view. The right brain sees the entire forest, and the left sees the individual trees. The right brain *synthesizes* information, and the left brain *evaluates* it. Although everyone is dominant on the right or the left, the goal is to improve communication and collaboration between the two hemispheres of the brain over a bridge that spans them: the *corpus callosum*. Working together, the two hemispheres produce unified experiences.

The main functions of the right brain are to shift attention to include the big picture and to notice complex social and emotional functioning. It is the high-powered emotional processor overseeing the capacity to read others, feel empathy, have self-reflection, and the capacity to self-soothe. It is the headquarters for seeing pictures in the mind, artistic talent, and musical ability. The right brain sees the context and patterns, so it is called an "anomaly detector." When the right side decides that new information has reached a critical mass, it revises its belief system. It responds and integrates the new information. Recollections about your life story are stored in social and emotional memory by the neurotransmitter acetylcholine in the right brain. The right brain also plays a big part in regulating the autonomic nervous system. If a child functions predominantly from

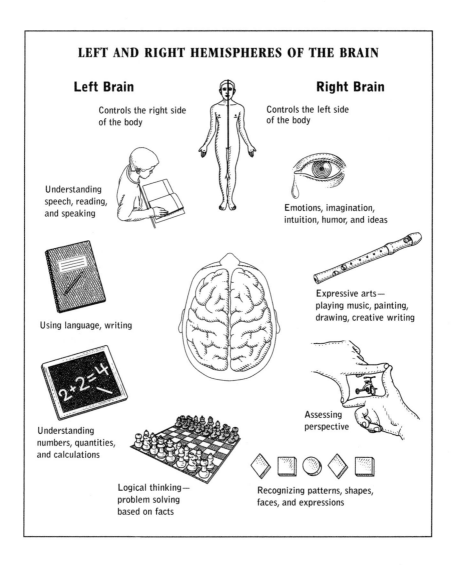

LEFT AND RIGHT HEMISPHERES OF THE BRAIN

Left Brain

Controls the right side of the body

Understanding speech, reading, and speaking

Using language, writing

Understanding numbers, quantities, and calculations

Logical thinking— problem solving based on facts

Right Brain

Controls the left side of the body

Emotions, imagination, intuition, humor, and ideas

Expressive arts— playing music, painting, drawing, creative writing

Assessing perspective

Recognizing patterns, shapes, faces, and expressions

his right brain he can be swamped, scattered, and will have limited language abilities. The left brain focuses on the individual details. Most children and adults are dominant on the left hemisphere. Dopamine is the main neurotransmitter for the left brain, which functions with short-term memory. Its main functions are language, interpreting, and rationalizing. The left brain condenses sensory input in order to make simple and speedy decisions. It is linear and logical, so it reduces flooding the brain with tons of information, but it tends to deny or distort what it doesn't want to see. Or it tries to make a square peg fit into the round hole it already knows. The left brain looks for links between cause and effect, it classifies, and it tends to judge things in terms of right and wrong.

In the United States, we often overvalue the logical left and diminish the complexity of the less verbal right brain. Evolutionary psychologists think we have evolved separate brain functions so we can use one brain region at a time without getting overloaded and distracted.

Let's look at what happens when the two sides communicate well. In conversation, the left brain will notice the words that are spoken: *what* is said. The right brain will register *how* something is said. The right brain picks up the emotional communication, facial expressions, tone, and gestures to add nuance, meaning, and associative links to the objective words. Together they collaborate to enhance understanding by synchronizing all levels of communication, verbal and nonverbal. Another way we see right and left brain cooperation is when a child is writing a paper. He uses his right brain to pick a subject he likes and to brainstorm topic ideas for the paper. Then he engages his left brain to make an outline and begin to logically organize his ideas.

The Whole Enchilada

"Never desert your own line of talent.
Be what nature intended for you,
and you will exceed."—Sydney Smith

Let's look at "the whole enchilada" and see how these four sections of the brain turn their activity up or down, like the flame in your gas fireplace, as your child grows and develops. Eighteen months is

Brain Facts

- The brain is born prematurely—it's only 25 percent developed at birth. We know that the frontal lobes, which manage both feelings and thinking, don't mature fully until about age thirty.

- Genes influence brain development, and they continue to be activated if the conditions are right as the brain develops and matures.

- Holding and soothing babies speeds their physical and emotional growth and development.

- The brain creates maps of what it needs to understand. When you are tapped on the shoulder, you know where your shoulder is because an internal map of your body has been created.

- Most of our brain functions unconsciously—outside of our awareness.

- It takes effort to be conscious.

- The brain divides input and stores it in separate places all over the brain. When we retrieve it, we have to rebuild it.

- The brain has separate functions and it is associative—one thing is connected to another.

- All senses have both a fast simple tract and a slow complex pathway.

- The brain is always torn between speed and accuracy.

a big turning point in a child's life. Several brain regions switch from one side to the other so she can reduce some functions and turn up others. The *right* brain, the *back* of the brain's amygdala, and the sympathetic nervous system mature first in babies and remain dominant for the first eighteen months. This gives kids high emotional reactivity to signal parents and find joy in life, and provides lots of get-up-and-go to learn to walk. At about a year and a half, *left* brain functioning, the *front* of the brain's hippocampus, and the parasympathetic nervous system increase their activity. This allows the child

Memories Are Made of This

Storing memories is one of the brain's most important functions. Children need to remember all sorts of diverse information, like recognizing friends, which dogs are friendly, the rules to games, how to tie their shoes—not to mention what they're taught in school. To avoid an overflow of information, the brain has evolved a complex but clever process of storing information and memories, using the short-term memory system and the long-term memory system. The short-term memory remembers what happens from one minute to the next. It holds snapshots of images, remembers up to seven numbers, letters, or words in a row, and it is good for quick thinking. Ninety-nine percent of these memories are forgotten. Long-term memory remembers facts, stories, and skills, like how to ride a bike. It also recognizes what's familiar and pairs emotions with experiences.

In general, extroverted children use their short-term memory more often and easily, while introverted children depend on their long-term memory. This is because of the location of the major brain areas used for each type of memory—short-term memory is located along outies' primary pathway, and long-term memory is located along innies' dominant pathway.

All memories must be reinforced and retrieved to be remembered. It may sound bizarre to outies, but innies often struggle to retrieve memories quickly because it takes longer and requires special techniques to effectively trigger their long-term memory. When required to retrieve learned information, their mind often feels blank. This can be especially frustrating for children who are called on by their teachers for on-the-spot answers.

to slow down for potty training, listening, and language development, which is aided by an improved memory.

However, the emotional and visual right hemisphere continues to be dominant through the first three years of life. As I have discussed, some children's right brains will remain dominant throughout their entire life. One fascinating way to detect a more right-brain-dominant

To help your innie prime his long-term memory pump, explain that memories are broken up like jigsaw puzzles and that the pieces are tucked all around his brain. Make it a game of hide-and-seek. Ask your child what he thinks about when you say a word like "kite." Can he find its puzzle piece and the memories attached? Associated memories could be seeing the color of the kite, and recalling the feeling of holding it and/or the thrill of finally getting it aloft.

Or suggest that he sit back, relax and let his mind wander, allowing any images, sounds, feelings, or other sensory keys to float into his mind. Explain to him that recalling the smell of the ocean, the taste of pizza, the feeling of skating, or the image of his cousin will unlock a whole chain of other memories. And whenever you ask your innie a question, give her time to fish for her thoughts and feelings. Say, "Think it over and let me know what bubbles up." If your innie can't remember where she placed something, encourage her to walk around the house. This will activate a different memory system that stores location.

To help innies strengthen their short-term memory, suggest that they connect an image with a word, number, or a name. Remember Jack by picturing Jack and Jill. Saying a new pal's name aloud and connecting it to a character in a movie or book will help it stay in short-term memory longer. Playing cards and other games that require the use of short-term memory can also be helpful. Although it requires lots of practice, your child will slowly learn to retrieve information in his memory banks faster.

child is that around the age of two or three, she may speak out loud to herself in order to communicate better with her left hemisphere to improve her language ability. An innie may be more hesitant to walk and talk due to her less activating sympathetic nervous system. An outie's less activating parasympathetic nervous system may have trouble slowing her down for listening and language development.

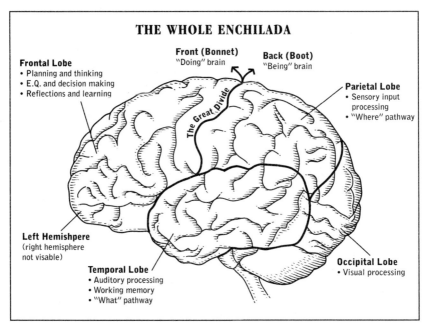

THE WHOLE ENCHILADA

Front (Bonnet)
"Doing" brain

Back (Boot)
"Being" brain

Frontal Lobe
• Planning and thinking
• E.Q. and decision making
• Reflections and learning

The Great Divide

Parietal Lobe
• Sensory input processing
• "Where" pathway

Left Hemishpere
(right hemisphere not visable)

Temporal Lobe
• Auditory processing
• Working memory
• "What" pathway

Occipital Lobe
• Visual processing

The brain can be divided into two hemispheres, right and left (only the left is visible here), connected by a main bridge, the corpus callosum. The Great Divide marks the line between the front and the back of the brain (the bonnet and the boot). The brain is also often described by the duties of the four main lobes: Temporal, Frontal, Parietal, and Occipital.

Although you can't change your child's hardwiring, you can help him integrate the four areas of his brain in a rather simple way. You can tell him your life story, and you can encourage him to tell his. Forming a narrative that makes sense and being able to share it weaves together these four parts of the brain. Sharing stories bridges the introverted personal world with other humans in the extroverted outside world. And it helps us reflect on and store our experiences in our memory banks. Bonds are deepened between people because we are enriched by hearing others' stories and gratified by having our own stories heard.

This has particular relevance to parents of innies. Outies live their lives acting in the outside world. They function based on current sensory information and old memories by responding with quick talking, thinking, and acting, and they rely on their short-term memory. They also need to talk and develop shared stories, but if they don't, they can still function adequately. However, they will lack some amount of self-reflection and a basic tool to build social skills: imitating other people.

Innies, however, live internally, and they need someone to draw them out. Without a parent who listens and reflects back to them, like an echo, what they are thinking, they can get lost in their own minds. Their thoughts and feelings may become disconnected. And they don't store their experiences in their dominant memory system: long-term memory. Innies in particular need to know that someone out there hears them: "I hear you—your thoughts and feelings are real. They are important, and you can organize and use them in the outside world." Innies also need to practice testing their inner perceptions in the outside world. This will strengthen their innate gifts and beef up the other areas of their brain.

The Heart of the Matter

- *Innies and outies travel different brain pathways and use opposite sides of the nervous system.*
- *Behaviors differ when kids are dominant in the back or front of the brain or on the left or right hemisphere.*
- *All children use less dominant regions of their brain, but it takes more effort and the results aren't as effective.*

CHAPTER 3

Introverts' Advantages in an Extroverted World

Learn to Highlight Your Child's Hidden Gifts

"Our culture made a virtue of our living only as extroverts. We discouraged the inner journey, the quest for a center. So we lost our center and have to find it again."—Anaïs Nin

J eannette, a mother of two, confided that she can't stand to watch her eight-year-old son, Colin, on the baseball field. He has just joined the team and only has a few games under his belt. "It frustrates me to watch him hang back while all his teammates rush onto the field," she says. She and her husband wonder if he has enough motivation. He didn't look aggressive enough when he stepped into the batter's box. Like Steve Martin's son in the movie *Parenthood*, Colin just limply waved the bat at the ball as it zipped past him.

Jeff, a single, divorced dad, is concerned about his eleven-year-old daughter. "Molly looks at her shoes and doesn't look people in the eye when she talks," he said. "She speaks slowly, and sometimes pauses when she's trying to find just the right word. I get nervous because I think kids will stop listening to what she's saying.

Boys Will Be . . . ?

All innies experience some discrimination, but boys who are innies face even more challenges than girls. Our culture isn't always thrilled with boys who are quiet, enjoy solitary activities like reading, and aren't aggressive. The myth is that being masculine, by definition, means being assertive, proactive, venturesome, and free of doubt. Anyone who bucks that trend is suspect. Just think about how many jabs were thrown at the children's television icon, the late Fred Rogers. "Mister Rogers" was often made the butt of jokes for being too feminine, too nice, or a homosexual (which he wasn't), when in fact his only "crime" was serving as a wonderful role model of a caring, compassionate man.

Research indicates that introverted girls are described as gentle, quiet, and thoughtful. Boys with the exact same qualities are described as weak, passive, and lazy. If you have a male innie, be sure you are helping him feel confident about his qualities and abilities. Encourage him to participate in activities that take advantage of innie strengths *and* have some cachet in the extroverted world. For example, suggest that he take lessons in the martial arts, join the photography or science club, or take up a musical instrument. I know one innie who proved to be very popular in high school because he was a fabulous dancer. He was in great demand at parties. Who knows? Your introverted son could grow up to be another Steven Spielberg, Bill Gates, Tiger Woods, or Tobey Maguire (all innies)!

Sometimes I jump in to finish her sentences. That's probably worse —she may not want to talk at all."

Many parents, aware that we live in an extroverted world, worry about their introverted children. And the fact is, introversion is devalued in our culture. Extroverted qualities like "the gift of gab" and the ability to "work a room" are prized in contemporary society. We value doing, getting out there, speaking up, winning, and achieving. One could argue that the United States was built by people who were go-getters who were able to adapt quickly to new groups and situations. So regardless of what being an introvert means to the individual, a child with that temperament is going to face some cultural bias.

Sociologists describe the North American cultural ideal as group acceptance, assertiveness, external accomplishment, and success. These standards of being active and "out there" have been integrated into every institution, school system, and virtually every other environment that an introverted child encounters.

More children at younger ages are spending time in group settings such as preschool and group day care. This is challenging for innies, who do better at home during their early years and adapt more successfully to group settings as they grow older. Many schools don't allow parents to stay and help their young children ease into the group experience; many parents of introverted children don't realize that they *should* stay and help the child adapt. With the huge emphasis on socializing, parents, and sometimes staff, too, think the paramount goal for all kids should be making friends and being popular—even when children are toddlers and preschoolers!

The extent to which a person fits into his culture inevitably affects his self-esteem. And the bias toward extroversion in American society is not lost on the perceptive innie child. I worked with the parents of a child who attended a prestigious preschool. The school made a sociogram of who played with whom in the class, and showed it to four-year-old Jill's parents. The director said that the sociogram revealed that Jill generally only played with one other child. They suggested that the parents help her with her lagging social skills. Jill said to her parents, "Miss Terry says that Hannah and I have to play with all the kids. But Hannah is the only other kid who knows about mummies, and she likes to play archaeologist with me. What were we doing wrong?"

Not all cultures are oriented toward extroverts. Researchers divide societies into "low context" and "high context" cultures. In low context cultures, the ideal is a focus on the external world of

Is There an Advantage to Temperament Variations?

The New York Times recently reported findings that appeared in *Neuroscience and Biobehavioral Reviews* that researchers in England, Germany, the Netherlands, France, and at the University of California, Berkeley, are honing in on proving a direct correlation between the neurobiology of the brain and personality traits. Researchers wondered why natural selection doesn't produce a standard personality in all species— why nature consistently supports a range of traits. To find out, they are studying how genes and environment shape various aspects of personality. They began with the observation that animals, like humans, have a similar range of traits; these are bundled into several personality dimensions, a central one being the introvert/extrovert continuum. They concluded that when humans and animals have a range of responses built into their genes, it expands their chances of survival during environmental variations. In Germany, Dr. Kees van Oers found that in lean food years, bold female chickadees fared better than hesitant females. But hesitant males

reality and tangible details with clear and direct communication preferred. The United States, Germany, and Switzerland are offered as examples of low context cultures. These cultures focus on people and things, quick decisions and actions, and social skills that reflect an effortless "hail-fellow-well-met" style. One should be able to accept what someone says without having to puzzle it out.

In high context cultures, however, discretion, nonverbal cues, and subtlety are valued. Examples of high context cultures are Japan, the Scandinavian countries, American Indian tribal groups, and China. These societies value the internal world of impressions, ideas, and feelings. Slower, more deliberate action and complex social behavior are preferred. People from such cultures are multi-faceted and, to the low context person, even mystifying. In a high context culture, one "look" might express a great deal.

had higher survival rates than bold males. During years of abundant food supplies, results were exactly the reverse. Van Oers concluded that when food is scarce, bold females can use their energy and drive to find food. Hesitant males don't fight as much, so they burn less fuel. In abundant times, bold males can fight *and* feed while hesitant females do fine staying out of the fray.

Studying animals allows researchers to analyze the impact of environment vs. genes on personality. With shorter life spans than humans, generations of such animals can be tracked far faster. "Human mothers will not let you just swap their infants at birth, which would be a great study to do," says Dr. Samuel Gosling, who studies hyenas.

All of these researchers are finding that personality variations in humans and animals derive largely from brain structure and function. And like humans, animals have consistent temperaments that remain stable over the course of their lives.

Research confirms that extroverted temperaments are the norm in most Western cultures. Since introverts focus on their internal world—a realm the typical extrovert has less access to—they appear mysterious to extroverts. This can unsettle the extrovert, who likes, and even expects, to know where someone else stands. Extroverts may view the introvert, even the introverted child, as unassertive, cool, passive, sneaky, or withholding. This sends the young innie the message that she is not behaving as she should be and that something is wrong with her.

Teacher and researcher Bonnie Golden, M.Ed., conducted a study to see whether extroverts have higher self-esteem because they fit the cultural norm. She asked 258 introverted and extroverted junior college students about their feelings of self-esteem in school, family relationships, friends, and internally. As expected, the extroverts expressed a higher sense of self-esteem. The central condition that raised self-esteem for extroverts was accomplishing goals. The central condition that raised self-esteem for introverts was *being appreciated.*

What does this mean for raising an introverted child? In her book about personality types, *Gifts Differing,* Isabel Myers observes that extroversion has come to be seen as achieving healthy socialization rather than simply as a style of temperament. The result, she says, is that in Western cultures a penalty is placed on introverts.

As a parent, your job is twofold. First, you need to reestablish the notion of introversion as a temperament rather than as a failure of extroversion. This is important so that your child is better able to accept herself for who she is; and she feels able to articulate her needs without feeling ashamed. Second—and this is what the coming chapters of this book address—you can help give your child the tools needed to flourish in an extroverted world.

Perhaps the most important thing you as a parent can do is to project your acceptance of your child—and his temperament. Paradoxically, feeling accepted for who they are, in all their introverted glory, grants innies the self-esteem needed to test out and develop extroverted skills. As the introverts themselves said in Golden's study, they need others to *understand* and *appreciate* who they are and what they have to offer.

What Introverts Offer Us

"Change your thoughts and you change your world."—Norman Vincent Peale

Although no two introverts are exactly alike, they do share similarities in the way they move through the world. Unfortunately, as we have seen, their way of moving through life is often misunderstood or devalued. But extroverts can learn a great deal by paying attention to introverts.

No doubt reflecting the fact that extroverts outnumber introverts by a three-to-one margin, American culture values doing over being. I think we can even safely say that our culture values *overdoing*. Introverts have the need to counterbalance doing with being. In this way, introverts can serve as anchors for the extroverts in their lives and offset the extroverted tendency to spin into action at a high velocity. Introverts remind us to stop and consider before acting. They also remind all of us to downshift, to enjoy hanging out, and to make time for reflection.

Introverts broaden the continuum of human behavior and show that there is more than one way to be. Without some introverted balance, extroverts can become too externalized and too dependent on others' opinions. Introverts can show extroverts the value of checking in with oneself. Innies remind all of us that each person has a valuable perspective to contribute. Extroverts can be so oriented toward others that they forget to pause and consider their own needs and beliefs.

Extroverts can at times react without reflection. Introverts demonstrate the importance of pausing to relish introspection; their deliberateness shows the benefits of taking time before acting. They remind us to slow down, conserve our energy, and restore ourselves. Even extroverts need to retreat from the hubbub occasionally, and introverts can show them how to do so in a way that feels safe and pleasurable.

Introverts enjoy focusing on one thing in depth, and they are able to create long-terms goals based on well-thought-out ideas. They like to assess the results and to revel in what they've accomplished, rather than racing on to the next challenge. Innies also show us how to be in the moment. They demonstrate how to savor the blush on a pear, the scent of honeysuckle, and the sound of birds singing a few notes in the garden. They remind us to be quiet and hear our internal world.

Helping Your Innie Child Reap Introvert Advantages

"Wisdom is the quality that keeps you from getting into situations where you need it."—Doug Larson

Because of the way they're hardwired, innie children are primed to enjoy the following twelve advantages. Parents can give these children a helping hand so that they can understand and use their potential strengths and brainpower. If they can embrace these advantages and learn to use them in positive ways, introverted children will be well on their way to forging a fulfilling life path.

1. Introverts Have Rich Inner Lives

"Do you believe in God?" seven-year-old Adam asks me when we meet. He goes on to say, "My family isn't religious, but my friend Kesah goes to church every Sunday." I respond to his interest in religion and say, "Yes, I do. Sounds like you are wondering about God and what other people believe. People all over the world have many different religious beliefs." "I'm still thinking about it," he says. I can almost see the little wheels turning inside his head. "I'm sure you will decide what you believe," I add.

Introverted children know they have an interior world. It is ever present and alive for them. Rather than constantly turning to others, they rely on their interior resources to guide them. In their private garden away from the material world they concentrate and puzzle out complex and intricate thoughts and feelings. This allows them to engage with the deeper aspects of life. They want to know what things mean, why something matters. They're not afraid of the big questions. They can step outside themselves and reflect on their own behavior. As with many things, it is a double-edged sword: This interiority gives them rich inner resources, but it can also lead to feeling isolated.

Innie children want to understand themselves and those around them, to know what makes people tick. They are observers and watch other kids. They are less vulnerable to peer pressure since their own internal thoughts and feelings serve as a base for them. They make decisions based on their own values and standards rather than running with the pack.

It's important for parents and other key people in introverts' lives to help them express their thoughts and ideas. Without the experience of talking with others, innies won't learn how to value, trust, and manage their interiority. Without enough interaction with similar-minded children or adults they begin to think that other kids don't share their experiences, that the tenor of their private thoughts separates them from others. Innie children will feel less alone if they are given the opportunity to share their thoughts and feelings with other children. When this happens, everybody benefits.

Cherish your innie's interiority. Chat with him about your thoughts and feelings. Ask for his responses and ideas, making sure to pause so he has enough breathing room to answer. Recognize that innies care about purpose, meaning, and feeling connected to others. Find ways for him to contribute by volunteering in an area of interest, hook him up with a pen pal in another country, or encourage him to give to a charity in some way that is comfortable to him. If you aren't religious, you can find a mentor or religious person for him to talk to about his spiritual thoughts and questions. Help him make sense of all he notices, affirm his appreciation of nature, reduce his sense of isolation, and give him a means of directing his compassion.

2. Innies Know How to Smell the Roses

Isabella's mother tells Marcie's dad, "All I ever hear is, 'I want to go over to Marcie's house, she has her very own room.'" Isabella, who shares a room with two noisy, extroverted sisters, loves the peace and quiet of Marcie's room. Marcie regards her bedroom as a sanctuary and can amuse herself there for hours: watching her two pet tropical fish, adding to her collection of nature drawings. At times, she enjoys sharing her retreat by having her best friends come over.

Isabella in particular loves to refuel in Marcie's calm and peaceful play space.

Innies show us how to "stop and smell the roses." Introverted children savor the little things, the details many people pass by without notice. There doesn't have to be a lot of bells and whistles for them to find something fascinating. Often they don't even need to leave home to keep themselves occupied and interested.

The classic film *To Kill a Mockingbird* opens with a leisurely shot that pans young Scout's tattered cigar box. We are invited into her inner sanctum. Inside the box are coins, marbles, crayons, beads, dolls, a harmonica, and a pocket watch. We immediately know that Scout values the small things in life; they are a comfort to her. (Mary Badham, the introverted actress who played Scout, said that working on this film was like having a transparent glass jar dropped over her—she felt stared at by everyone. She never acted in another film.)

Innies remind us that we really don't need so many fancy material things; they enjoy a slower pace and focusing on life's simple joys. Validate your innie's ability to savor a leisurely walk, a sprint through the water sprinkler, building blanket tents in the living room, watching *Lady and the Tramp* for the umpteenth time, or staying home and coloring. Let yourself slow down from time to time so that you can enjoy this with her. Introverted children remind us that real life is in these moments.

3. Innies Have a Love of Learning

"Do you know what the rings of Saturn are made of?" Justin asks me as he enters my office. The week before we had looked at pictures of Saturn together in a science book. "I think the Jet Propulsion Laboratory in Pasadena has pictures on their Web site," I offer. "Want to look?" "Yeah," he says, with uncharacteristic excitement. We lean forward and "ooh" and "aah" over the incredible close-up images of the rings. Eight-year-old Justin asks informed, intelligent questions about their composition. From his questions, I learn a lot about Saturn myself.

Ironically, Justin's parents brought him to see me because they were worried about his intelligence. Although he wasn't doing so well in school—he had trouble tolerating the intense stimulation of his classroom's extroverted style—it was obvious that he had a deep thirst for knowledge.

In general, a high percentage of introverted children grow up to attend college. Here, they may begin to enjoy learning in a whole new way, as their learning styles are better suited to higher education. College work rewards many innie strengths, such as learning by listening to lectures, taking essay exams, analyzing complex issues, being self-motivated, and choosing one's own course of study. College study also requires good reading and writing skills, and many innies are good writers. Often they keep journals or do other kinds of writing without anyone knowing about it (the proverbial novel kept in the drawer). They usually enjoy reading as well. Innie children, for instance, may like to read aloud (if not under pressure), read silently to themselves, and be read to (or listen to a book on tape).

Support your innie's love of learning. Introverts need lots of information to feed their brains. They are continually comparing and contrasting what they are learning with their own personal reactions—that internal voice is always chatting away. Without compelling data to fuel their thoughts they can become bored, self-critical, or even depressed. They need lots of relevant input to satisfy their curiosity and interests.

Sign up your very young innie for a library card and take him to the library for story hour. Visit your local branch regularly, allowing plenty of time to select books. Discuss with your child the books he reads and the movies he sees. Let him see that books and movies are not just time-passers, but that they broaden his world and serve as a link to others. Pay attention to what interests him, and help him find materials on that topic. Like all kids, innies may prefer informal learning to sitting in a classroom. They often surprise others—even their teachers—by knowing a lot about a variety of subjects. I have worked with several introverted children under the age of five who knew enough about dinosaurs to narrate a Discovery Channel documentary. They could tell me if the Stegosaurus and Allosaurus were from the Jurassic or Cretaceous period, if they were carnivores or herbivores, how they raised their young, and who their main enemies were. When an introverted child starts talking about a favorite subject, it's like turning on an information fountain.

4. Introverts Think Outside the Box

When six-year-old Tia and her mother moved to a new apartment, Tia was afraid at night and had difficulty sleeping in her new room. She and her mom discussed the problem, and as a solution, they decided that Mom would sleep in Tia's top bunk for a week. At week's end, Tia still cried and couldn't settle in. Her mother was beginning to feel frustrated and discouraged. Tia was walking through the living room when she quietly said, "Could we change bedrooms? I think it could help me." Her mother was surprised, since she had picked the brighter, more spacious room for her daughter. But she began to realize that the room Tia wanted was smaller and closer to the center of the apartment. Perhaps she would feel safer there. They switched bedrooms and, sure enough, Tia easily drifted off. Her mother was amazed that Tia had come up with the suggestion. She happily returned to her own bed.

Introverted children are creative problem solvers. I am always impressed when I ask them for their ideas. They take in all sorts of input, think about it for a while, and finally come up with innovative answers. They assess data they hadn't even realized they had observed. With sufficient processing time, they can make comparisons and anticipate patterns. They analyze the patterns within the context of their own subjective thoughts and impressions to arrive at complex conclusions. They come up with fresh, original, out-of-the-box ideas.

I asked Tia's mother whether she had praised Tia for her idea. She replied, "I told her that it was such a good idea—and that I was glad that she had thought of it and asked me to change rooms with her." I congratulated her for listening to Tia and following through on her solution to the problem.

Encourage your innie child's original thinking by asking her opinion on different matters. Ask her about a dilemma you face. What solutions does she see? Help her to access her *own* problem-solving abilities when she is upset. This, of course, is when it's hardest. Help her develop creative routes to innovative thought. Ask her to draw a picture or make up a story, poem, puppet show, or song about what's bothering her. Let her see that the process itself can yield interesting results.

This is a great way to get a glimpse of your introverted child's fascinating interior world. And paying attention to questions your child raises may have benefits for *you*. For example, Edwin Land, the man who founded and headed the Polaroid Corporation from 1937 to 1982, was inspired to develop the instant camera by his three-year-old daughter. She had asked him a precocious question, particularly for the time: "Why can't I see the picture you just took of me?" He pondered this puzzle and solved it within an hour—leading to this lucrative invention.

5. Introverts Excel in the Creative Arts

Creativity is a first cousin to out-of-the-box thinking and interiority. I always put out art supplies for my introverted clients—adults and children. It offers a way to express what's inside, without all that exhausting talk. One little girl, aged five, made me a miniature book about her life: ten pages of detailed colored-pencil sketches, stapled together. Each page had an intricate scene from her day: waking up, eating breakfast, being at school, eating dinner, playing with her dog, Sammy, watching TV, and bedtime. Her book included the cast of characters in her life: her family, friends, teachers, and, of course, Sammy. Many innies are writers, artists, dancers, actors, musicians, or are creative in other ways. My office walls are lined with drawings, paintings, photographs, ceramic pieces, poems, and stitch work given to me over the years by introverted clients.

The nostalgic, whimsical artist Mary Engelbreit is a typical creative innie. At age eleven she announced that she wanted to be an artist when she grew up. At school she was frustrated that teachers and students didn't really discuss books in depth. She spent hours in solitude and sketched in between reading books. She copied other artists and taught herself to draw. Her mother said Mary was relentless; it was obvious that she would use her talent someday. She skipped college and took a full-time job at the local artist supply store, the Art Mart, where she was exposed to artists and the local art community. The high school guidance counselor, appalled, said, "Oh no, you can't do that!" Today Engelbreit heads a successful company based on her artistic talents.

Creativity is about seeing—not necessarily seeing more, but from another perspective. The creative person takes in bits of the world around him and rearranges those pieces in his own inner world to form something novel or innovative.

Encourage your innie child's creativity. Make art supplies available, even if they're messy; musical instruments, though they're noisy. Allow for freedom and expression without criticism. Suggest that your child write about an experience he reacted strongly to. Offer dance, singing, acting, or music lessons. Take him to museums, concerts, flea markets, plays—a variety of places so that he gets to see all the incredible ways people express their creativity.

6. Introverts Have a High Emotional IQ

It's always a revelation to listen to introverted children describe their feelings. Darin, aged six, related this: "I was sad at school because my friend Molly wouldn't play with me at lunch. She wanted to play with the girls. I went off by myself for a while. Then I asked Joey if he wanted to play ball. He said yes." It's hard to find many adults who could manage rejection that well. Darin felt his feelings, calmed himself down, and evaluated the situation. He could then take the risk of approaching another friend. He had the resilience to hop over some common playground potholes to find a playmate.

Since introverted children tend to have delayed emotional responses, parents may not grasp how well their innie child knows his own feelings. And the innie himself may not know this unless he articulates those feelings. When something happens, the child may outwardly appear calm, cool, or even hesitant. Internally, he is pausing to integrate his complex thoughts and feelings. His ability to tolerate time alone allows him to mull over the nuances of his reaction. He likes to understand an event before reacting to it. He will then noodle out a plan of action, anticipating the potential consequences. As a rule, introverted children have intense emotional outbursts only if they are stressed, tired, or hungry, or if they feel threatened.

Because innies are aware of their own feelings, they usually have empathy for other children. They can slip easily into another person's shoes. When they ask you about yours or others' feelings, be honest with them so as not to invalidate their perceptions. As in: "It was very considerate of you, Nate, to ask me if my feelings were hurt when you said you wanted to talk to Dad alone. I was fine about it, but thanks for asking." Innies tend to develop a sense of morality and ethics early in life; they may be wise before their years. Contrary to assumptions people make about introverts, they work well in groups.

Acknowledge your innie's emotional muscle. Emotional IQ is crucial to success, because so much in life requires dealing with others. Remember, however, that the brain's emotional center is the last part to fully develop, so these skills need to be nurtured over a longer period of time. If your child is generous, acknowledge it. Let him know that empathy is a good quality to have, in boys as well as girls. Our world is in short enough supply of empathetic people as it is.

7. Introverts Are Gifted at the Art of Conversation

Ten-year-old Marta is looking at my bookshelves. "I notice you like books," she says. "What are your favorites? Do you read any more than once?" "Well, yes," I respond. "I read most of them quite a few times. I have lots of favorites—what are yours?" "Two of my favorite books are *The Giver* and *Sarah, Plain and Tall*. Have you read them?" "Yes, and I liked them, too. Why do you like them?" As we discuss favorite books, our exchange deepens and becomes richer than those I usually have with many adults.

This may be the most surprising of the introvert's gifts. It's a shocker to discover that introverted children, often tongue-tied at school or parties, can be hidden masters of the art of conversation. They enjoy listening. They are trustworthy, reliable, and direct. They ask questions. They don't interrupt. They make insightful comments. They keep confidences. They remember what their friends say. They pick up cues.

Innies often have good relationships with other family members. As they grow into their teen and adult years, they can become a central figure (albeit sometimes behind the scenes) in their family. Their calming energy soothes anxious people and helps them settle down. They excel in the one-on-one relationship—often choosing careers that rely on it.

Help your innie child enhance her conversational abilities. Compliment her ability to listen, ask questions, remember what people say, and engage in back-and-forth conversation. Point out the difference between light social chat and true conversation, noting that honest, open dialogue is the cornerstone of lasting friendships. Innies need to know that the ability to be interested and interesting in conversation is a fine quality that maintains deep friendships. Help your innie child find friends who can discuss topics at more complex levels.

8. Introverts Enjoy Their Own Company

Tina's dad comes home after a business trip, and Tina's sister and brother rush out to give him a hug. Tina, engrossed in her seventh-grade science project on whales, doesn't hear all the commotion. A bit later, her dad peeks his head into her room. She smiles. "Hi, Dad, when did you get home?" "A while ago. I just wanted to say hi. Talk to ya later." Tina's dad knows that she's immersed in her project and will join the family when she's ready.

Innies enjoy solitude. They don't need outside action in order to keep busy and engaged. Introverted children have a great capacity to concentrate deeply, to the point of shutting out the world. They savor becoming completely absorbed in a project, book, or movie. Remember, they receive "hap hits" when they are concentrating.

Let your innie know that the capacity to enjoy one's own company is a gift. It's very freeing not to constantly need other people. It's a key component of independence. It's also the linchpin to many of the desirable occupations in which introverts excel. Keep teaching your introverted child how to assess and balance her social time. Acknowledge that she may wish she could stay better fueled when around other people and activities. You can remind her that she can join her friends another time.

9. Introverts Are Refreshingly Modest

"I don't want to be on TV," Sadie, one of the introverted children I work with, said out of the blue. We were playing with her Strawberry Shortcake dolls. Living in Los Angeles, I see many kids in the industry. I asked, "Did someone ask you to be on TV?" "No, but the kids at school were saying they want to be on TV. And when I said I didn't, they said I was weird. It doesn't sound fun to me— too many hot lights and too much nerves." "It's good that you're thinking about what you feel comfortable doing," I laughed. "And you're certainly not weird."

In our age of celebrity, it seems everyone is hankering after every bit of the limelight. Being humble seems to have gone out of style. The current fad of reality TV makes it look like anyone could be and should be on TV. When I hear so many of the kids I counsel say that their life's ambition is to be on TV, I am chilled to the bone. It dismays me that fame and attention are goals in and of themselves. Today many children are forced into flashy, competitive activities like sports or cheerleading so that their parents can brag about them. Saying "I am best" is mistaken for self-esteem. What we get are competitive children who are easily discouraged if they aren't the best. Children are on sports teams, dancing teams, singing teams, science teams, and academic teams. Parents clap wildly when they perform. Children receive boatloads of gold medals for ordinary achievements.

So it's a good thing that we have a few innies who aren't always seeking the spotlight. They enjoy being in the background. They don't mind being part of the audience as opposed to on the stage. They are reserved and don't like too much attention and stimulation. They can tolerate attention—when the conditions are right. But most of the time, an innie will feel like disappearing because attention feels uncomfortable. She may actually feel physical or emotional pain if she is focused on too much or pushed into high-pressured situations.

Appreciate your innie's reluctance to be the center of attention. Let her know that it's more than okay to enjoy being out of the limelight. But remember that innies do like being recognized for their accomplishments, especially if they think they deserve it. It's a good quality to appreciate being acknowledged for work well done in private. And the irony is that being modest actually reflects and increases self-confidence.

10. Introverts Develop Healthy Habits

"See my cast? Want to sign it?" Jonathan shows me his white plaster-covered arm with colorful ink names and doodles drawn on it. "Two more weeks and it will be sawed off. It's kinda fun to see if I can do everything with my other hand." I add my name to his cast. His mother says, "I can't believe how well Jonathan is handling this broken arm. Last year when his brother broke his thumb, he got out the yard clippers and cut off his own cast—he didn't want to miss basketball practice!"

We hear a lot about type A behavior and less about what researchers categorize as type B. Type As are dominant on the sympathetic nervous system—the flight-fright-fight part. Overusing their system is like driving your car hard and fast. If you gun your engine and drive eighty miles an hour, smash on your brakes, and screech to a halt, in no time at all you will wear out your car. Extroverts may have trouble slowing down so as to balance and restore their systems. They may tend toward higher blood pressure and pulse rate. Since introverts are dominant on the braking side of the nervous system, they don't burn out their bodies so quickly. They keep their car idling, starting and stopping slowly. This is one reason why introverts are often blessed with longevity.

New medical research shows that particular personality traits influence health choices. Such studies indicate that qualities like conscientiousness, dependability, persistence, flexibility, thinking before acting, truthfulness, and a lack of vanity create a healthier person. These traits encompass the ability to say no to oneself. Innies are more disciplined and manage illness better than extroverts because they will slow down, practice self-reliance, and limit themselves. They also avoid risky behavior, which is a leading cause of accidental injury and death in young people.

Congratulate your innie child on the healthy choices he makes that promote well-being. Many times introverted children will say they want to go to bed early. Encourage this—your child will know when he needs to recharge. Innie children will often eat healthier if they understand why their bodies need certain foods. As they may need to eat smaller portions more often to sustain their energy throughout the day, encourage flexibility in eating schedules.

11. Introverts Are Good Citizens

"Alicia is excited about driving, isn't she?" I am asking my eight-year-old grandson, Christopher, about his sixteen-year-old sister. "Yep," he says. "What do you think about becoming older and learning to drive?" I ask. "Well, that there are lots of rules, and so I think it's pretty scary and dangerous," he says. "I may be like Aunt Kristen [our youngest daughter] and not drive until I'm older." "That might be a good idea," I say, "or you may change your mind." "I doubt it," he says. Since Kristen is still a cautious driver, I wonder

The (Neurological) Path Most Taken

As we found in Chapter 2, the brain develops connections through the use and reuse of pathways; over time, the well-worn path draws more of the neurological traffic. Watching highly stimulating (including violent) TV or movies or playing repetitive video games triggers the same dopamine routes over and over. These are on a fast track to quick-reward left-brain pathways. In his book *The New Brain*, leading brain researcher Richard Restak, M.D., expresses his concern about how the modern age is *rewiring* the brain. Everything has become so fast. Dr. Restak wonders whether people will be able to devote the time required to master a subject or a skill. He talks about the "ten-year rule," noting that "it takes *at least* ten years of practice and giving attention to nuances to become an expert at anything." Innie children have the advantages of curiosity and the ability to notice nuances, and they get "hap hits" from concentrating on deeper meanings for longer times. Without those "hap hits" they won't learn to prize their brain-power. Even innies can become addicted to the dopamine neural pathways that give cocaine-like feel-good shots. We need to teach introverted children to appreciate their abilities and encourage their willingness to learn.

Our job as parents is to let our introverted children know that there are advantages to their temperament, despite the messages they may receive from the culture at large. You can do this by affirming your child's strengths and by helping him or her to build on them rather than try to change them or to hide them.

what Christopher will be like in the future. I have the reassuring feeling that he'll grow up to respect rules and take things like driving seriously.

Your introverted child will also likely grow up to be a valuable citizen. Despite the fact that the stereotypical criminal is described as a "loner," research shows that extroverts, who run on high-octane dopamine rewards, actually raise more of a ruckus in society. They seek thrills and excitement. Proportionately, they are arrested and divorced more often; they become workaholics, alcoholics, gambling addicts, and act out in various antisocial ways with greater frequency. The difference may come down to physiology as much as morals. All that stimulation and the energy drain of such dramatic actions is simply too much for most introverts to manage. So crime wouldn't pay.

Apart from the energy question, however, introverts generally have strong internal values; they are often religious and are guided by their own interior compasses. They see the bigger human picture and want to do the right thing. They appreciate courtesy and like to be polite. They can say no to themselves. They think before acting and are aware of consequences. They can anticipate what could happen if they did something wrong. They think about what they say and value words, so they are often honest. They become solid citizens.

Acknowledge qualities that contribute to your innie's mature choices. In his new book, *American Mania: When More Is Not Enough,* UCLA researcher Peter C. Whybrow claims that humans are becoming addicted to a reward-driven and demand-driven culture. He also states that combining dopamine-pathway dominance with a consuming society leads to a situation where people feel they need more, more, and more. The result is greed and anxiety. Innies, however, look for calm interludes and are able to consider the personal and community implications of their choices.

12. Introverts Are Good Friends

Ethan and Dylan, both innies, became friends in preschool. They loved to make up imaginary adventures, play computer games, and banded together as spies who sleuthed out bad guys. They once turned a fallen tree trunk into a pretend elephant that they would ride throughout India. In first grade Dylan moved away. The boys e-mailed and wrote letters to each other. They visited on weekends and during the summer holidays. With the help of their families, they were able to maintain their friendship throughout their elementary school years.

Innies are loyal, caring, sensitive to others' feelings, and good listeners, all of which make a good friend. They take time to forge connections, but once they do it's for the long haul. They are not prone to the kind of conflicts or competitions that can mar childhood friendships. And because they're *not* everybody's friends, they are motivated to keep in touch once they find a special companion.

The Heart of the Matter

- *Introverted children are undervalued in our extroverted world.*
- *They need to be told about their hidden gifts.*
- *Extroverts need to appreciate and practice using their introverted side.*

PART II

Raising Introverted Children with Roots and Wings

"It's only with the heart that one can see rightly; what is essential is invisible to the eyes."
—Antoine de Saint-Exupéry

CHAPTER 4

Building Emotional Resilience

Establishing Strong Bonds with Your Child Will Provide Him a Secure Foundation

"With anything young and tender the most important part of the task is the beginning of it."—Plato

Many parents find innies quite confounding. They may seem unpredictable (at least, until you understand their patterns). One mother expressed surprise after she and her daughter took a weeklong trip to a farm. "I thought she'd revel in the quiet, but she didn't stop talking!" It's not always easy to know what your innie child wants. We invited our introverted grandson to pick a theme park he'd like to visit for a weekend adventure. He left us speechless by saying, "I'd rather just stay overnight at your house." A father told me, "We say that our daughter is 'barn sour.' She reminds us of a horse soured on sauntering down the trail, itching to turn around and trot back to the cozy barn." Indeed, after a single outing or errand, perhaps only the first on your long to-do list, many innies are ready to switch gears and return home.

Some innies may not overtly express a lot of affection, and these children can be misunderstood. "My other children need me more than my son does," one mother told me. But in fact, innies very much value and need one-on-one time with their parents. Another boy, whose parents thought he was perfectly happy and self-sufficient, confided to me, "I wish I had more time alone with my mom or dad." I hear a lot of comments like that from the introverted children I meet. It's easy to take their seeming independence at face value, especially when other children are clamoring for attention.

The innie temperament can certainly pose a challenge, particularly for extroverted parents. Perhaps you love parties, and your son hates them. You like to be out and about, and your daughter is a determined homebody. You are full of energy, and your child tires easily. But innie children can also be trying for *introverted* parents. Perhaps when you were young, you hated feeling overwhelmed by groups. Does seeing your child hang back in crowds make you uncomfortable and push your buttons? The truth is, every child has traits we like, along with some traits that spark concern or make us anxious, and, yes, qualities we just plain don't like. After all, being the parent of any child requires us to stretch ourselves.

In this chapter, we explore the underlying emotional issues related to raising an introverted child. We discuss how to be attuned to your child's needs, and how to provide a solid foundation. As with any child, the important thing is to work from a place of acceptance and to strive to understand how the world looks from her eyes. For it is through observing and listening that you'll learn how to support your child and to create an environment in which she'll thrive.

Creating a "Hardiness Zone"

In the gardening world, a Hardiness Zone is an area within a larger climate zone where conditions provide a good fit for the particular plants that grow there. When your introverted child is in a growing environment that is well suited to him, he will flourish. Parenting becomes easier for you. Your child is happier. The important thing is to provide the four key elements that innies need in order to create their own Hardiness Zone—the interpersonal equivalent of sun, shade, soil, and moisture. First, you can ensure that you have a strong bond with your child. Second, you can teach him how to work with (rather than against) his own temperament. Third, you can establish a flexible relationship with your child that acknowledges his feelings and supports his brainpower so that he develops his full potential. The fourth element is providing a home "refueling" station where he can recharge.

In giving your innie these four ingredients, you are giving her a sturdy foundation, confidence in her abilities, and a degree of self-sufficiency. For an introvert, trying to be an extrovert uses up tons of fuel. It's not long before she's running on empty. You can reduce the resulting energy crash-and-dive and help her keep to a steady, comfortable course.

Establishing Deep Roots

> *"To be rooted is perhaps the most important*
> *and least recognized need of the human soul."*
> —*Simone Weil*

Human beings are born with disorganized brains and helpless bodies. We begin to gain control over our bodies in the first year, but it is not until we are well into our third decade that our brains are fully developed. We humans manage to survive this less-than-auspicious beginning because nature has evolved so that infants instinctively seek bonds with their parents. This inborn drive compels the human baby to seek closeness and comfort from her immediate caretakers. Infants need parents not only to give them food and protect them from saber-toothed tigers, but also to help integrate and organize their brains.

Children also build their view of themselves according to how their parents treat them. This is called *internalizing*. Children take in, or "incorporate," the way they are treated. This, in turn, builds their sense of an *internal caretaker*. This is how the child keeps his sense of you, the parent, inside of him as a kind of emotional bulwark. As your child experiences a satisfying enough relationship with you and establishes his internal caretaker, he builds a sense of "we-ness" that is the foundation of his self-esteem. This interior base of acceptance and care allows innies to feel self-confident as they set out into a broader world that doesn't necessarily understand them.

Your attachment with your innie is crucial because it affects how her brain develops. In psychology, there has been a great deal of research on "attachment theory." The quality of the bond between parents and their young child has a strong correlation with her future emotional health. Secure bonds support brain complexity, strengthen emotional fortitude, build strong social skills, and enable a child to make use of her innate brainpower. They ensure a hardiness and resilience in the face of life's adversity.

Stranger anxiety and *separation anxiety* are two universal reactions that reflect how humans bond. Infants may show fear, wariness, clinginess, and tears around unfamiliar people. This is a healthy stage that indicates that the child is developing a good connection to his parents. Parents can help the little one by reassuring him, being friendly to appropriate strangers, and by realizing that this stage will pass. Introverted children may stay in this stage a bit longer, and parents may need to serve as bridges for their toddler or child and tell others that he will warm up as he gets to know them.

Separation anxiety is triggered when a parent moves out of visible range. It can start at about six months and generally peaks at around age two. Separating from loved ones is scary for children at certain ages and is an ongoing issue throughout life. Like stranger anxiety, it may occur under many conditions, disappear and reappear unpredictably, and have different degrees of intensity. Separation anxiety can crop up when a child goes on a sleepover, learns a new skill such as reading, or goes on a vacation. It can resurface with an older child if there's a divorce or if the child faces any important transition. Again, innies may have a particularly strong reaction to separation. These episodes can be reduced by preparation—alerting your child about upcoming transitions and separations—and handling them in a kind but matter-of-fact way.

The deep roots you establish with your innie will help her to manage in the outside world as she grows up. For example, my daughter Kristen used her bond with her own daughter, Emily, to create bridges to strangers. When passersby smiled at Emily, Kristen smiled back and said, "My little one has delayed smiles, so she'll be smiling at you in a few minutes." Strangers usually laughed and smiled back. This kind of action made the world seem friendlier to Emily. As she grows up, her strong bond with her mother and these bridging experiences become internalized. Later on, Emily's own internal caretaker may remind her, "I have delayed smiles so I better speed up this smile."

Nurturing Interdependence

> *"I never saw a discontented tree. They grip the
> ground as though they liked it."—John Muir*

Parents I work with often feel overwhelmed and aren't sure where to direct their energies. Every aspect of child rearing seems so important. What should they focus on? Understanding what your innie needs makes your job easier and more enjoyable. Knowing innie vulnerabilities relieves the pressure of guesswork. You can be prepared for trouble spots and reduce the urge to blame your child or to experience those awful pangs of parenting guilt. And as for potential behavior problems in the future, you can nip them in the bud.

Every child shows hints and signs of his natural bent. Within your child's behaviors and moods are clues for how best to parent him. Observing your introverted child's patterns and noting how your child responds are important ways for you to learn how to meet his needs. Things are not always what they seem at first glance. For example, parents may think their introverted child is highly dependent because he is sensitive or cautious. On the other hand, if an innie tends to be withdrawn or internally focused, he may seem more independent. However, this may or may not be true. Once he's made his initial assessment of a situation, the cautious child may be quite independent. And the internally focused child may long to be more connected to his parents but simply not know how to tell you what he needs. As you understand your innie's energy patterns—learn to read his or her needs for connection and solitude, and establish good lines of communication with your child—you will be able to decode subtle signals with increasing ease.

Child rearing is a paradox: A child only develops wings and becomes independent if he has established strong roots of *de*pendence with you. Your child was born with his own little seeds to grow to independence and maturity through his attachment to you. The seemingly opposing capacities of dependence and independence ultimately lead to the most mature relational ability: interdependence.

Here are four vital things you can do to forge close bonds with your innie:

- **Offer the assurance of proximity.** Although your innie may be in another room or seem to be oblivious as to the presence of family members, she is actually highly attuned to her parents' whereabouts. She is calmed by your proximity. You are available if needed. (Talking on the phone is the quickest way to be reminded that a young child needs you. The moment you start talking, your previously happily occupied child suddenly needs your attention so as to be reassured that you know she's there.)
- **Provide a safe haven.** Your innie looks to family members who are familiar, reliable, calm, and caring in order to experience

them as safe havens. Loud voices, tension, and overt fighting undermine this perception of safety. The innie child seeks the comfort of predictability from the parent in order to build trust.

- **Teach your innie how to engage and disengage.** This is the delicate dance that underlies all human relationships: engaging and disengaging. Parents teach innies that interacting is fun through enjoyable, affirming engagement—eye contact, conversation, and connection. Disengagement (looking away, quiet time, release) allows the child space to appreciate her or his separateness.

    Real communication requires this back-and-forth flow. Without it, interactions are awkward, stilted, and one-sided. You may have talked with someone and noticed a lack of flow. It's uncomfortable. The ability to engage and disengage establishes the rhythms of relating. This helps children learn to be together and apart, to give and to take, and to communicate in a two-way exchange.

- **Offer a portable yet secure base.** You and your child play, talk, have fun, and enjoy each other's company. Such experiences, repeated again and again, help in the creation of your child's internal caretaker, which gives her emotional self-sufficiency. They also help her develop a basic sense of self-confidence. Other relationships and learning experiences build on this core sense of self, culminating in an internal sense of security. As she grows up, your child will refer to this built-in secure base and take it wherever she goes. Innies in particular must have a sturdy, internal foundation as they confront a world where they need to adapt.

Child development experts say the capacity for interdependence is built through particular moments in a parent/child relationship, such as when a child is hurt or needs comfort or when parents leave and return. Can the child ask for help and reassurance? Can she acknowledge your leaving and perhaps cry? When the two of you reunite, can she reconnect with you? Can she seek comfort? These moments heighten her need for you to be a safe, trustworthy person. If you and your child have a good bond, that trust is confirmed. The trust that's built up enables you to help her overcome the innie's natural reluctance to venture out into the world. A positive bond develops both aspects of interdependence—dependence and independence—so that your innie can trust others and feel secure in herself.

Teach the Importance of Temperament

"We have all come on different ships but we're in the same boat now."—Dr. Martin Luther King Jr.

Speak with your children about temperament. Even very young children can understand that people are born with unique personalities. Explain that part of temperament is about where someone gets his energy and where he focuses his attention—inside himself or outside himself. Understanding the idea of temperament will help your child weather any perceived criticisms of his introverted nature; this way he knows there's a reason for his responses and needs, and he won't take things as personally. Give him the tools he needs to gauge other people's temperaments. Accepting that others are different in *their* own way will enhance his people skills and tolerance.

One good way to broach the topic of temperament is to talk about favorite book or movie characters. Is Spider-Man an innie or an outie? What about Harry Potter? How about Ron and Hermione? Are any of the Baudelaire orphans in the *Series of Unfortunate Events* books an innie? What about the characters in Charles Schulz's *Peanuts* cartoons?

With younger children, you can read books that feature characters with clear temperament types like the Winnie-the-Pooh stories.

Innies and Children's Literature: Do They Dominate?

One place where innies may be in the majority is the children's bookshelf. Many protagonists in children's literature are innies. Why? In part, I'd say this is because they make interesting and complex characters. Literature comes alive when a story is depicted through the eyes of a thoughtful, observant character with a rich inner life. I would add that the authors of children's literature tend to be innies (creating an entire imaginary world is a quintessential innie task), and they write for a majority of readers who are, themselves, innies. It's the same for movies with children as the protagonists.

Who are some innies who live on the page? Harry Potter and his friend, studious Hermione Granger. Violet (the brainy inventor) and Klaus (the nonstop reader) in Lemony Snicket's *A Series of Unfortunate Events* books. Roald Dahl's heroes, like modest Charlie in *Charlie and the Chocolate Factory* and thoughtful Matilda, stuck in a family of loudmouths, in *Matilda*.

Some extroverts I can think of include Lucy in *Peanuts*, Tigger in *Winnie-the-Pooh*, Ariel in *The Little Mermaid*, Samwise Gamgee in *The Lord of the Rings*, Ron Weasley in the *Harry Potter* books, along with Dennis the Menace, Eloise, and Tom Sawyer.

Discuss how the various characters act. What words would best describe each of them? What makes each unique? How do Christopher Robin and his friends in the Hundred Acre Wood help one another with their different temperaments? Ask your child if he thinks he is more like Eeyore, Pooh, Christopher Robin, Tigger, Kanga or Roo, Piglet or Owl.

Another way to help your child understand temperament is to ask her to think about her friends and teachers. Are any of them introverts? Help her develop concrete examples to support her

Temperament and Energy

A core difference between innies and outies is the source of their energy: where their *oomph* comes from and how they replenish it. When energy is flagging, kids are more prone to meltdowns, crankiness, indecisiveness, and self-centeredness. Come to think of it, so is anyone.

Picture yourself with a lightbulb affixed to the top of your head. Now imagine that this is connected to a battery, and the battery to a charger. The energy from the charger is flowing into the battery. The battery illuminates the lightbulb. It lights up. Consider what recharges the battery, and what depletes it. An outie replenishes his recharger by being wrapped up in activity. When he is quietly reflecting, energy flows out, leaving the lightbulb dim. Conversely, an innie gets recharged by quiet solo time. When he's out with lots of people, he loses energy and therefore brightness.

Explain to your innie how personal energy works. This will give her a tangible reason for why she needs breaks. Ask her to imagine the lightbulb on top of her head. What's the wattage right now? Is it bright, medium, or barely glowing? Point out when she is refueled, "Oh, I see that your bulb is bright." When her energy shifts from high to low you can say, "It looks like your bulb is barely lit right now." Explain how taking a relaxing break rekindles the bulb. And how energy level has an affect on her mood and inclination to be with other people.

Note to parents: Take notice of the relative glow of *your* personal lightbulb. Parenting requires a lot of energy and effort!

opinions and offer positive feedback: "I see what you mean, Kylie. Your friend Max is very quiet when he goes to new places with us. I saw how you helped him by holding his hand." It will build your child's confidence to know that she can accurately "read" temperament. Plus, knowing what to expect in a friend's behavior reduces an introverted child's energy outlay. Acknowledge her capacity to notice other children's behavior and use her ability to help them. Don't condone any ridiculing of other people. Lead by example, and be open to other points of view. Acknowledge that she may not like all the ways people's differences manifest themselves.

Helping Innies Be Innies

"A child is the root of the heart."
—*Carolina Maria de Jesus*

Often parents of introverts think that they should encourage extroverted traits in their children. Not only is this impossible, like planting a tulip bulb and expecting a rose to miraculously poke out of the soil, but it's counterproductive. In their classic book *Please Understand Me,* psychologist David Keirsey and coauthor Marilyn Bates caution that introverted children are particularly vulnerable to damage if they are forced to behave as extroverts. Innies are frequently misunderstood, and they are often pressured to function outside of their comfort zones. They aren't designed to be racy sports cars. They can't sustain an outgoing, energetic, and chatty extroverting style all the time. Too much extroverting overloads their system and reduces their physical and emotional energy. Innies are reliable station wagons. But without downtime, they have no resources left to develop their natural introverted gifts.

The messages innies receive from their families are crucial. If they get the message that they are bad, defective, or should be more outgoing, they will feel shame about who they are. They will retreat into themselves and conclude that the negative reactions they receive from outside are correct. In order to build a positive view of herself, an innie needs to feel accepted and appreciated in her own family.

One aspect of temperament is how someone gives and receives love. Parents often don't understand why their child doesn't feel loved by them. They know they love their child. But telling a child "I love you" isn't always the best way to convey that message. You need to give your child love in the language he understands. Conveying your love to your child is vitally important. Introverted children may be more subdued in how they receive and express love. But their apparent nonchalance can be deceptive.

As with everything else, expressing love to your innie is a matter of balance—and no doubt trial and error. A parent who races up with a big bear hug may be experienced as too intense, and the child may retreat. Something more subtle and private, like taking his hand or smiling or even offering a surreptitious wink, can convey your warmth without overstimulating or embarrassing your child. Some innies like hugs only at certain times. Your child may want to be hugged when he's tired. Or he may *absolutely not* want to be hugged when he's tired. Some like to kiss or be kissed, and others may not. Some like sitting on your lap facing outward and some may prefer sitting so they can see your face. And of course these preferences change with the years. Pay attention to how your introverted child responds to physical affection. A family discussion about how people like to give and receive love teaches children that not everyone is the same. Parents often express love as it was expressed to them, or as they wish it had been. But expressing love that is nourishing and supportive to your child requires that you know how and what makes him feel loved.

Demonstrate to your child that you enjoy who she is and tell her that you love her. A child may feel loved by a parent when they share special times together, as when Mom or Dad reads her a story. Another child may feel special if the whole family takes part, perhaps each person taking a character and reading that same story as a play. Acknowledging your innie for a personal quality can be a powerful way of communicating love. As in: "I noticed how well you pick out birthday gifts, Samantha. You always know what someone will like." One child may be keen on a dinner out with just one parent. Another may want the entire family to go to the park. Often we make assumptions about what a child likes without actually asking. Or we bend to majority rule, and the quieter child isn't heard.

Children also feel loved when their needs are met. One way for you to meet your innie's needs is by creating a nourishing home turf. With innies, however, it rarely works to take a one-size-fits-all approach to home life. Remember the story of *Goldilocks and the Three Bears*? This classic tale captures the flavor of what it's like to raise innies. It can be challenging to find the soft shirt that is "just right," to determine how much recharging time is the right amount, or assess what is enough activity without too much stimulation.

Working *with* Innies' Emotions

> *"Pain is inevitable. Suffering is optional."*
> —*Anonymous*

One could argue that American culture values thinking over feeling. Peoples' emotions are unpredictable and therefore often inconvenient. Many people wonder why we humans have feelings at all, thinking we might be better off if we were all like *Star Trek*'s Mr. Spock and relied solely on reason. But reason in isolation ignores what real relationships require. Without the input from feelings, thinking alone leads to relationship problems and poor decisions. This is why you can't *think* your way out of ingrained habits like overeating, smoking, or being a workaholic. You need to understand your emotions and grapple with them before you can haul yourself out of your rut.

On a very basic level, feelings make us human. They also help us in three specific ways. First, emotions are electrical energy ebbing and flowing inside of our brain and body in response to our internal and external worlds. The energy connects and integrates the five levels of the brain. It moves messages to coordinate the different systems throughout your body. Second, these emotional messages reveal practical, internal information about yourself and others. Knowing your own feelings enhances your ability to form and maintain relationships. Your feelings tell you what feels good and what feels bad. Third, your emotions serve as a compass for guiding the decisions you make. They tell you what feels *right*.

Emotions have important jobs to do. Sadness helps process loss and encourages others to comfort us. Fear tells us that we need to protect ourselves or that we need reassurance. Anger signals the need for boundaries. (For example: Molly says, "Rebecca took my Lego and won't give it back. I don't like it." "Yeah, I bet that made you mad," Molly's mom replies. "Next time Rebecca starts to grab your toy you tell her, 'No.'" Molly's anger signals her to take care of herself and tell her friend no.) Guilt says we need to make reparations. Shame says we shouldn't do something. Pain says we need to do something to take care of ourselves. Feelings show children how to earn the real rewards of life: establishing and maintaining healthy relationships, discovering personal meaning, and finding satisfaction. Feelings steer them in the right direction by informing them when an experience is painful, sad, enjoyable, satisfying, scary, or irritating. Emotions guide them toward what they need and away from what is harmful.

Unfortunately, many of us grew up in families that denied or talked us out of our feelings. We didn't learn to manage our own feelings, let alone teach our children to do so. But you can learn a few ways to help your child manage his feelings. With introverted children, their dominant neurological pathway travels to the front of the brain, the site of complex emotional abilities. This gives them a natural ability to tap into their emotional IQ. Many other children will need to work harder to develop emotional awareness. Some children will never develop emotional intelligence.

Innies need parents and caregivers to notice and name their emotions. Otherwise they won't know what they are feeling—and therefore know how to use these emotions constructively. Feelings need to be named and validated. If you teach your innie to pay attention to what she is feeling, she learns to value and trust her emotional gifts. Without your help, an innie can lose touch with her own feelings or become overwhelmed by them. But you can help her acknowledge, feel, and use the signals from her emotional reserves.

Feelings as a Resource

Timmy reaches out to pet a dog he doesn't know. It snaps at him. He feels afraid and pulls his hand away. He registers the experience: "That dog looked friendly, but he snapped at me. It scared me. Next time I want to pet a dog, I need to ask the owner before I stick out my hand." He tucks this knowledge away—remember, innies in particular store negative experiences.

Feelings guide innies in their interactions with the outside world. For example, it's through feelings that innies notice that they enjoy socializing, even though it takes energy. Amy reflects: "I had so much fun playing at Maddie's. I hope we have another playdate soon." Emotions highlight important relationships. Kesha thinks: "My birthday wasn't as much fun without Grandpa. I'll have Mom get him to come next time we have a party."

Too many children today don't learn to feel their feelings. Rather, they learn early on to shift away from uncomfortable feelings—to quickly change the mental channel, so to speak. They don't learn to regulate their feelings. Regulating feelings means to keep them in a range that's manageable. Without regulation, many young people either look for fake highs or fall into deep lows. Extroverts in particular can get habituated to highs. Some routes to fake highs include overeating, overdoing, taking drugs, running on adrenaline, engaging in risky behavior, feeling superior, and seeking approval. Introverts can get stuck in lows. Some examples of lows include being overly dependent, wallowing in guilt or shame, becoming depressed or apathetic, overeating, taking drugs, or feeling hopeless.

Signposts to Guide Innies Through their Emotional Terrain

As you know, innies have a rich interior life, but as parents it can be hard to read them. It will help to know that innies . . .

- May get overwhelmed by their internal thoughts and feelings, and become frozen or withdrawn. Encourage them to express their feelings, and make sure they don't feel you're judging them.

- May be sensitive to others' feelings and have empathy (especially right-brained innies). Validate their warmth and talent.

- Take longer to *know* what they are feeling. Remind them that they will be clearer about what they feel later.

- Are drained by intense feelings, anger, and conflict. Help them understand that these can't be avoided and that sometimes conflict is worth the energy.

- May feel overstimulated by the kind of excitement that extroverts seek out. Reassure them that they can enjoy excitement in small doses.

- May feel anxious about trying anything new and avoid the unknown. Help them learn to tolerate being uncomfortable. Remind them that feeling anxiety is a part of life. It will pass if they take a break, breathe, relax, and gently tell themselves to calm down and take it slow.

Being alive means that we will feel pain at times. Pain deepens our experience of life. Children need to learn to tolerate and process their feelings. You can help your child learn to self-soothe to ease painful feelings. Since emotions are energy, they naturally flow through us. If we notice their cues and feel them, they recede.

You can *externally* balance the ebbs and flows of your child's emotions by calming her down when she is upset. And you can encourage her when she is discouraged. This teaches her how to *internally* right herself when her own emotional balance is wavering. The ability to do so is a pivotal skill in the process of growing up.

Help Innies Express Their Feelings

One tool that can help your introverted child learn to express and value his feelings is called "reflective listening." You can listen to him describe his feelings and, like a mirror, reflect back what he is expressing. Do this with both pleasant and unpleasant emotions. Acknowledging and restating his thoughts and emotions will help your child "see" what he is feeling. He can correct you if you didn't quite get it or catch every nuance. The feelings take on a new clarity, and he can now learn to cope with them.

The process also builds trust between you and your child. Feeling understood is a very powerful experience, particularly for someone who may be focused on the internal. Innies are sensitive and perceptive about how you respond to what they say. As you become more comfortable with his feelings (and, as often happens when you express emotion, with your own feelings), you will see him open up. He will also, over time, have greater control over his feelings and his behavior.

Steps To Reflective Listening:
1. Be accepting and respectful: All feelings are okay.
   "I know you are so mad at your sister."
   • Acknowledge limits on behavior.
   "But you can't grab the truck out of her hands."
   • Listen and pay close attention to what she is saying. Maintain good eye contact. Don't interrupt.
   "I know she took your truck without asking."

2. Acknowledge her feelings without judgment by responding in neutral ways.
   "I see. And then what happened?"

- Reflect what she is saying and feeling.
  "It sounds as if you feel like she doesn't listen to you and that you are helpless to protect your toys from her."
- Name her feelings.
  "That sounds so frustrating. She didn't even ask you if she could borrow it."

3. Acknowledge her needs and wishes. Problem-solve only after feelings have been acknowledged.
  "Do you want me to help you talk to Tiffany about taking your toys without asking?"

Weathering Relationship Upsets

All relationships have ups and downs and disagreements that need repair. When you provide a model for repairing hurt or angry feelings, innies learn that relationships have bumps in them, and that it's okay. "I'm sorry I was grumpy yesterday. I snapped at you, and the reason was my being frustrated that I'm late with my project at work. I'm sorry." All children get angry with their parents, and all parents get angry with their children. It's painful when your child says hurtful things to you, but it builds a stronger relationship when he feels safe enough to express those negative feelings. You don't have to agree. Yet, if you listen and understand his viewpoint, he will learn that he can be truthful and assertive.

Innies may not notice that they are angry for a while. And they dread the energy outlay of fighting, so they tend to hold in angry feelings. They're more likely to withdraw then to engage in arguments.

Innies need to practice dealing with conflict in a safe environment. Otherwise they can't use their anger to protect them in the outside world. Listening to your child's upsets and helping her to repair disagreements gives her important relational tools. Repairing doesn't necessarily mean that she gets her way. It is acknowledging her view, apologizing if you did something hurtful, explaining a misunderstanding and/or deciding how to negotiate a limit. ("I know you want to stay up as late as your cousin Liz. I'm afraid you need to hit the hay earlier than she does. Did you think because we had company tonight that you might be able to stay up later? I'm sorry about the confusion. What if we ask Liz to read you a story before you go to bed?") Listening and negotiating misunderstandings shows your innie how to work through conflicts. It also encourages her to speak up in the world. And you are modeling how to apologize, a skill that is crucial in relationships.

If Your Innie Is Upset
DON'T:
• Try to reason with him.
• Contradict him.
• Defend yourself or others.
• Minimize or dismiss her concerns.

DO:
• Validate her concern.
• Try to see the situation from her point of view.
• Make a date to discuss the issue again.
• Apologize for hurt feelings and misunderstandings.

Sometimes your innie just won't like a rule you make or a limit you set. Just let her vent.

Stop-Sign Emotions

Shame and guilt are emotions that come easily to innies. As I discussed in Chapter 2, their side of the nervous system houses these feelings. These are stop-sign emotions that serve to shut children down. Without them, they wouldn't know right from wrong. When used sparingly, they help to socialize kids. Shame says, "Stop doing that." Guilt says, "You did something wrong, and you need to make amends."

Outies usually need more vigorous signs to stop their behavior. Innies only need a hint to inhibit them (unless they have been treated too harshly or they have learned to ignore you). If not overused, shame and guilt lead to self-discovery and growth. However, harmful shame makes kids feel horrible about who they are. They feel humiliated and angry. Harmful guilt makes kids feel as though everything were their fault. Ideally, these stop signs serve as a moral reality check but not a constant source of anxiety and self-abasement.

Here's how to distinguish between useful and detrimental inhibiting emotions:

Beneficial Shame
- *Dad won't like me taking his camera without asking.*
- *I'm not happy with my performance; I can do better.*
- *Some things are right to do, and others are wrong.*
- *I want to help my family get along better.*

Harmful Shame
- *I am a rotten person.*
- *I can't do anything right.*
- *I hate everyone.*
- *People are no good.*
- *I can't do anything. I'm helpless and hopeless.*

Beneficial Guilt
- *I did something wrong; I need to apologize.*
- *I need to make it up to my friend.*
- *I feel bad about what I did.*

Harmful Guilt
- *It is my fault that Mom feels bad.*
- *I should never say anything that upsets my dad.*
- *Problems are usually my fault.*

Daniel Goleman, Ph.D., popularized and explained the concept of a sophisticated ability to know one's own emotions and empathize with others' feelings. He integrated a wide variety of research on the topic, and in 1995 published his book entitled *Emotional Intelligence,* which provided a name for a kind of psychological intuition and perceptiveness readers could recognize. Innies are hardwired to have emotional intelligence. But they can't develop it without help from their parents to name and validate their feelings and to remind them that they have delayed emotional reactions. When introverted children's emotions are reflected back to them, they can use this natural resource to guide their decisions, maintain long-term relationships, enrich their daily experiences, notice what sparks their interest, and keep their motivation on track. Without their emotional signaling system, innies can be flooded by their feelings, become overwhelmed, and then shut down.

With the emotional foundation you provide and your continued attention to the world of emotion, you can help your child develop his natural ability to self-reflect, learn to handle his feelings, respond appropriately to stress, and harness his ample intellectual gifts.

The Heart of the Matter

- *Innies build their confidence from a deep bond with you.*
- *Emotions organize and integrate all areas of your innie's brain.*
- *Encourage your innie to tune into her emotional compass.*

CHAPTER 5

The Care and Feeding of Innies

Predictable Routines Energize Innies So They Can Flourish

"The environment is the extended body. It must be peaceful."

—Deepak Chopra

In the previous chapter, we talked about the big picture issues—parenting your introverted child in a way that enhances his confidence and self-esteem and helps you build a strong, lasting bond with him. In this chapter and the next, we'll look at ways to meet the everyday challenges of life with an innie: setting up routines, keeping him fed, dealing with discipline, and the like. We'll look at ways you can use your knowledge of your child's temperament to guide you through the innumerable family decisions you confront day in, day out. For example, you'll learn how to gauge your child's energy status and slip in little breaks that allow him to regroup. It's all part of the nitty-gritty of raising children today: negotiating the realm of new media; claiming private spaces; finding safe and wholesome ways to play.

Introvert-Friendly Routines

*"A garden dies quickly without a loving
gardener to keep it alive."*—May Sarton

Home routines provide the frame for family life, and innies in particular thrive on routines. Knowing what's coming reduces their energy consumption and, when necessary, eases them into extroverting. Creating regular morning, after-school, and evening schedules shape a predictable innie-friendly world where rules are known and surprises kept to a minimum. She knows: "I go to bed at eight on school nights and nine on the weekends." Make a note of her liveliest time of day and her slowest. (Innies are often sluggish in the morning, and it can take a while for them to get going.) Notice what conditions seem to bring out the best in your child as well as the conditions that bring out the worst. You can organize her day around the need for structure, private time, and the inevitable dips and peaks in energy.

If your innie's routine is disrupted, he may drag his heels, become disoriented, or pitch a fit. Make an effort to keep things consistent whenever you can, and, when there's a change in routine, explain it clearly: "Kathleen is picking you up from school today. But you'll still have your piano lesson, like you usually do on Tuesdays." Alternatively, let your innie assume a role that helps maintain a sense of continuity: "Dad is going out of town on business in two days. How about you and I make a card to stick in his suitcase?" Incidentally, the preference for a calm environment and predictable schedule is unlikely to change as your innie gets older. It goes with the temperament!

Discuss all changes and transitions in advance. If your child is going to sleep at someone else's house, have her try out the sleeping bag beforehand. A younger innie can sleep at home in her travel crib before trying it out at a relative's home. Often innies need to revise the image that they hold in their head before they can adapt to something new. "We are going to the park," you say. Who could complain about that? Well, be sure that your innie is picturing the same park you are, or else there could be a meltdown. As your child gets a bit older, you can broaden your repertoire and use other tools like the kitchen timer, calendars, and stickers to prepare her for upcoming events and changes. "The school fair is on Saturday. Let's put a sticker on the calendar." Letting her affix the sticker helps settle it in her mind and gives her a sense of being an active participant as opposed to feeling that events merely "happen" to her. I used to say to my daughters, "In one Flintstone"—meaning a half-hour episode—"it will be time to go." We had agreed that one cartoon unit was fair warning.

Learning New Skills

Another kind of transition that shakes up routine is the learning of a new skill; a big accomplishment invariably brings about a big change. Innies need special attention to their pacing when they take a developmental leap. For instance, when a child is edging toward a major advance such as learning to walk, he may stop talking or his ability to talk may regress. His level of speech will return as soon as he becomes steady on his feet.

As children grow, they usually need to have a new skill under their belt before tackling another one. This is particularly true of introverts, because they integrate more complexity at one time and they are using more energy to do it. If your innie is concentrating on learning to read, he may not be able to learn to ride a two-wheeler at the same time. As soon as the new skill is automatic, he will be ready for another challenge. Assure your child that new skills improve with practice. And remember to anticipate that changes in routine, learning new skills, and facing unfamiliar events will require lots of energy. Help your innie be prepared and be sure her energy reserves have been refilled.

When faced with a significant new challenge, an innie will probably drag his feet. This is the introvert's way of modulating the stimulation and regulating how much new information he has to

Help Create an Innie Haven

Here are a few ways to create some private time and space for your innie:

- Develop a coming home ritual: perhaps it will include picking up the mail, changing clothes, fixing a snack, or sitting and reflecting for ten minutes as a way of relaxing and breathing in home.

- Discuss your home with your child. What are his thoughts and feelings about it? Help him define for himself what makes an ideal sanctuary for him.

- Ask him what he likes or doesn't like about his bedroom. How would he create his ideal bedroom?

- Make sure your child has a quiet place for homework. She may want to be near you if it's quiet. Be sure she has an interruption-free zone.

- If he shares a bedroom, build a dividing wall (inexpensive lattice, or curtains sold to divide rooms, will do the trick) or create a private alcove. Negotiate private time for innies when they can be in their

process. Don't push. Give him the time he needs. Let him watch—innies learn by observing. Ask him what he notices that interests him, and present him with opportunities to take the next step. Let's say children are going down a slide, something your child has never done. Ask him when he's ready to join in. If he demurs, ask if he would like you to go down it with him first. The more your innie is allowed to ease into new situations and the more routes you provide for entrance, the more easily he will be able to adapt. Doing something with you first can be like a trial run.

Whenever possible, break the learning of new skills into bite-sized bits and take an easy pace. This uses less energy, allows for breaks, and enables your child to build confidence as she sees her progress. Also, innies perform better when they are less pressured. For example, shared room alone for private time, and allow no interruptions. Make a sign for the door: CHILLING—WILL EMERGE WHEN REALLY COOL.

- Be sure your introverted middle schooler or teen has privacy. Allow innies to shut their door. Require all family members to knock when a door is closed. I saw an innie teen in my practice who had her own room with a communal TV in it. Her three siblings were allowed to come in and watch TV whenever they wanted. She and I negotiated with her parents to allow her sibs only limited TV viewing when she was at her after-school job.

- Let your innie teen decorate his room according to his own taste. It's a safe, easy, and painless way to give your innie autonomy. Many innies are highly visual and are soothed and regenerated by beauty. Beauty is in the eye of the beholder, of course. One innie who wants to be an astronomer painted her room black and scattered glowing stars around the ceiling.

Morgan had to memorize the poem "The Midnight Ride of Paul Revere" to recite in front of her class. She practiced the poem in quarters while looking at a picture of trees. For two nights she rehearsed a quarter of the poem by saying it out loud for ten minutes right before bed. Every two days she added a new section, until two days before the performance, when she practiced the whole thing. (Remember, innies store what happens during the day into their long-term memory while sleeping at night. Looking at a picture helps them store information into their visual memory—which is easier to retrieve.)

Renewable Private Spaces

Innies are notoriously protective of their space. The introvert's experience of space goes beyond the notion of having her own room or a place to store her things. Rather, innies are highly sensitive about closeness and proximity. "Don't touch my seat, and don't look out my car window," Terri, a little innie, said to her sister Maggie on a car trip. And what physical contact innies can tolerate alters with their moods. They can run up and hug you one day and pull away from physical touch another. One afternoon my innie granddaughter, Emily, wasn't feeling well, and I sat next to her on the sofa. She started to slide my arm around her. Then she stopped herself and drew away. Later, when she became accustomed to me sitting near her, she leaned against me. Indeed, there are times when innies feel that even someone just looking at them is intruding on their space.

Predictably, home is profoundly important to introverted children. When her mother pulls into the driveway of their blue Cape Cod house, Emily throws up her arms and yells, "Home!" In that one enthusiastic utterance, she is expressing at once her joy at returning to her familiar retreat, her relief that a busy outing is over, and the proprietary sense that the house is *hers*.

Innies need to feel a sense of security and safety at home. They are deeply affected by their surroundings and do best when home is harmonious, tidy, quiet, airy, and filled with pleasing scents, comfy furniture, good lighting, soothing colors, and views of the outdoors.

While they enjoy being around family, innies also need a place of their own where they can keep energy demands to a minimum and refuel. If he doesn't have his own room, your innie could claim a certain nook where he is protected from the incursions of siblings or other family members. Innies love cozy spots like a playhouse, the storage space under the stairs, a tree house, a tent pitched in a bedroom, an attic, a corner of the porch, or any other small, discrete space. One little innie I know has a pink fabric playhouse cottage in her bedroom. She pops in and out of it all day long—taking little recharging breaks. A tween innie I know has a special armchair where he curls up to read.

How to Eat Like an Innie

"Talk to your children while they are eating; what you say will stay even after you are gone."—Nez Percé saying

Innies must stay fueled to keep their energy levels high. Keeping up with the demands of an extroverted world is demanding enough without adding the weariness that comes from being hungry into the equation. Our culture has its "three square meals" rule, but innies require a constant caloric inflow throughout the day.

When it comes to behavioral issues, parents tend to look at any number of possible causes before considering nutrition. I often raise questions about eating with parents because I find hunger is the most common cause of meltdowns—in innies of *all* ages.

Many innies are picky eaters. I was a picky eater, and my innie grandson is a picky eater. Family lore has it that his innie father was a picky eater. We have all survived so far; none of us have starved to death. But pickiness makes eating a fertile ground for power struggles. Don't get pulled into one. Introduce a couple of new items each week and don't make a big deal of it. If she eats it, great. If not, move on. She may like it later. Innies may respond well to explanations about why their bodies need food and water. As your child grows older, you can show him books about the body and explain why the rest-and-digest side of the nervous system needs fuel to burn.

Food for Thought
- Know that not all innies love to eat, and they often eat slowly.
- Read children's nutrition books with your innie and talk about why certain foods are important for energy to play and work.
- Teach your child to notice the feeling of hunger and low blood sugar.
- Be aware that innies may be more sensitive to different smells and tastes.

Crash and Burn

Hypoglycemia is a medical condition that has drifted in and out of fashion. It is often minimized by physicians. But it is a real problem for many innies, especially in the empty-calorie world of high sugar and simple carbohydrates that we live in today. Innie children *must* have protein and complex carbohydrates, and their tanks need to be constantly topped off. If children don't have enough of the right kinds of foods, their energy plummets, glucose dips, and oxygen traveling to the brain is depleted. In short, they crash and burn.

I know exactly what this feels like. It can happen without warning. It feels as if all the life force has plunged to your feet. Suddenly, your body is *soooo* heavy. Your head is fuzzy. You have to sit down. When this happens to your innie, she loses energy, gets droopy, and can't think or learn. What causes this? Blood sugar zooms up if we eat too much sugar and carbs and then drops like a rock. Or, it can occur just because we have run out of food to metabolize, like Audrey, the alien plant in the movie *Little Shop of Horrors*. And like Audrey's, the innie's system is always saying, "Feed me, feed me." The best way to maintain blood sugar levels is by eating frequently and consuming protein and complex carbohydrates together— for example, putting nuts on your oatmeal and using whole grain bread for turkey sandwiches, etc. If you give your child a sweet, make sure that she has eaten protein beforehand, or that she has some with it.

- Serve good healthy food early in the day, as innies tend to eat better then.
- Keep healthy snacks within reach; innies are usually grazers.
- Don't get into a power match over food. Save her meal or snack and if she doesn't eat it, remove it without comment. Try again with a healthy choice later. Innies can withdraw and become stubborn when they feel pushed.
- Never use food as a reward or punishment.

Some of the common symptoms of hypoglycemia include: feeling awful after eating, fatigue, looking pale, insomnia, agitation, mood swings, depression, sweating, heart palpitations, headaches, lack of motivation, dizziness, and irritability. If it's extreme, someone can tremble, throw up, or faint.

How to Battle Low Blood Sugar:

- Grazing, or eating small meals all day. (I usually finish breakfast by about lunchtime.)
- Eating protein and complex carbs first thing in the morning.
- Carrying protein snacks (nuts, cheese and crackers, protein bars).
- Reducing intake of sugar and simple carbohydrates.
- Eating sweets and carbs *with* or *after* protein.
- Teaching your child to gauge how he feels so that he will learn to manage his sugar level (and it doesn't become a power struggle with you).
- Explaining to your child that she may need to eat when she doesn't feel hungry.

For more information, contact the Hypoglycemia Support Foundation, www.hypoglycemia.org.

Eating Out

Innies often lose their appetites in crowded or noisy restaurants. The commotion, unfamiliar food, the rush or the wait affect their ability to take in food. They may eat better at home, having small snacks or being able to nibble finger foods at meals. Don't expect your innie to be a big eater in any crowded situation like a family celebration. It may work better to feed him at home first, and when you're out, let him snack off your plate or just have a small dish.

Off to Sleep

"The baby's temperament shapes her patterns of sleeping and waking from the start."—T. Berry Brazelton, M.D.

Many children I see in my practice don't get enough sleep. I find that if innies don't get at least eight hours of sleep each night, they won't recharge energy. And they will have more difficulty storing what they have learned during the day into their long-term memory. Since innies predominate on the rest-and-digest side of the nervous system, they need more rest than outies. Teens in particular need plenty of rest—just when they're least inclined to take it.

Test-Drive the Opposite System

Innies and outies both need to use the nondominant side of their nervous systems. For instance, exercising gives innies energy from the outie side of the nervous system. Sleep, on the other hand, uses the innie side of the nervous system, and it restores outies in many ways: emotional, cognitive, physical healing, proper digestion, and other conserving functions.

Sleep is an ongoing challenge throughout life for introverted children. Acetylcholine is our major neurotransmitter, and, in conjunction with other chemicals, it switches dream and alert cycles on and off. Acetylcholine ebbs and flows like all neurotransmitters, and, since innies are sensitive to its changes, it impacts their sleep cycles. Innies need the right amount to go to dreamland—and stay there. If too much acetylcholine is released, it causes sleepiness. And if an innie's fight-and-flight mechanism has been activated, he can have trouble calming down from the buzzing, anxiety-producing chemicals. Innies' active minds can be hard to switch off.

Another reason sleep may not come easily is that it also represents a central psychological issue: separation from parents. Sleep can trigger lots of fears, especially in younger children. As a result, many kids have trouble falling or staying asleep. A child needs to achieve the ability to soothe herself back to sleep when she wakes up—which happens at least four or five times a night. The ability to sleep through the night is an accomplishment that involves the maturity of the child's nervous system.

Giving Your Innie a Restful Retreat

- At each age range, set an appropriate bedtime that your child knows and can predict.
- Develop bedtime rituals: singing, rocking, reading, rhymes, and *short* quiet games. For older kids, reading or quiet talking.
- Remember that at each new stage of a child's development, sleep patterns usually change. Expect sleep disruptions during stressful periods, new experiences, family changes, and during touch points in a child's development. Gently ease your child into putting himself back to sleep.
- Innies can wake up if they are hungry or too hot or cold. Studies show that innies sleep better if their hands and/or feet are covered at night. Christopher, my innie grandson, wore his Big Bird slippers to bed every night until he was about three.
- Encourage your innie to take something comforting, like a blanket or stuffed animal, to bed to hold. As innies grow older, they may need gentle music to get out of their busy minds. Extroverts usually need all outside stimuli reduced.
- Respond to your child's fears calmly and with respect. Help your child look for monsters in dark corners or under the bed. I used to sweep a baseball bat beneath my daughter's bed and wave it in her closet to clear out those pesky gremlins.
- Make sure that bedtime doesn't get dragged out. Two requests—and that's it. For younger kids, make some "Bedtime Request" coupons that read: "Drink of Water," "Go to the Bathroom," or "Blow Me a Kiss." Give your child two a night and then say, "Oh no. You already used up your two coupons. Night, night."

Delicate Discipline

"Without discipline, there's no life at all."
—*Katharine Hepburn*

Discipline prepares children to be independent adults. It's not always comfortable—for either of you—but it's necessary. A parent has but a short window of opportunity in which to influence a child. Interestingly, the number-one way that children learn about discipline is through observing their parents' behavior; kids respond more to what you *do* than what you *say*. During the short time span you have with your children, you can model self-control, make good choices, and think independently while also respecting authority. You can demonstrate one of life's most important lessons: that responsibility is the price of independence. In *Gifts Differing*, Isabel Myers highlights the importance of *self*-discipline, which she calls good judgment: "the ability to choose the better alternative and act accordingly." If these building blocks aren't established early, it makes life harder as the child grows up.

Introverted children have hardwiring built in for self-discipline. They can say no to themselves, they evaluate situations, and, as they pause to think before acting, they naturally make choices about their behavior. If they aren't treated badly, it's easy for them to develop self-discipline. They only need delicate discipline to guide them in the right direction.

The Discipline Continuum

The degree to which children are disciplined runs the gamut. On one end of the continuum are children who lack discipline altogether. Without discipline, children don't have to face the consequences of their actions. As a result, they don't learn to connect their own choices and actions to what happens in their own lives. The message they get is that everything they do is acceptable.

If something goes wrong, they may blame others for their problems. On the other side of the scale are children who are *over*disciplined. Too much discipline and the wind gets taken out of a child's sails. She lacks confidence and may feel like a failure. She gives up easily.

Positive discipline means maintaining a good balance between not too much and not too little. Fortunately, for you as a parent, introverted children tend to be amenable to discipline. Innies are wired so as to put the brakes on their behavior. As they take their time before acting and speaking, they rarely speak or act impulsively. Particularly in comparison to other children, they understand consequence. They are observant and perceptive about what's going on around them. They have a strong, often precocious, sense of morality. That said, they're still children and do need to test their boundaries from time to time. They will make errors of judgment. And they are very strong willed.

Discipline is quite different for innies and outies. Innies' basic hardwiring is built to inhibit their behavior. Innies usually want to please their parents, and they feel shame and guilt easily. Outies are wired to let their "fur fly." They want outside approval but not always from their parents. If outies don't receive enough stimulation they may get into mischief to stir up some excitement. They may actually enjoy conflict because the stimulation is exciting for them. Since outies can be impulsive, they need firm, consistent limits. They aren't as impacted by shame and guilt as introverted children are.

Most innies only need encouragement, support, and a few well-chosen limits. Usually just explaining to an innie does the trick. "Hon, I have a headache, could you take a break from your electric guitar for a bit tonight?" They tend to be able to adjust easily to others (the why of this is explained in Chapter 2) and naturally restrict themselves without feeling resentful. They usually need more help with the opposite behaviors—to disagree or take risks.

Two common problems innies have is taking on too much responsibility and easily feeling guilty, even for things that aren't their fault or over which they have no control. I don't know how many innies have told me that if a teacher reported that an item was missing from the classroom they would feel guilty—while knowing full well that they didn't take it. This is another reason to be thoughtful and delicate with your discipline.

Keep an eye out for your innie taking too much responsibility for an accident, for instance. If she becomes guilt-ridden about a mishap, she may not be able to let herself off the hook without your help. For instance, if she accidentally stepped on her dog's foot, she may be very upset and angry with herself. She doesn't need more harsh words or any discipline. She will be more careful in the future. If a child isn't remorseful or upset when he or she hurts a pet or another child, then you need to apply some discipline. Set limits that will guide your child, not necessarily constrain or discourage her. It can be a delicate balance.

Built-in Stop Signs

Since innies are naturally inhibited and can imagine the future consequences of their actions, they are often reluctant to engage in destructive behaviors like driving fast, shoplifting, or other illegal activities. This is a good thing. They also feel uncomfortable with too many "jolt juice" chemicals released by risky behavior surging through their veins. Outies don't have the same built-in stop signs, and they enjoy the surging of those exciting chemicals. This is why they may not give a second thought to doing something daring, or, on the far end, even illegal. So although the downside of innies' behavior might be too much compliance, the upside is that they are actually more sensible than extroverts about risky behavior. Innies with good self-esteem who have heard more encouraging than critical words are more likely to conform when appropriate—a quality in short supply in today's world—and to stand up for themselves when necessary. They can follow award-winning actress Helen Hunt's example; she refers to herself as a "daring introvert." She says she may hang back at times, but she uses her chutzpah when she needs to leave her comfort zone behind.

Remember that trusting relationships are central to building an introverted child's self-confidence. Unless he learns that relationships are valuable and enjoyable, an introverted child may tend to stay in his shell. A sure way to end up with an overly shy and/or insecure introverted child is to treat him harshly—and that includes disciplining him too harshly. Physical punishment or other demeaning means of punishment teach children that aggression solves problems. Every child development study out there shows that hitting, shaming, spanking, teasing, or comparing children are poisonous to their growth. Moreover, that kind of discipline doesn't even work. Parenting is tough; everyone gets testy at times. But if you often have trouble with your temper, read up on the topic and consider taking an anger management course.

Controlling vs. Cooperating

Many parents think they need to have power and control over a child's behavior. They may not be conscious of this, but power and control wears many guises: blaming, commanding, lecturing, making comparisons, using sarcasm, acting the martyr, and making threats.

The opposite of control is cooperation, where both parent and child drop their claim on power and control. The best way for a parent to win a child's cooperation is to send him the message that he is capable. Cooperating with the family reinforces that sense of competence. This, in turn, builds self-esteem and confidence in his ability to contribute and deal with others.

Even when you know the value of cooperation and the futility of trying to control a child, it's still difficult not to get drawn into a power match. First of all, children are hardwired to flex their autonomy muscles at certain ages. We all know about the "terrible twos," but four and a half is a less well-known flexing period. Also, ages six, eight, thirteen, and seventeen will truly test your parenting skills. In phases like these in particular, struggles for control flare up quite easily. And while the introverted child may *seem* mild-mannered, he likes to do things *his* way. It's that old, defiant drummer he's marching to. He's also more likely to become recalcitrant when he feels helpless, overwhelmed, angry, or frightened. However, it takes two to tangle. As the parent, you can learn not to take the bait.

How to Keep Above the Fray

- *Remember that you are the adult.* Even if you don't feel like it, take yourself out of the power struggle. Stop arguing. If a power struggle has developed, it means you aren't acknowledging your child's feelings and viewpoint. Step back and take a deep breath. Think about what is going on and ask, "Why are we deadlocked?"
- *Cool off.* Take another deep breath and look at the big picture. Ask yourself, "Why can't I let go?" Your child is depending on you to keep a level head.
- *Think about your next move.* Focus on what you will do, not on what you are trying to get your child to do.
- *Put what's happening in perspective.* "I know you are mad and frustrated, but I'm sorry—there's no more dessert tonight. Hey, but guess what? Tomorrow after dinner—another dessert!"

Making the Switch to Cooperation

- *Articulate the problem.* "We can't seem to get out of the door on time in the morning. The result is that I'm cranky and you are late for school and upset."
- *Ask your innie to help find solutions.* "What do you think are some possible ways to speed things up? Let's see what we might be able to do." If he can't come up with any suggestions, prompt him with some of your ideas. In this instance they might include getting up earlier, laying out clothes ahead of time, fixing lunch and breakfast the night before, and not turning on the TV in the morning.
- *Evaluate how things are going in a few days.* Make it clear that you're in this together.
- *Send your innie a note.* "Hey, I think we're doing better. We were on time three days in a row!"

Mastering (Innie-Style) Meltdowns

"Children aren't happy with nothing to ignore,
and that's what parents were created for."
—*Ogden Nash*

All children go through certain ages (like "the terrible twos") and stages (growth spurts) where they melt down more easily than at other times. Around the age of four or five, many innies who have been easy, even as two-year-olds, start to have stronger and more clear-cut wants that should be addressed. At that point, they may try begging, whining, withdrawing, and refusing to speak to you when things don't go their way. Then there are just plain bad days. Your child doesn't feel well, he wants his way, he feels backed into a corner, or he is flooded with feelings . . . and the result is a full-fledged temper tantrum. Outies tend to externalize, and blame or get angry with someone—probably most often a parent—for their troubles. Innies tend to *in*ternalize, so they're more likely to withdraw, go limp, or tune you out rather than pitch a fit—but it can happen.

These are the moments that try parents' souls. When a child is in the throes of a tantrum, it seems that anything you do or say simply escalates the crisis. When tempers flare, take a little break—a kind of momentary time-out to calm yourself. Then you can put on your sleuthing hat and try to pin down the culprit. Innies are most likely to succumb to flare-ups when they are overscheduled, overstimulated, tired, or hungry. Ask yourself, was something too much (i.e., too much visual "stim," too many people around, too much change, too much sugar)? Was something too little (i.e., too little rest, low blood sugar, not enough recharging time)? Acknowledge your child's feelings. You can say, "I know you want that toy, but I'm not going to buy it." No excuses, exceptions, or explanations. Only offer alternatives *after* he calms down. Take a few deep breaths. This too shall pass. Yes, your child will grow up.

If you have been out and about for a while and your innie is bored, tired, hungry, hot/cold, overwhelmed by stimuli, or feeling confined, she may start squirming, fussing, demanding toys or a snack, or whining in an ear-splitting pitch. Of course it's best not to let things get that far, but now that it has, your best bet is distraction. Make a silly face, sing a song, point out something of interest with great enthusiasm. If at all possible, leave, especially if you're in a noisy, public place. Keep focused on your child and ignore any prying, disapproving stares. Calm your own temper and jettison any embarrassment you may feel. Every parent has dealt with a fussy child. Next time, stop conflagrations before they happen by anticipating how long your child can shop, walk without a stroller, or go without eating, and plan your outing accordingly.

Big-Kid Attitude

Older innies can present their own special brand of meltdowns. Sometimes innies have been easy children, and when their hormones start surging it's a shock. It may seem like some moody alien has invaded your formerly sweet child's body. Where did your cutie-pie go? It can be quite a loss. Your tween begins to give you what I called my daughter's "fish eye" (a cold stare), sulk, stop speaking to you, give you clipped one-word responses in an irritated tone, roll her eyes behind your back, and get a "tude" (that's a bad attitude, for the uninitiated). Charming . . .

Luckily, I have lived long enough to see my formerly fish-eyed daughter get the same cold stare from her own tween. Choose which battles to take on as your innie teen goes through these irritating stages. Remember that finding parents "oh so annoying, stupid, silly, and dumb" has a purpose. Tweens and teens are preparing for their scary upcoming leap from the nest. It helps them to leave if they can knock you off your pedestal. They are trying to achieve autonomy and independence. But it's also okay to say, "Hey, cool your jets." "Rewind that response and spit out a friendlier one." "Go back into your room and come out when the 'tude is gone." A sense of humor is your best ally during these stages.

I am now working with a very sulky introverted teen named Rachael. Her mother has reacted to normal "teen-tude" by becoming hurt and angry. "She was such a sweet child," her mom says wistfully. So now Rachael, driven by normal growing pains, has dug in her heels. The battle for autonomy is on, and so far, Rachael is winning. She's very withdrawn. She's rude to her mother. She stares at me with cold eyes. I have encouraged her mom not to take her daughter's budding independence personally. It doesn't mean she hasn't been a good parent—in fact, the opposite. Rachael is showing normal behavior for a teen. I have talked to Rachael about her feelings—they are normal. It's developmentally correct that she's sick of her parents. The positive result of acknowledging these feelings is that mother and daughter are getting along much better.

The Heart of the Matter

- *Innies flourish in a home that is safe, structured, and predictable.*
- *Routine increases your innie's ability to conserve and reserve his energy.*
- *Inviting innies to cooperate promotes self-competence.*

CHAPTER 6

Play, Conversation, and the Art of Relaxation

Encourage Daily Chats, Creative Play, Decision-Making Steps, and Stress-Busting Skills

"Perhaps imagination is only intelligence having fun."

—George Scialabba

Sometimes adults see play as frivolous—what your child does *after* he finishes his homework, music lessons, and his other scheduled activities. But play is the *work* of childhood. Play is how kids learn, reduce stress, explore, imagine, and try out roles and social behaviors. Contemporary American culture devalues play and overvalues achievement in children. So many children today aren't getting enough authentic, unstructured play with parents and friends. Real play—in my book, anyway—involves dirt, water, trees, parks, playgrounds, paints, stacking blocks, and pretending. Play is the freedom to build and create, to ask "What if . . . ?" and to act "as if" in a kid-safe environment.

With their rich interior lives, innies in particular need the roominess play provides to practice interacting with things, people, and new concepts before they use them in the real world. Through play innies can test out their ideas, expand their language skills, work out emotional conflicts, practice new social behaviors, and learn to solve problems. For innies' play is usually a low-fuel-consuming activity that gives them "hap hits." It teaches innies that interacting with the outside world is fun, while allowing them to soothe themselves with comforting, predictable rituals they create themselves. Innies concentrate and become fully engaged in their play so they tend to learn a great deal from it.

Best Bets for Playing

Appropriate play is crucial to brain development. By nature, right-brained innies may be particularly playful, but all children's brains develop through play. Innies need substantial mind food, not empty calories—they need *enriching* play. Leading brain researcher Antonio Demasio has expressed concern about the fact that we are raising children with faster and faster-thinking left brains without integrating the emotional and moral centers in the right brain. As a result, the logical left brain is overused, and the more associative right brain is underused. Many children today are playing fast-paced, aggressive, goal-oriented electronic games on their Game Boys, computers, or TVs, along with other battery-operated toys with built-in responses. Such games and toys require no human interaction and little imagination. Studies show that dopamine overstimulation in the left brain builds rigid brain pathways that teach kids to expect quick rewards and zaps of powerful "hap hits." This increases impulsiveness. It also trains children to go for the quick source of stimulation and satisfaction rather than attempt anything where the rewards come more slowly. (For more on how to manage video games, see page 121.)

Children do better with toys and activities that offer them the freedom to explore, imagine, build, and observe. To this end, I suggest

Playing with Your Child

When you play with your child, you are strengthening your emotional bond. It's a good way to spend time together. But not all play styles are equal. Researchers have found that children demonstrate less creativity when parents direct the play or make the rules. Children, especially innies, act out their internal lives when given room to play spontaneously. They'll be thrilled to have your company, but they don't need you to do everything for them!

DO:

- Offer some guidance on which materials to use. "Shall we see what we can do with the blocks now?"
- Ask open-ended questions. "Your building looks cool. What are you making?"
- Allow your child to direct the play. Follow his lead.

DON'T:

- Make specific suggestions, like: "Let's use those blocks to make a bridge."
- Guess what she is making; she may feel judged or pressured.
- Give orders or take charge of the play.

choosing open-ended playthings and activities, such as blocks and other construction toys, dolls, and art supplies. The great outdoors also offers children myriad opportunities to use their imagination—rocks, sticks, leaves, and flowers can all be turned into toys, and kids can derive hours of pleasure from watching bugs and animals. Most innies find that nature restores their energy, and they tend to seek it out. It can be slow-paced and a nourishing and subtle teacher. I remember a valuable lesson I learned about life when my friend Sharon and I built a fort out of bamboo and old chunks of wood in the river bottom near our homes. We had a terrific rainstorm and, when Sharon and I went to check on the fort, we saw that every last stick had been swept away. I remember feeling awed by the power of nature. We lamented our loss and then rebuilt our fort on higher ground. As I have mentioned, innies' brains flash back and rewind their experiences. During this review, innies can apply the lessons learned. I never forgot the destructive power and the resilience nature showed me in that river bottom. Remembering this helped me later in life to rebuild after losing homes in two major earthquakes and a fire.

Play provides a fresh viewpoint, which develops a child's social and cognitive skills. Play also provides room to succeed or fail in safety. With play, innies are protected from consequences as they practice for real life. Innies like to be prepared; they don't like to be caught unawares. An innie's preplanning part of the brain thinks through and imagines alternatives. Rehearsing uses less energy *and* prepares a child for action in the real world.

An Innie Playbook

Tailoring play for innies develops their unique talents. Innies can be overwhelmed by too many supplies, toys, or playmates. On the other hand, they can be underwhelmed by toys that don't require thinking, creativity, or problem solving. Here are a few tips:

- Keep some toys in the closet and rotate them so that there are always new things to try but never too many at once.
- Select basic toys, such as stuffed animals, Legos, tea sets, trucks, Play-Doh, crayons, and paper that leave room for the imagination. Innies tend to be creative, and abstract thinking comes easily to them. Innies can use these basic toys, such as building blocks, to replicate in the real world any idea they come up with internally.

- Innies like one-on-one play. Provide your child with opportunities for playing with another child or an adult with whom he's comfortable.
- Encourage her observing skills. The natural ability to perceive what others don't notice is one of the greatest advantages innies possess. Later in life many innies will use this ability in their careers as writers, scientists, psychologists, or teachers, to name but a few jobs requiring observation skills. Give your child a disposable camera or spy toys, and play games like charades and Guess Who?
- Innies find water play soothing. Give your child plenty of bath toys, funnels, sponges, pitchers, pouring cups, and tub appliqués. Finger paints and watercolors are also favorites.
- Find toys that fit your innie's particular interests, whether animals, soldiers, woodworking, music, or dolls.
- Acting in plays, writing songs and stories, artwork, ceramics, and doing craft projects are ways tweens and teens play. Learning card, and other, games teaches valuable social skills such as winning and losing and playing by the rules.

Those Electronic Houseguests

*"I find TV very educational. Every time someone switches it on,
I go into another room and read a book."—Groucho Marx*

There are several things to consider when thinking about children and the media. (By media I mean any TV programs, DVDs, videos, radio, newspapers, magazines, video games, computer games, or the Internet.) One is the content, another is the medium itself, and a third is what your child is missing out on while she is involved with the media. You needn't be fearful of the media. It's part of our world, and there is a place for what it offers. Innies can

Screens, Screens Everywhere

Parents these days are concerned about electronic media's influence on their kids, particularly since it seems to be everywhere. While it certainly has some downsides, there are some upsides as well. The key is to limit screen time and to make sure your kids discuss what they are seeing with you. For instance, encourage them to use their judgment skills to assess how advertisers try to manipulate them.

Negative Aspects of Electronic Media:

• It's mesmerizing, addictive, and overstimulating.

• It reduces imagination and creativity.

• It shortens one's attention span.

• It reduces time for reading and other activities.

Positive Aspects of Electronic Media:

• It takes innies out of their active minds.

• It relaxes them.

• It sometimes depicts other countries, other interests, and other ways to live.

use the media to get out of their own heads. It affords them new input and gives them a break from their active minds for a while. They find most forms of media relaxing for this reason. Many innies listen to the radio or music, or watch TV to help them go to sleep. Innies, unlike many outies, actually learn through using the media. They like the science, animal, and history channels, for instance. Often they do research on the Internet. Most innies (including adults) love to be read to, so they enjoy books on tape.

But media intake has to be monitored. When it comes to TV, kids are bombarded with crass, often manipulative, commercials targeted

- It sometimes teaches about history, nature, science, and culture.
- It may expand imagination and storytelling ability, if discussed with others.

What You Can Do:

- Limit screen time to one or two hours a day.
- Play a video game with your kids, making it an interactive experience rather than just electronic solitaire.
- Discuss the differences between real life and TV.
- Talk to your child about violence on TV, explaining that it is make-believe rather than a reflection of real life.
- Talk to your child about commercials on TV, explaining that you don't have to buy something simply because it looks cool or because someone else says you should have it.
- Finally, ask your child what he has seen related to particular issues or events. Children often know more than you think they do about world events. It's important that they are able to discuss their knowledge and ideas with someone close to them.

right at them. And, while there are some good shows on television, it's also rife with crude, violent, and frightening images and disturbing story lines. Children need adults to watch with them so they can intervene, if needed, and respond to any questions their kids might have. It's important to discuss with your innie the shows, games, and other media they interact with—they need help to digest all the data they have taken in.

Remember, introverted children are very perceptive. Sometimes they've only picked up fragments of information. This can be more confusing and upsetting than having all the facts before them. The problem is that they might not know how to introduce the topic or to know what questions to ask.

I met with the family of a six-year-old boy soon after the attacks of September 11, 2001. I asked the parents whether they had talked about these events with their son. They said, "Oh, he doesn't know much about it. We keep the TV news off." I said, "You'd probably be surprised by what he *does* know." Sure enough, they were stunned to discover his familiarity with terms like *terrorist, suicide,* and *hijack.* Once he started talking about it, he asked questions about how the pieces of the story that he knew so far all fit together.

Children need to have the chance to talk about these things with parents. Knowledge about the problems in the world can weigh heavily on a small child, especially a quiet, insightful introvert. She needs to be able to ask questions and to have her view corrected or enlarged. Otherwise, she'll mull it over in her busy little head, ad infinitum. And that's a lot for a child to deal with.

The Importance of Chat Time

"It would be so nice if something made sense for a change."—From the film Alice in Wonderland

Talk for at least fifteen minutes each day with your innie. Chatting is a powerful linking tool with innies, showing that you are a partner and affirming their place on the family team. It gives your child "hap hits" and develops her trust in you and her understanding of her mind. Listen to what she says, mull it over, and respond with an open attitude. Ask questions with curiosity. "What happened at recess?" "What did you learn today that you never knew before?" "Why do you think Susie likes to play with you?" Don't interrogate, judge, or attempt to fix the child's problems or feelings. Ask what she thinks she can do to solve her own problems.

Chat Crafters

Sometimes it's hard to get a conversation started or, once you begin, to keep it going. Here are a few tips for getting your innie to open up.

- Avoid yes and no questions—Ask the "w" questions: why, where, what, or who?

- Ask for specifics—What was the most fun thing you did at school today?

- Ask for details—How did your butterfly presentation go?

Try playful role-playing: "If you had that to do over again, what would you do?"

When you listen to your innie, it helps him practice sharing his inner world with others. He needs you to engage in conversation and discuss what's on both your minds. It draws him out and reduces the possibility that he will get stuck in his head. With daily chats, innies learn they have interesting things to say. He needs a safe interaction, in which you listen without discounting his thoughts, feelings, perceptions, and questions. He will learn, "My ideas are worth listening to." Dialogue is a powerful strategy to affirm, broaden, and encourage even very young innies.

Chat time is a good time to snuggle. Relaxing together during bath time, bedtime, or just lazing around is a good time for an innie to surprise you with what's on his mind. Casual talking, asking questions without pressure, and thinking about something together free him up. Learn what kinds of topics pull him out—sometimes if you share something, he'll open up.

One of my clients just started up a fifteen-minute chat time with her seven-year-old daughter, Elise. The two are both innies and have a prickly relationship. The mother doesn't like to play, and she

Book It

Most innies love to read. In an online survey of introverts, when asked what they remembered as their favorite childhood pastime, they listed reading first. They enjoyed going on imaginary adventures and getting to know the characters in the stories.

Use your innie's love of reading as a means of getting closer. One way to do this is to read the same book and discuss it together. Or ask your child to tell you about what he is reading. Why does he like this book and not that one? Discuss books you have enjoyed.

The touching film *One True Thing* portrays the gulf between an outie mother (housewife) and an innie daughter (writer) played by Meryl Streep and Renée Zellweger, respectively. The mother suggests that she and her daughter form a book club—just the two of them. Through discussing the books together, the daughter's eyes are opened to a new view of her mother's interior world.

Innies love to be read to—many tell me it's their most pleasant memory from their childhood. Choose a book you'll both love, and round out your chat time with a story or a chapter of a novel. Discuss the plotline and the characters. When you encounter something in your daily life that reminds you of the book, mention it.

expects Elise to be an adult. After much urging on my part and dangling the carrot of reduced spats, the mom finally instituted a chat time. So every night before lights out, they rest on Elise's bed and muse about their days. It's a time of casual unhurried conversation. The mother is surprised that her daughter will now casually say, "We can talk about that tonight during chat time." Elise is sharing more about her life with her mom and even asking for advice. Their tiffs are fewer.

Making Up One Mind at a Time

"I must have a prodigious quantity of mind;
it takes me as much as a week, sometimes,
to make it up." —*Mark Twain*

"Let me think about it," is the innie mantra. Innies can't make instant decisions like outies can. Their longer brain pathway requires time to combine and formulate lots of information before they are ready to reach a decision. Usually they need a quiet environment, time, and space to percolate. In fact, introverted children can become overwhelmed when asked to make on-the-spot decisions. Yet decisions, no matter how small, crop up all the time. Remind your child that it's okay to take some time to decide. Teach her that decisions need not be so overwhelming. Once you break them down into a few steps, they become more manageable. Also tell her that, like most things, decision making gets easier with practice. Plus each decision, even a seemingly trivial one, presents the chance to make a choice, take a stand, or resolve a problem.

Discuss the issue at hand with your innie and over the course of the conversation, gently ask, "What are you torn about? What are the positives and negatives of each possible choice? What is your 'gut' feeling? Are there any past decisions that could serve as a useful model? Are there mistakes you want to avoid making again?" Acknowledge her struggle by saying something like, "It's hard to make a choice, I know." In most instances, you can sleep on the decision; things often look clearer in the morning. Then it's time to decide and make a plan. Ask her to think back on a decision she made that turned out well. Remind your child that there are no perfect decisions. There are simply the best choices one can make with the information available. Also, reassure her that few decisions are cast in stone.

How to Help Your Innie Make Up His Mind

Innies can become good decision makers. Role-playing the steps to make a decision is a good way to practice:

- Ask your child what makes the decision difficult for him.
  "I want to go to the camp, but I am afraid."
- Tell him to write down the pros and cons.

Pros:

- It might be fun.
  - Caleb and Nathan are going.
  - There are horses and campfires.

Cons:

- I've never been there before.
- It's a whole week away from home.
- It might not be fun.
- There might be bullies there.

The Art of Relaxing (and Revving Up)

Every day, introverted children face frustrating, anxiety-producing, and potentially disappointing situations, such as new developmental tasks, school pressures, and uncertainties in friendships. As parents, we need to balance teaching our children to ask for assistance and helping them learn to manage frustration by themselves. The good news is innies can learn to calm themselves down, which is

- Ask what possible solutions he sees. Throw out a few if he can't think of any.
  - I could talk with Nathan's brother, who went last year, and get a better sense of what it's like.
  - I could plan to talk on the phone or write home.
  - I could see if my friends could be in the same cabin as me.
  - I could take some special things from home.
  - I can tell the counselor or my friends if someone bullies me.
  - It might have some fun and some not-so-fun activities, and I can deal with that.
  - If it turns out to be really awful, Mom and Dad could come get me.

- Let him sleep on it.
- Encourage him to make a preliminary decision and see how it feels. He can discuss further concerns or ideas that arise.
- Make a plan. Congratulate him on his choice.

important because they can't resolve a problem without first calming down. The earlier children learn to soothe themselves, the better they will be able to tackle whatever comes their way.

Start early to reinforce your child's self-soothing abilities. When a child gets frustrated, it's tempting to try to fix the problem yourself rather than reinforcing her ability to calm herself. Instead, give her a little room to try to handle things. When she figures out a way to remedy the situation, or makes another attempt despite getting discouraged, you can pat her on the back and say something like, "You got yourself on top of this. Good for you," or "Boy, those word problems were difficult. I'm glad you stuck it out."

Armchair Traveling

Here's an exercise that will teach your child how to take a mini-vacation in her mind and come back relaxed and refreshed. Have her sit in a comfortable position. Suggest that she imagine a peaceful scene, such as a sunny, flower-filled meadow, the beach, or wherever she feels most relaxed. Tell her to focus on the scene for a few minutes and start to pretend that she's really there. Remind her to feel the sun, the breeze, the temperature of the air, and to hear the waves or the wind moving through the grass. Have her practice this a few times. Let her know that this place is always there for her. When she is tense, she can take a short relaxation trip to it.

Quick and Easy Stress Busters

- Hum (anything).
- Buy lip balm in peppermint or another scent your child likes—sniffing it will make her more alert.
- Shake like a wet dog.
- Kick a ball (outside) or throw Nerf balls.
- Rip up paper or a magazine (what you would recycle anyway).
- Put on lively music and dance any which way.
- Pet or play with an animal.

Since innies tend to be anxious before attempting something new, help your child develop the tools to manage anxiety. Teach him to anticipate what could happen and practice how to respond. This will calm him and give him confidence. It will also streamline that let-me-think-about-it-before-I-say-or-do-anything process. Practice various ways the situation might go and keep rewriting the possibilities of what could happen. This will help your child recognize that life does surprise us at times—but he needn't fear those surprises. Help him to hone the tools needed to handle the unexpected. When you do something assertive, discuss it with your child. You can say, "I was a little nervous when I had to ask the dry cleaner to re-clean my coat. How do you think it went?" Innies need to know that we all face doubt in our dealings with others. Such discussions will instill a positive internal voice: "I can manage like Mom."

Revving Up

Sometimes innies need to be reminded to rev up. Give your innie a nudge from time to time so that he'll get his muscles moving. When he's playing quietly in his room, the thought of physical activity may not look so appealing. You may need to jog his memory in order to realize that he does, in fact, like doing things like riding his bike, playing catch with his sister, or taking a brisk walk with the dog. Have him write "What I Like to Do" on colored three-by-five cards (color is always more invigorating than plain white). If he can't think of what to do, he can look through the cards. You can also get him in the habit of picturing what he wants to do before he embarks on doing it. This can serve as a motivator, a way of priming the pleasure center.

Quick and Easy Engine Revvers
- Be a windmill. Show your child how to shake her hands and feet and swing her arms around to increase circulation and boost her energy level.
- Invite your innie to sing with you at the top of her lungs, or suggest she blast a few notes in the shower if she prefers private crooning.
- Put on some music and dance around the room with or beside your innie. Or ask him to teach you the latest steps.
- Be silly and laugh together. Watch an old comedy film like the Marx Brothers' *Monkey Business*—laughter is the greatest energizer.

- Have your innie swing, spin, or jump on a small trampoline. Bike riding and skating are great; innies love the freedom. Ping-Pong or badminton are good revver-uppers, too.

The Heart of the Matter

- *Play is an energy-saving way for innies to test new skills.*
- *Innies need time to mull over complex input before making decisions.*
- *Daily chat time helps innies make sense of their experiences.*

PART III

Family
Variations

"Having children is a lot like making a movie.

There are a lot of the same worries.

Will it have legs? Will it go wide?

How will it do domestically? What if it goes foreign?"

—Meryl Streep

CHAPTER 7

The Family Temperament Tango

Increase Family Harmony by Validating and Appreciating Each Member's Footwork

"Children have never been good at listening to their elders, but they have never failed to imitate them."—James Baldwin

Introverted children are strong family people—they want to have good relationships with their families. Arguably, they have more at stake than most: Because their social circle is often smaller, they may focus more on their families. I have often noticed that innies, even children, are their family's behind-the-scenes "go to" people—the undeclared hub that the family revolves around and whose opinions hold added weight. In their own, often subtle, way, they support and encourage family members and attempt to smooth out conflicts. They come to be depended upon for their observations, their loyalty, and their sense of what's right.

The family inner circle serves as a training ground for your introverted child to become comfortable in relationships. Children watch how adults interact. They learn from you. Strong, positive relationships boost your innie's belief that relating is worth the energy outlay.

Encourage family members to take the Temperament Quiz on page 16 in Chapter 1. See what people say about their scores. What do they think about other family members' results? Do the scores reflect how people act in the family? Assessing the whole family's temperament could be fun and enlightening. Kids—especially innies—can observe and say the darndest things. . . .

The Range of Family Temperaments

"I believe that basically people are people,

it's our differences that charm, delight,

and frighten us."—Agnes Newton Keith

I have a friend, a fellow introverted psychologist, who is married to another introverted psychologist. They spawned two introverted daughters. Randy laughs about their favorite family outing: They trek over to their preferred bookstore and each selects a book. They then grab a quick bite and go home and read by the fire. Pretty exciting, eh? It is unusual for everyone in the family to be an introvert with such similar interests. But it certainly streamlines those discussions of what to do on a free night!

When people share temperaments, they enjoy a special understanding that comes from seeing the world in similar ways. This leads to an environment that is predictable, congenial, and easily creates a sense of belonging. A child and a parent who are alike may develop a special bond. Their goals mesh and they communicate easily. Too many similarities, however, can become constricting, reinforce weaknesses, or create rigid patterns. People who are alike can also step on each other's toes; alas, similarities sometimes breed contempt.

The truth is that looking at our kids and seeing ourselves in them *or* seeing traits alien to us can push our buttons in different ways. A family that I see in therapy has three children who are outies and one son who is a classic innie. They are very active and frequently travel. When they enter a new hotel room or visit a site, the introverted son hangs back. He doesn't race around, expressing his excitement with his siblings. His parents conclude that he doesn't appreciate the trip. Sometimes his folks feel frustrated and think he's spoiled. His mother asks me, "Why isn't he excited? Why doesn't he join in?" Needless to say, this prompted a conversation about temperament. Now they know that his way of exploring may not look like theirs.

Adjust your child-rearing expectations to your child's temperament. Remember, too, that you and your spouse have temperaments that will have an affect on your child. Keep an eye out for temperament-based stumbling blocks in your relationships with your children, innie and outie.

Innie Parents with Innie Kids

An innie parent and an innie child can enjoy simple pleasures like lazing around and watching a video, reading books side by side on the couch, or kicking back together and drawing all afternoon while they listen to the rain tapping on the roof. They easily fall into sync. They may value and share each other's interests and know each other well. But this cozy congeniality can have a downside: Sometimes they may have trouble getting themselves up and out of the house and can get stuck in a rut. Then they don't expand their social circle or stretch themselves in unfamiliar experiences.

Some parents recall feeling isolated as innie children themselves. As a result, they may be concerned that their children are introverts and may attempt to change them. Here is how one introverted dad describes it: "I worry that Jordon is too much like me. I know he keeps a lot inside. I try to give him space to talk. Maybe I should push him to be more outgoing. Every time I think that, I remember

Single Parents

If the innie parent is single, the child may become a partner rather than his or her child. Innies are good listeners, they are often wise, and they like intimate relationships. This can lead to trouble if they become what is termed a "parental child." Children who are pushed into an adult role too early don't get a chance to be kids. They skip over developmental milestones. Becoming too merged with a parent or parents erodes an innie child's confidence and reinforces his natural hesitation. Later it will be harder for such children to grow up and fly the coop. If they do leave the nest and marry—and many don't—it will be hard for them to manage adult life and parenting because of the early deficits. If you are a single parent, make sure you develop your own adult support network. Don't talk about too many adult problems with your child. Encourage your innie to have other friends, especially one or two peers. Enjoy the dynamic of parent and child with your innie—it's best for both of you.

how shut down I felt when my parents pressured me as a kid. I try to let him know it's okay to be introverted, that I know what it's like."

Outie Parents with Outie Kids

Outie children and extroverted parents love to be on the go. They play hard, work hard, revel in the glow of the spotlight, and remain loyal to their pack. They enjoy having people around, engaging in lively, flowing discussions and good-spirited arguing. They love feedback, achievements, and rewards, and they are usually competitive. People like them, and they like other people. They make life fun. I have a number of clients who are outies with outie kids—many have year-round passes to Disneyland. However, they can overdo it and lose track of the richer aspects of life. They may not pause to listen to themselves or to others. If they don't learn to balance their outgoing ways, the years of extroverting can wear them out. If no one in the family—or no life crisis—slows them down, they can be vulnerable to physical or emotional burnout at midlife. And they won't necessarily develop self-reflection or the ability to savor the slower pleasures of life. They may expect that everyone thinks and behaves as they do. An outie raised by outies can grow up lacking a sense of individuality and be overly dependent on external praise.

That's why it's very important for outie parents to help their outie kids practice using the innie side of their system. Developing an appreciation for others' differences and increasing their capacity for empathy will enhance their intimate relationships. Encouraging outie children to pause and reflect improves their decision-making abilities and helps them focus and achieve more long-term goals. Building their internal resources helps extroverts lessen their need for external approval.

Innie Parents with Outie Kids

An innie parent with an extroverted child feels she has a tiger by the tail. This is how Jacqueline Bouvier felt upon marrying into the wild and woolly Kennedy clan and having her two children. She had much in common with her introverted daughter, Caroline, but felt concerned about her extroverted son, John. Several of her biographers report that she worked hard to curtail his hankering for high-risk behaviors. Innies may find their outie children hyperactive, loud, demanding, noisy, superficial, and overpowering. They may feel pressured to squeeze more into a day than they can really manage. They can have trouble setting limits because they get worn out long before their child is ready to rest.

The outie's urge to stay active, coupled with irritation if he misses out on anything, can make an innie parent feel like she's on a constant, speeding merry-go-round: "You said in a half hour we could go. Is it time yet? What can I do till it is?" The outie's verbal barrage can flood the parent's brain and it will slam shut: "Stop, I can't *think*!" The parent, who longs for more quiet time and more intimate relating, can end up feeling used by her child: "Irina only wants my taxi services and my social secretary skills."

Conversely, an outie child with an innie parent can feel stifled—a sentiment the parent may pick up on: "My extroverted daughter gets frustrated by my quiet personality," one innie father confesses. "She feels I am too distant. She is hurt, because I don't attend all of her dance competitions. On the positive side, I think she likes the way I trust her and listen to her, and that I give her privacy. Sometimes I feel inadequate and wish I had more get-up-and-go, the way she'd like me to be. It scares me when I'm with her and feel like my energy is being sucked right out of my bone marrow. I try to cover up my irritation, but sometimes I wonder, 'Doesn't she ever stop talking?'"

Outie Parents with Innie Kids

An extroverted parent may wonder what is wrong with her introverted child. "I worry about my daughter, Gaby," says one mother of an eleven-year-old girl. "She seems happy with a couple of friends, but I wish she were more popular. She spends a lot of time alone. When I was her age, I was active in sports, clubs, and school events. I worry that I'm doing something wrong as a mom. Or I think that maybe Gaby is physically ill, or depressed, or that she has a more serious problem like being autistic. I wish she'd talk to me more."

Outie parents can wear themselves out investing their energies trying to convert their innie into an outgoing child. It's a losing proposition. An introverted child may also make an outie parent restless. He may feel that his innie child's slow-as-molasses-in-January pace keeps him from getting things done. He may be uncomfortable with the innie's in-depth curiosity and the unnerving questions she asks. For innies will doggedly pursue questions outies don't give a second thought to—questions that demand reflection, stir up uncomfortable feelings, or require research to learn. This can intimidate or annoy the outie parent: "Just get on with it, you don't need to know that." "Why can't she just go with the flow?" " We don't have time to stop to read about that."

In their rush to get things done, many outie parents may not make time for conversations with their children. They may communicate in chitchat that doesn't give innies enough time to answer. The innie child ends up feeling that her parents aren't interested in what she has to say. Outie parents are usually energetic; they fly around, accomplishing things and having fun. They feel like good parents; their kids "do" a lot. But an innie can wilt on the vine when parents don't adjust to her pace.

Outie parents may misunderstand their child's need to process information before making a decision. "For heaven's sake, just decide!" Delayed emotional reactions puzzle them, too. An innie's slowness worries extroverted parents who equate speed with smarts. They may also feel insulted if the child doesn't reveal her feelings: "Why didn't you tell me you didn't have a good time at Jen's? You never tell me anything."

An outie parent may unknowingly intrude on his innie. He might barge into her room without knocking, or interrupt and start talking while the child is still trying to acclimate to his presence. Innies feel discombobulated when suddenly brought out of deep concentration. An outie parent can take it personally if he doesn't understand his child's hardwiring. Unless he understands the innie's need for space and privacy, he may feel rejected or think the child doesn't love him.

Since innies don't offer the same energy kick, sadly, some outie parents become less interested in their innie—and prefer outie kids. "Robbie is fun, I like his spunk." "Peter is so slow, I start feeling like I'm dragging a bag of potatoes around behind me. All I say to him is, 'Hurry up' all day long."

There is a flip side. As Gaby's mom puts it, "I think she is relieved because I am friendly and can grease the social wheels for her. Our conversations flow best when we do something like take a walk, eat together, go for a drive, or work together in the garden. I can tolerate the pauses and silences more easily."

Innie Parents with Outie and Innie Kids

Having children with differing temperaments can be quite a challenge, especially for a single parent. You may feel constantly torn and unable to meet your two (or more) children's individual needs. It will be crucial to find extroverted adults and friends for your outie child to spend extroverting time with. You will need to help your outie meet his need for out-in-the-world adventure.

You and your innie will likely interact with more ease. There's no need to feel guilty about this; you may have an easy spark of unspoken knowing between you. Your outie may sense the difference and wonder why his sibling enjoys more rapport with you. He may feel you are withdrawn and not very exciting. It's important to discuss these temperament differences in your family.

Thirteen-year-old Alison, a left-brained outie, has a right-brained innie mother and younger sister. The sister and their father, also an innie but left-brained like Alison, had a much easier time communicating about upsetting conflicts in the family. Alison could also talk about how she sometimes felt left out of the relationship between her mom and her sister. Luckily, her mother was fine with Alison talking out these frustrations with her father. In order to help Alison find balance for her introverted home life, they arranged for her to join a soccer team and Girl Scout troop, and to go on outings with her friends. She also spent time with an extroverted grandparent.

Outie Parents with Innie and Outie Kids

In a family with extroverted parents and kids with mixed temperaments, the innie child may feel like the "odd kid out," the one who is slower to get going, who prefers to stay home, who needs peace and quiet to recharge. This can work out fine if the family is understanding and accepting of the innie's needs. In fact, family members may come to rely upon the innie sibling as an island of calm amid the general din of the household. Because innies tend to be cooperative and invested in family harmony, they can become the stealth family referee, listening, dispensing family wisdom, and generally serving as the family compass.

However, if the family is less aware and accepting of differences, the innie may feel isolated or overlooked. I have heard from numerous innies who grew up in outie families and felt excluded, pressured to be more extroverted, or even ganged up on to the point where they became the family scapegoat. In general, innies try to accommodate other family members, and this can leave them vulnerable to being teased or taken advantage of. Unfortunately, many of my innie clients were mistreated by siblings, and their parents did not intervene.

Parents set the tone for how kids are treated in a family. Don't let more aggressive siblings gang up on innies. Tap into your innie's talents and let her demonstrate them to her siblings. For example, invite your innie to tell other family members about one of her hobbies. Point out her strengths to the other family members. "Boy, Samantha is a really good listener, isn't she?" "Did you notice the great idea Dakota came up with?" Acknowledge and value that child's contributions to the behind-the-scenes running of the family. An innie can balance a family of outies, but she will need adult help.

Differences Are Not Flaws

When different temperaments coexist in the family, awareness and flexibility are required. A child who differs from you may likely require you to learn new skills and perhaps spend more energy parenting him. Differences suggest counterbalanced strengths, and you can admire your child's: "Zachary is so outgoing, and I was never that social," or, "Rachael can amuse herself with a book all day. I couldn't sit still for ten minutes!" You can take the opportunity to learn from your child's differences. If you're an extrovert, for instance, see if you can tune out the world and focus on making your private place in the house a true haven.

Within a family, different temperaments lend balance, variety, and diverse perspectives. I know that my extroverted husband can give me a nudge to get out and go places, just the way that I can (for a while, at least) get him to slow down. But differences can cause misunderstandings. Introverted children can feel like fish out of water in a family of extroverts. Conversely, extroverted kids can be made to feel like noisy, superficial balls of energy in a family of innies. "I always felt too loud and in the way," says one extrovert—now a comedian—who grew up in a family of introverts. Modeling this level of understanding offers your children an enduring legacy.

Parenting Challenges . . . by Temperament

Parenting has its stumbling blocks no matter *what* your temperament. Here are some specific hurdles that innies and outies face.

Challenges for Introverted Parents
- Focusing on so many external things: children, a job, the house, etc.
- Constantly bumping up against that energy limit
- Situations when you're responsible for multiple children
- Feeling that you are not doing enough for the family
- Not having enough time to think things through
- Feeling on the spot when asked for decisions
- Focusing so much emotional and cognitive energy outward that there's not enough for your own interests
- Understanding highly extroverted kids
- Being around extremely chatty kids for long periods of time

Challenges for Extroverted Parents
- Feeling isolated at home with children
- Needing to let go of external rewards that drive many outies
- Worrying that your kids don't have enough friends or activities
- Overdoing it—saying yes to too many outside demands
- Giving more attention to outsiders than to your own family
- Staying quiet and listening when children are speaking
- Understanding introverted children's needs for downtime to recharge

The Key Word Is Enjoy

"Laughter is the fireworks of the soul."
—*Josh Billings*

Individuality brings spice to the life of a family. Every member of your family came wrapped in a package—just like the presents we open on holidays—and each has hidden gifts waiting to be discovered. In large part, children learn about themselves from how their families treat them. Many families attempt to build their identity by saying, "We are all alike." But no family is made up of members who are completely alike. And trying to institute an ideal of conformity doesn't promote healthy individual development. It's important to recognize each member's unique talents and what each has to offer.

One of the best ways to do things is through fun. Laughter and good times bring families together and teach innies the rewards of relating. They also create a storehouse of positive, warm memories from which to draw. Try to plan outings or activities that your innie will enjoy. Innies enjoy places we often think of as for adults, such as quiet parks, gardens, and nature sanctuaries. Innies love to hear about their family genealogy; they like to visit a parent's childhood home, look at old family pictures, and visit cemeteries where their ancestors were buried. They enjoy small, less tiring, and often quirky museums, like an old car or plane museum, their town's historical museums, famous writers' homes such as the writer Jack London's Wolf House (now old ruins). They might want to investigate historical places such as a stagecoach museum, ride a canal boat, watch cranes and bulldozers at work, or go to an adult art museum and visit one exhibit—especially if it has audio tapes that tell about the artist.

And sometimes they'll want to stay home when the whole family goes on an outing. That's okay, too.

Simple Pleasures

Here are some things I've enjoyed doing with my family. See if they spark some ideas for you and your family.

- Taking a bag of pennies to a fountain or pond and giving each person a few to wish on. Have your kids share pennies with any other children who happen to be there.

- Feeding ducks, birds, or (if there's a farm nearby) goats.

- Taking a walk around the block and having each person point out what they like best about different yards and houses. You might not have known you had such varied tastes!

- Collecting leaves, pods, and twigs and decorating the dinner table for a festive meal.

- Going fishing. Each child can document the trip with a disposable camera.

Make Everyone Count

"Cooperation is spelled with two letters. WE."
—*George M. Verity*

Innies like to be appreciated and needed. If they're not treated harshly, they tend to be naturally cooperative—most of the time, of course. Encourage each member's contribution to the family. Ask for your children's opinions and ideas, and come up with age-appropriate ways for them to help out. All kids love to do real jobs; it makes them feel grown-up. Ask your two- or three-year-old innie to empty the clothes dryer, give the cat dry food, or dust the tables with a dust cloth or feather duster. Two-year-old Emily had the biggest smile on her face I had ever seen as she staggered in one Sunday morning lugging the newspaper, which was about as big as

- Creating a family fun night and making a collage that describes the outing.
- Letting each child be in charge of planning and (if old enough) cooking, or helping to cook, dinner once a week.
- Making papier-mâché masks of one another. We decorate them and hang them in the hallway or along the staircase wall.

I have introverted clients now in their fifties and sixties who remember cooking with a grandparent, making crafts with their mom, or learning to knit from an aunt. These small moments mean a lot to innies—although you may not know it for years! Pack every child's memory bank with fun times, a spirit of cooperation, and a sense of belonging on the family team. Innies will wear your family identity like a badge of pride.

she was. Contributing to the family tells your child, "You are capable. You can contribute. We need you."

Our grandson, age eight, enjoys the suds-and-warm-water-play of washing a few dishes. He was annoyed with us once recently when he came over to visit and we hadn't left the dirty dishes for him to do!

Ways for Innies to Help Out

Give a preschooler a job around the house: dusting, tearing lettuce for salad, throwing away trash, setting the table, and washing spoons.

Have school-aged innies help with more advanced chores: cooking, folding, and delivering laundry, gathering dirty clothes, taking sheets off the bed, and making their own lunches. Acknowledge a good job (it doesn't need to be perfect) and make an effort to ensure the experience is pleasant and cooperative. (You wash, and I'll dry; you stack the dishes, and I'll put them away.) Be sure your innie has a say in some of the chores selected for her, and change chores every few months.

Discuss with your child a problem you are having and ask for suggestions: Innies of all ages reflect on their experiences. They are gifted observers and insightful problem solvers. They can imagine impending situations and replay their past experiences. But an innie's insights can remain buried underground unless someone asks for his reflections. He won't even know he has this valuable advantage! Ask him for his thoughts and suggestions about daily family problems.

Start asking him early. One of my clients asked her six-year-old son, Leo, if he had any secrets for easing a nervous tummy before talking in front of a group. Leo said, "Well, I can lend you my worry stone. You tuck it in your pocket. Anytime you start to feel butterflies in your tummy, you rub the smooth coolness. It really helps." Leo's mom had no idea he was using this trick when he had to speak in front of his class! Remember to give your innie time to think about the problem. Acknowledge any idea he gives you (even if you don't use it). "Thanks, I think the worry stone will help me, and I'll think of you."

Discuss with your child a problem that another child is having and ask for suggestions: I often ask introverted children and teens I work with about problems they have had, or a problem they still struggle with. I ask what they think I should suggest to *other* kids or parents who are having a similar problem. For instance, I'll say, "Devon is seven and he doesn't talk much. Any ideas about what might help him?" "I had that problem when I was young," says twelve-year-old Jon. "My dad and I started walking around the block and talking every other night. The walking seemed to help me talk. I talk much easier now." Jon pauses to think and continues: "Another thing that helped me when I was younger was the 'Penny for Your Thoughts Bank' my mom made for me. I jotted down an important thought, idea, or question and slipped it into the bank. Later when mom and I talked I could fish one out for discussion. That way I didn't lose my thoughts and Mom gave me pennies for my wishing bank." "Thanks, Jon," I say. "I am going to share your ideas with Devon."

I asked seventeen-year-old Trisha for some teen dating advice: "Sharat wants to go to the prom but she doesn't have a date, and she doesn't want to go with a big group. Any ideas?" "Well," Trisha said, "I helped on the prom refreshment committee and by the time the prom rolled around, I knew so many kids I felt okay going alone. We took turns manning the goody table. It was fun to be in a group, but I wasn't tied down. We could leave after our half-hour shift. We all hung together though. I know girls who ask their best friends to go to the prom. One of my friends asked her friend's brother, who was a quiet college guy. He hadn't gone to his own prom and so he had fun going to hers." "Thanks," I said. "Those are good ideas, I'll pass them on."

Share Your Life Stories

"Plant magic in a child's mind."
—*Thomas W. Phelan*

We've explored the importance of conversation with your introverted child. But sometimes we forget the importance of talking *to* our children, of telling them our life stories, and sharing our opinions and thoughts. Here's an example that shows how hungry an innie might be to learn more about others' inner lives.

I have been working with twelve-year-old Jennifer for the better part of a year. She always looks glum as she reluctantly enters my office and flops down in the glider chair, ignoring the art supplies laid out for her. She twists her long hair around her finger and occasionally peers up at me with challenging eyes. She responds to every question I ask with "Yes," "No," and her favorite, "I don't know."

Jennifer's parents want her to be outgoing like her brothers and sister. "She's just lazy," her mother tells me. "She doesn't want to do anything." The truth is that Jennifer, the only introvert in the family, is starving for deeper interaction. Yet she is so defensive that it's hard to get through to her. I buy preteen magazines and we talk about the pictures. I ask her what she likes, what she doesn't like. I ask her to show me how to use my cell phone. She does a good job of teaching me (no small thing—I'm technically impaired). She's pleasant and cordial, but I still have the feeling that I'm bumping against some wall.

One day I bring in a book of family history questions that people use to interview their relatives. I pick two questions to ask her, and she picks two questions to ask me. She surprises me and picks "Did your grandparents tell you any family stories?" So I talk. I tell her how my grandmother described the choppy crossing on the *Scandinavia* from Denmark to the United States. She listens and asks more questions. Then she tells me that she enjoyed reading Laura Ingalls Wilder's books when she was young. We are having a real conversation. Something has shifted between us.

In trying to bring out a reticent innie, many parents make the mistake of assuming that it's most important that *she* talk. They try to chip information out of their child, as if with a pickax. But communication goes two ways. Often, introverted children need the opportunity to ask *the other person* questions rather than be put on the spot. This offers a way out of her mind and a way into other people's experiences. For other peoples' lives interest her. And listening to another person's story builds her confidence so that she feels more comfortable talking.

Adult Anchors

"The ultimate test of a relationship is to disagree but to hold hands."—Alexandra Penney

A well-functioning family, like a well-planned garden, should conform to a few basic design principles. One is that every garden has an anchor—a focal point that establishes harmony between all the various elements. Family relationships follow similar psychological design rules. Countless studies have shown that the parents' relationship functions as an anchor for the family, lending stability.

The strength of the parents' bond is the foundation for building all other family relationships. Children learn about compatibility, caring behaviors, mutual respect, and problem solving from the examples their parents have set. Families today come in many configurations, but one fact holds true. It isn't *who they are,* it's how parents *treat each other* that sets the stage for what their children learn about relating. All relationships have differences. It is the way those differences are handled that teaches children how to value family.

Keep your adult relationship well nourished by planning date nights and child-free weekends and by going out with other couples. Appreciate small moments you share together—remarking on a cute thing your child does, telling a joke you heard at work, or simply enjoying the fleeting moments when you are actually alone. Remember that in long-term relationships we like each other better on some days than on others. Handling disagreements with respect, humor, and openness is vital to a relationship. And you don't have to remove yourselves from the rest of the family in order to do it. Negotiating differences provides a great example for your children to learn from. Innies are often wary of conflict. It helps them feel safe to see that their parents can handle some friction and still enjoy each other's company.

A solid partnership creates a sturdy but flexible bridge that can span temperament differences. There's room for all family variations. You and your partner will represent different points on the temperament continuum; even if you're both innies or outies, you have different salient aspects to your personalities. Your introverted child, perhaps more than your other kids, will notice how you and your partner behave. Innies watch how their parents act around each other, and they notice subtle social cues. They will internalize the relational skills they observe in the family. Later, they can pack them up and take them along with them to use in their own social lives. It's a great gift you can give them.

A Special Family Issue: Adoption

Nothing reveals more about the power of genetics than adoption. Children who are adopted often have different temperaments from those in their new family. For this reason, it's important to pay special attention to your adopted child's traits. Interestingly, it's often easier for adoptive parents to appreciate different temperaments. Biological parents of introverted children may feel shame or guilt about their children's inward nature. Adoptive parents usually don't feel responsible for temperament. One extroverted mom I worked with said to me, "If Dan had been my biological child I would have felt it was my fault he is so quiet, but since he's adopted I feel like it's his natural personality. My biological daughter is very outgoing."

In a study of identical twins raised apart, researchers found that one child was raised in a family of professors and that she was a voracious reader. When they located her twin sister, they found that she was a con-

In the Case of Divorce

"We're frightened of what makes us different."

—Anne Rice

Even if it's better for the parents in the long run, divorce is very stressful for all children. It shakes up their world—after all, the only one they know—like a major earthquake. Innies thrive on the familiar family routine that doesn't demand too much energy. Even in families with severe problems such as neglect, abuse, addiction, and violence, the relief an introverted child feels at the end of the confrontations may pale beside the sense of disruption. Separation and divorce jars his or her sense of safety. It requires tons of outward energy to adjust to the new family constellation.

stant reader, too. The surprise was that she was raised in a family with little interest in reading. Yet in grade school, of her own volition, she took three buses to get to her town's main library.

Some children are adopted by parents who had a particular vision of the child who would fill what they perceived as a hole in their family. Such parents may feel disappointment in a child who is temperamentally different from what they had expected. Pay attention for clues to your child's interests and inborn talents.

Energy mismatches are common in adoptive families. Innie parents can also be quite shocked by an extroverted child's outgoing personality and energy level. Pair them up with energetic friends or relatives who love being on the go. One skiing family I know adopted an indoor-loving child. They now let him enjoy cozy weekends with his grandparents when they head for the mountains.

In the meantime, parents are preoccupied, anxious, and often living on frayed nerves. Innies can register this tension and become depressed or conclude that any family problems are their fault. In coal mines, canaries were once used to warn of dangerous fumes that humans could not detect. Innies are like these canaries in the mines: They sense unexpressed difficulties long before other members of the family may be aware. An introverted child may not show her reaction to the family upheaval, or the reaction may be delayed, but count on this: She is having one.

Provide Stability During Divorce

- Don't put your innie in between you and your spouse—he identifies with and feels loyal to both of you.
- Understand that innies have delayed reactions, and it may take a long time to process the change.

- Take the high road in disputes with your ex—your innie will respect you for this when she is older.
- Discuss the divorce (at an appropriate age level) and be sure he knows it isn't his fault.
- Ask what he is feeling and what concerns he has, and troubleshoot the problems: "We can talk on the phone at night when you are at Dad's."
- Keep daily routines as normal as possible.
- Visiting two homes can be stressful for innies because they tend to be homebodies. Ask your child how you can help him feather each nest.
- Keep a calendar with stickers for younger innies or notation for older innies that shows when they will be where. Include trips, school events, doctors' appointments, and other info both parents should have.
- Acknowledge that while your innie wishes you would get back together, that isn't going to happen.
- Don't have your innie spy on the other parent or fight your battles with a parent.
- Remind him that in time everyone will adjust to the change and eventually feel better.

Innies place a premium on family life. A harmonious family setting where family members recognize and appreciate differences will serve as your innie's refuge and provide emotional ballast for her forays out into the larger world.

The Heart of the Matter

- *Innies value family relationships.*
- *Coping with temperament matches and mismatches teaches valuable skills.*
- *Acknowledge and appreciate all temperaments in the family.*

CHAPTER 8

Improving Sibling Relationships

Encourage Understanding, Establish Boundaries, and Dampen Rivalry

"If a plant is to unfold its specific nature to the full, it must first be able to grow in the soil in which it is planted."—Carl Jung

Sibling relationships are in many ways a microcosm of the social world. Through them, innies learn to respond to the challenges of social interactions—as well as to reap the rewards. Temperament-savvy parenting can help create an environment that makes room for differences, so the rewards outweigh the clashes.

When Siblings Clash

Most of us have the expectation—often in spite of our own experience—that brothers and sisters should naturally enjoy each other's company. Research shows that often they don't. Actually, only a small percentage of siblings maintain close relationships into adulthood. This is due to many factors besides temperament, of course. But temperament does loom large and can affect how siblings interact, how much they play together, their need for personal space, and how they view one another.

Learning to see your kids through the lens of temperament will help you set realistic expectations—which will in turn enable you to be a more effective referee. Help your kids understand and appreciate their temperaments by focusing on each child's personal strengths. Try a playful approach: "Hi, Nate. I'd like to introduce you to your sister, Judith. She loves horses and reading Junie B. Jones books. Judith, this is your brother Nate, and he loves baseball and Superman. I wonder what you two could find to play for the next hour that you both like. Maybe horses with capes would do the trick?" I'm kidding about that introduction, but serious that it does help to adopt a neutral viewpoint. Don't join the fray and become yet another fighting sibling. I see parents doing that all the time. Encourage kids to find common ground. The reality is, it's usually not too far away.

It is vitally important to teach an outie how to respectfully ask his innie sister or brother for playtime. Remind your outie that innies are like deep-sea divers. They plunge into the depths of their mind, fascinated by the watery world. They need a few minutes to come up, or else they'll get the bends. They may need time to shift into a dual play mode. Teach your outie to ask, "Do you want to play in a few minutes?" or, "After you finish your homework, do you want to play catch?" Help him see that he's more likely to secure a playmate by slowing down to his sibling's pace, as opposed to rushing in and startling her. It also helps if outies, always full of lots of good ideas, occasionally learn to ask the innie sib for suggestions about what she wants to play once in a while. Suggest that your outie invite his innie sibling to teach him about her interests. Explain to outies that innies need to have downtime and that setting a start and stop time can be useful.

Innies and outies have different tolerances for how long they can play together. Innies often enjoy their differently wired sibling's spontaneous, energetic personality—in small doses. You may need to step in to be sure that innies aren't drained by too much sibling togetherness. I see parents who expect their children to play together *all the time*—and then share a bedroom, too!

Encourage your outie to blow off some steam, perhaps with some outdoor play or indoor Nerf ball tossing. Then help him learn to enjoy quiet time. You can suggest that he read, listen to music, or do some artwork not too far from the rest of the family's activity. If alone in his room, he may want to keep the door open. Help him ease into enjoying time and space alone, perhaps starting with fifteen minutes every few days and increasing the time. This establishes a pattern so that he can enjoy alone time all his life.

Remind your outie that innies need privacy. The outie should know that if his sister is deep into a fascinating book, project, or hobby, she may ignore her siblings. Help your outie learn not to take this personally.

Make Use of Outie Skills

Explain to innies that outies get charged up around other people and activities. Encourage innies to utilize their outie sibling's snappy verbal skills. If an innie is dealing with an obnoxious, teasing schoolmate, she can ask her outie sib for quick comebacks. The outie brother can help her test out the retorts. Outies usually enjoy being the family scout. They like to be the first to sit on Santa's lap and thus can introduce innie sibs to new places, like a Halloween haunted house, or, in their teen years, act as the trailblazer in all kinds of adventures. Outies also make good mouthpieces. They can speak up for their innie siblings occasionally, for instance when returning something to a store or asking an adult for a favor.

Invite your outie's pals over; let the innie sibling decide if she wants to be included. Set aside time for outies to play alone so they can practice and expand their ability to enjoy solitude. Observe how the dynamics play out. For example, two innies may need private shared playtime without outies being around. Generally, outies like to play in groups with louder roughhousing. They often tease more. Parents need to help keep the volume at a moderate pitch so that innies aren't overwhelmed and don't withdraw or melt down.

Establish Boundaries

"Certain springs are tapped only when
we are alone."—Anne Morrow Lindbergh

One of the gifts of having an innie in the family is that he can teach lessons about the need for respecting personal space. Innies may be compliant about many issues—but *not* about their territory. They want, even need, a low-stimulation place that doesn't gobble up their energy and where they know where things are.

I am constantly shocked by the lack of boundaries in many families today. One innie client says, "Mom popped into my room whenever she wanted; she never knocked. I never could relax." In many families, children and adults aren't expected to knock before entering another person's bedroom. Nor are they asked to be quiet if another child is studying. One of my innie clients tells me about how many times her twin takes her shoes without asking. She is afraid to speak up since she wants to avoid causing trouble—but she hates it. Parents may laugh off such behavior, but it's very important to know how an introverted child feels. If she feels she has no control over anything, she may become more passive or close down completely.

Establishing family boundaries helps everyone feel safe. Make it clear that you expect everyone to respect others' property and space by following rules like knocking before entering, borrowing only with permission, and not interrupting when others are working or studying. This in itself will curtail numerous sibling tussles;

when kids have the security of family boundaries, they have better relationships. Children will also learn to function better in the outside world.

Parents can set an example of how to safeguard an innie's "space bubble"—the privacy he needs to process and recharge. Give him a sign to put on his door that reads, RECHARGING! or RETURNING TO PLANET EARTH AT . . . with a clock to set for his "return" time. If he doesn't have his own room, let him use your room at times, or find another cozy, secluded spot. If he is tired, stressed, or hungry he may need longer in his decompression tank. If outies are always in his space and in his face, there will be trouble.

Make sure siblings understand temperament-based needs. Outies often feel frustrated by innie siblings who want to stay in their room. They can feel hurt or rejected—angry that their own personal "live-in energy source" doesn't want to hook up. Once they see this as a different physical need, it reduces the tendency to take it personally. You can also explain that when an innie feels more comfortable, she is more inclined to interact with outie siblings.

Rivalry and Its Discontents

"The best way to raise a successful garden
is by trowel and error."—Anonymous

There are some thorny aspects of temperamental difference—competition, dominance and submission, and jealousy—that are not often talked about. We live in a dog-eat-dog culture where children are expected to be outwardly competitive. In certain instances, such as on the playing field, competitiveness can be constructive. Sports can be a healthy way to redirect aggression. But competitiveness as a global outlook sees other people as rivals. It divides people and promotes an attitude of "everyone for himself."

Competition discourages what actually builds loving relationships, which is a sense that we are all in this life together.

I believe that healthy competition is always *within* oneself—not *against* others. With *external* competition, the goal is to be the best or to win. As a motivator, it will always be discouraging, since there is always someone better than you. *Internal* competition, however, is within your control. It is directed toward your own achievement; it provides encouragement because you are challenging yourself to improve your own skills. This is achievable. A person—child or adult—can always learn and improve. Internal competition is built upon and promotes good self-esteem.

Competition between siblings can be destructive. To some extent it is natural, but parents should not compare siblings or pit them against one another. If parents have a theoretical ideal child that everyone is trying to become, every child will feel he is missing the mark. And if a child does somehow get the idea that he is the best, he will feel intense pressure to maintain that position. This is very damaging to innies, who often drive themselves very hard.

An innie should never be pushed to act like another child. Since introverts frequently internalize their problems, they often think they ought do better or be better than they are. They may already feel inferior because of the pressure to act more like the extroverted norm. Adding more demands to compete with siblings can be debilitating. Innies may give up or dig in their heels. Instead, point out each child's strengths and don't create expectations that all children should be the same. Encourage cooperation and the development of qualities vital to creating a satisfying adult life, including generosity, helpfulness, sensitivity, humor, adaptability, and concern for others. You have influence—maybe more than you think—with your introverted children. Use it to acknowledge and nurture their innate advantages.

Make the Most of Your Kids' Strengths

As bird, animal, and human studies on temperament show, extroverts tend to be more dominant and introverts tend to be more submissive.

The Dark Heart of Envy

"Envy is a kind of praise."—John Gay

Many innies feel that they should be outies and may envy an outie sibling who has many friends and "seems to have everything so easy." An innie may sense that her parents and relatives prefer the outie. It's helpful to tell her that it's normal to feel jealous of a sibling. Since outies are more outgoing, they may be easier for some friends and relatives to relate to. Tell her that you can understand why she wishes things were easier—as it seems with her sibling. Then remind her about what's easier for her; innies may not see their own strong points. Discuss what is difficult for her sibling; that her brother or sister struggles, too, may not be immediately apparent. You can also relate what you learned from your siblings or people you were close to during childhood. Certainly you can empathize with these feelings.

On the outie side, many are jealous that an innie sibling never seems to get into trouble. I recently talked with an extroverted twelve-year-old. He thinks his parents are unfair to him. I can see why he thinks so—he gets into more trouble than his introverted sib. As we talked, I was able to point out where he had choices about his behavior. There were instances when he made decisions that led him to break rules. If he didn't want to get into trouble so often, he could make other choices. This is the positive use of jealousy—it can motivate us to make better decisions.

Check in with yourself and make sure that you and your partner are showing individual appreciation to each child in the family—the surest way to minimize that envious green shine in the eyes.

Extroverts fight more, and innies are more reluctant. Within the safety of the family, kids of all temperaments can learn to value their strengths and soften their limitations. Left-brained extroverts, for

Temperament and Twins

Twins don't necessarily share temperaments. It's natural to compare and contrast twins, and tempting to make assumptions. But it's important not to slot them into rigid roles. This tendency is exaggerated when parents force twins to be together too much; becoming the opposite of one's twin may seem like the only way to feel like an individual. Or the family, without realizing it, encourages opposing traits. Twins are quickly labeled: Brianna is the studious one, and Bethany is the live wire.

Balance your responses to your twins to reduce the likelihood of each becoming an extreme. If a child is more introverted, don't let his outie twin speak for him too often or overshadow him. Point out innie advantages. For example, "Boy, Jeremy, you really calmed Jake down. You're good at that." Twins shouldn't always be together. Innie twins can become enmeshed or too dependent on each other; they need to develop separate playmates, interests, and identities. Parents need to establish individual relationships with each twin. Take each out separately to run errands or have "just the two of us" dates. Help your innie branch out and develop her own preferences, interests, and hobbies.

example, tend to see the world as right or wrong or black and white. We all know that few things are ever that simple. Such children often become frustrated and blame others. However, when all-or-nothing views are toned down into nuance grays and the child's aggression is well directed, this temperament can grow into fine leadership skills. You can acknowledge positive uses of dominance, such as an extroverted child's using his gifts to lead the pack. "James, you come up with so many good ideas. I see why kids like to go along with you. I'm glad you lead them toward constructive activities."

Acknowledge your innie's quiet leadership skills. Most innies won't show their keen ability to influence others unless they have to, when nothing else is working. Studies show that innies, even in preschool, look for solutions to conflicts. Outies tend to argue to try to win conflicts. Point out your innie's subtle talents. "Rebecca, I know you don't like to speak up in groups, but I noticed what you said when Zach and Sam were fighting. You thought of a good way for each of them to get part of what they wanted. Good for you, your suggestion helped the whole group get back on track." Many innies head up large companies—you just never hear about them!

Bicker Busting

"Differences are sources of strength for us—so long
as they aren't used against us."—Jean Baker Miller

Remember that your introverted child relies on home for comfort. It is his refueling station, his sanctuary. Promote harmony among siblings at home by intervening early in conflicts. Too much tension is hard on all children, but especially on innies, who are highly sensitive to atmosphere. Even minor disputes, like what to have for dinner, can build up. Consider each child's preferences . . . and be sure to include your own once in a while: "Okay, Max. We'll have pizza tonight. But tomorrow we're having chicken." Innies will feel included and encouraged rather than left out and unseen. And they learn the important lesson that they can speak up and discuss their own wants and needs.

All children feel safest when they know you are in charge and make the family rules. Innies, especially, feel most secure in a predictable family setting where conflicts are handled in a reasonable and fair manner. The pursuit of harmony doesn't mean that problems are swept under the carpet or that irritations are expected to magically disappear. Nor does it suggest you go to the other extreme and react harshly to sibling conflicts in order to snuff them out. In general, outies require more rules and stricter consequences than innies, since they are less inhibited. You can loosen the reins a bit with innies as they may be permanently stymied by too many rules and restrictions. Discuss these differences so that outies don't feel picked on.

Innies, adaptable and conflict-avoidant, may be reluctant to stand up for themselves. Frankly, it takes too much effort for them. If you see your innie standing his ground, acknowledge it. "Matt, I liked the way you said no when Julie wanted you to give her your candy. Good for you!" There are, however, times to step in. If your innie has a bossy brother or sister, he might just go along with them: "Oh, it's okay. I don't mind watching the Mr. Magoo movie again." It's up to parents to encourage fair play and say, "I notice that Peter usually goes along with your movie choices, so this time it is his turn." "Today it's Brett's turn to pick the movie, and from now on take turns choosing." In this way, innies know they have backing should they decide to expend the extra fuel it requires and speak up and hold their own. And more dominant siblings will learn an important lesson about listening to others, compromising, and negotiating.

It may at times frustrate innies to have to negotiate space and energy with their brothers and sisters. But children that learn to work out differences with their siblings will bring those skills to relationships throughout their lives.

The Heart of the Matter

- *Expect sibling temperament clashes.*
- *Encourage everyone in the family to learn from each child's strengths.*
- *Never allow one sibling to make fun of, hurt, or harass another.*

CHAPTER 9

Extending the Family Tree

Cultivate Close Relationships with Grandparents, Other Family Members, Friends, and Caregivers

"If you have knowledge, let others light their candles at it."—Margaret Fuller

Close bonds with extended family members are enriching for all children—and especially for innies, who are family-oriented and invest in enduring relationships. Strong relationships with grandparents, uncles and aunts, godparents, and parents' close friends can provide no-strings-attached love, a sense of place, a feeling of family connection, and windows into other times and worlds. In his classic child-rearing book *Touchpoints,* T. Berry Brazelton, M.D., argues that children pay a terrible price for the loss of intergenerational connection. He recommends treasuring the continuity and family tradition that extended family affords. Introverted children can grow up feeling unseen, and many feel like outsiders in today's in-your-face culture.

It needn't be this way. A good relationship with special relatives or friends can assure your child that she matters. These figures can

The Gift of Grandparents (and Other Special Adults)

"To everything there is a season."—Ecclesiastes 3:1

Several years ago, I interviewed thirty introverted adults about their relationships with their grandparents. What quickly became obvious was that innies drew on these relationships, whether good or bad, to widen their worlds. As we've seen, research shows that introverted children appreciate differences. Most people I interviewed learned from and valued the possibilities reflected in their grandparents' tastes, interests, and styles of interacting. For example, Marcia, an artist I interviewed, told me,

> *"My grandmother raised and loved red cabbage roses. She decorated her whole house with them, right down to the floor covering. I loved them, too. On hot days I used to lie on her cool linoleum floor in the sunroom. It had gigantic candy-pink and apple-red cabbage roses spreading across the shimmery blue background. No one else in my family loved their plush petals like my granny and I did. My brother and sister teased me for wanting my whole room decorated in a lush rose theme."*

This connection was very meaningful to Marcia. She felt different from others in her family, and her grandmother gave her permission to be herself. Today she is the only artist in her family, and, indeed, her warm home is festooned with red and pink cabbage rose blossoms.

provide mooring as children grow up and are tossed about by the challenges of life. They can convey family lore, help to broaden a child's view of her parents, and demonstrate that there isn't just *one* way to be but rather *many* ways of being.

Innies find the rich tapestries of their elders' worlds fascinating. At their best, grandparents* offer them family history, hobbies, unique interests, playful attitudes, and learning experiences. Innies are little sponges looking for all sorts of information to absorb. They recognize the value of a grandparent's history, wisdom, and knowledge. For grandparents of any temperament, sharing themselves and their gifts with their grandchildren gives them an opportunity to remain young at heart. They can appreciate and evolve new aspects of their personalities through seeing themselves, via their grandchildren, with a fresh lens.

Introverted and extroverted grandparents have different strong points and offer their grandkids different growing experiences. Let's take a look at those differences.

Innie Grandparents— Breathing-Room Relatives

> *"What matters most is what we learn from living."—Doris Lessing*

Innie grandparents provide breathing space in the life of an introverted child. Older relatives can often afford to be patient. They are frequently in the position to do what many busy parents don't have time to do—they can, as teens say, "chill." This can be a lifesaver for innies, as well as good practice for outies. A grandparent's companionship can be a sanctuary for introverted children: They enjoy a slower pace, they value the smaller joys of life, and are generally gentle and understanding. Innie grandparents may not realize what good role models they can be.

---

* For the purpose of simplicity (and because the relationship is often special) I focus on the grandparent/grandchild relationship in this chapter. But much of what I say pertains to other close familial and friendly relationships.

Ask your child's innie grandparent to share an interest, hobby, or anything he enjoys with your child. Growing up, one of my daughters enjoyed gardening with my husband's parents. As they weeded and watered, they told stories and discussed the issues they were facing. If your parents don't have an obvious hobby to share with your child, you can start things off by telling your parents about a few of your child's interests. "Addy loves mermaids. Do you think you could take her to the library to find some stories about mermaids? She would love it."

Introverted grandparents can provide a wonderful open dreaming space where innies can play with their imaginations.

Recently, our innie grandson and I were eating lunch and musing about where the tooth fairy lives. Christopher had just lost his second front tooth, and the topic was very much on his mind. We decided that she lives in Fairy World with ten thousand other tooth fairies. We agreed that a pretty large staff of fairies would be required; after all, they would have to cover *all* the children who are losing *all* their teeth in countries all over the world. Chris wondered how the tooth fairy is able to silently slip the tooth out from under his pillow and slip the money in without waking him up. Perhaps, he decided, stretching his imagination, she has some special powers so that she can whisper "Poof!" and the tooth comes out, and then another magic "Poof!" and the money slides in.

It took us several hours of "what-iffing" to come up with a behind-the-scenes narrative we liked about the tooth fairy's life. Musing time is scarce today. Taking a stroll around the block, checking out the ants, noticing the colors of the fallen leaves, smelling roses, saying hi to neighbors, and looking at how other homes are decorated can be a wonderful experience that enriches an introverted child's soul.

Strong Points of Innie Grandparents:
• Understand the energy needs of innies.
• Focus on one grandchild at a time.
• Help the child value his inner world.
• Encourage the child to explore her interests.

- Enjoy in-depth conversations.
- Allow sufficient time to make joint decisions.

"Hardy Perennial" Outie Grandparents

*"People would have more leisure time
if it weren't for all the leisure-time
activities that use it up."—Peg Bracken*

Many outies love to shoot the breeze with anyone, even strangers. They are the hardy perennials of the social world. They find interacting with others effortless. However, since they rely so much on the outside world, they are more sensitive to perceived rejection. As grandparents, they may have trouble understanding that children have different temperaments, and thus may feel rejected by an innie.

June, a client of mine, had a new granddaughter, Karin. One day June said, "She doesn't like me." I asked her to tell me what happened to make her think this. She said, "Karin turned her head away and wouldn't look at me." To me, this suggested that Karin was in the stranger-anxiety phase of babyhood. "I can see why you thought that, but this is normal at eight months," I told her. "Karin is just showing that she has made a healthy connection with her parents. She sees that your face looks different from theirs. It's a good sign. Don't take it personally. She'll be past this stage soon." Later, Karin showed signs of being somewhat introverted. Over time, June learned to calm her expectations and wait for Karin to come to her. She stopped regarding Karin's hiding behind her parents as a reflection of her feelings toward her. As Karin got older, she learned to enjoy June's enthusiasm and fun-loving personality.

Innies will certainly enjoy an outie's ideas, activities, and zest. They'll enjoy learning about their grandparents' lives and going on adventures with them—as long as it doesn't get to be too much. Innie grandchildren can teach outies to slow down and notice things. Outies may think that everyone enjoy's life in the same ways—or should. You can explain that your child is different, and that a slow walk around the lake and feeding the ducks would appeal to him most. If an outie grandparent wants to take her innie grandchild on a special outing, suggest something of interest to both of them, because many outie grandparents may pick something to do without first finding out if their grandchild is keen on it, too. One outie client I had took his innie grandchild whale watching without asking the parents if he got seasick. Let us just say that he won't make that mistake again.

Strong Points of Outie Grandparents:
• Come up with lots of fun things to do
• Are friendly and enthusiastic
• Are spontaneous
• Can manage more grandchildren for a longer period
• Appreciate outie children's spunk and energy
• Show warmth and love and give compliments

Constructing a Sturdy Span

"I loved their home. Everything smelled older, worn but safe; the food aroma had baked itself into the furniture."—Susan Strasberg

For numerous reasons, some grandparents are reluctant to create a relationship with their grandchildren. Perhaps they had intrusive in-laws when they were raising their children, and they don't want to repeat what happened to them. They may be hesitant, shy, or anxious about the responsibility. Or they may think past conflicts

Forgive Your Parents

Sometimes it is the parents who stand in the way of a strong relationship between grandparent and grandchild. There are many reasons for this. It can be painful to realize that a parent may be better at *grandparenting* than he or she was at *parenting*. I have seen adults continue to hold grudges against their parents instead of realizing that their parents were flawed, grieving about what they have missed during childhood, and not accepting their parents for who they are today.

Unless your parents are extremely self-involved, mentally ill (and not being treated), alcoholic (and not in recovery), or traumatizing in any other way, try to forgive them for past misdeeds. Many of us have parents who were disappointing, stressed-out, overwhelmed, or less than enlightened about child rearing. Try to let go of old wounds and appreciate that they may have grown. Give your children that gift. They will remember the example you set now when *they* grow up and have children.

One situation I've observed is parents who are jealous of their children's relationships with grandparents and other relatives. This is really tragic. It will eventually harm the parent's own relationship with the child as that child grows up. I have had many clients tell me that their parents barred them from having relationships with their grandparents or other relatives, and they still resent it. It's good practice to "share" your child when he is young because children are only borrowed; you will need to share him more and more anyway as he grows up. Grandparents and others provide children with other role models from which to learn. They give children the opportunity to love *more*, not *less*. Your children will thank you for it.

are still at play, not know they are needed or important, or perhaps they are just insecure about today's newfangled equipment. Even after four grandchildren, we still have trouble getting the fancy stroller upright and then collapsed again. Some grandparents may need to get the thumbs-up signal from the parents before pursuing a close relationship with a grandchild.

Since, even today, mothers are still usually the child's gatekeeper, the father's parents may not enjoy the easy access the mother's parents do. If the father's mother has trouble letting go of her son, it sometimes causes territorial problems, and their daughter-in-law doesn't feel as generous with the children. Blended families only complicate these kinds of matters.

One of my clients, Keri, was very hurt when her introverted mom suddenly no longer wanted to babysit for her three children. I encouraged Keri to talk to her mom in a nondefensive way and ask why. Keri's mom told her that she felt confident and safe with her two introverted granddaughters, but when her extroverted grandson, Jake, who is quite a handful for anyone, was there she felt scared and out of control. She was worried that she wouldn't be able to handle him, and that Jake might get hurt. Keri's hurt disappeared. Now they only leave all three kids when Keri's dad can help out. They also began to arrange for each child to visit alone with Grandma more often. The bonds between Keri's mom and her grandchildren grew stronger.

Here are a few ways to strengthen the bridge that spans the generations:

- Realize that the more loving relationships your child has, the better.
- Tell your parents that you appreciate their efforts to understand your children.
- If you do things differently from your parents, acknowledge that things have changed since they were parents and that you value their ability to learn new ways.
- Discuss the notion of temperament with them, specifically as it relates to your innie child. Let them know how much their affection and interest means to your innie. Encourage them to take the Temperament Quiz on page 16 and share how they feel temperament has affected their own lives.

- Explain that innies react differently around people they don't know or don't often see, and in groups. You can discuss what your innie might need from them to feel comfortable.
- Encourage your child to send cards, e-mails, and artwork to his grandparents.
- Be sure to acknowledge gifts: "Andy loved the book you sent him."
- Keep communication flowing.

Shake a Little, Grow a Lot

"The key to change . . . is to let go of fear."
—Rosanne Cash

Miracle-Gro has a product called Shake 'n Feed Continuous Release Plant Food. The ad for it in *Southern Living* magazine reads, "Shake a Little, Grow a Lot." It recommends shaking the nutrients onto plants and flowers, and voilà!, they'll grow beautifully. This ad could apply to grandparents, too.

Sometimes you need to teach an old sage new tricks. If you have grandparents or other relatives who expect all children to be outgoing, thrive in groups, and generally behave like good little extroverts, explain that you reach an innie via the three Rs: release, read, and relate, as I explain below.

I recently worked with Ellen and Dan, the parents of an extremely bright, highly sensitive five-year-old innie named Zara. Dan's parents expected all the grandchildren in the family to act more or less the same. They should be talkative, offer a kiss when greeted, enjoy noisy family gatherings, gobble up all the food on their plates, and jump for joy over gifts. But in actuality, at parties, Zara was overwhelmed by the noise, the kissing, and the pressure to be gregarious. When visiting her grandparents, she often succumbed to a meltdown. Dan's parents criticized Dan and Ellen for what they called "babying" Zara.

Closing the Distance

These days most grandchildren—except for the lucky few—live far away from their grandparents. It takes effort, but you can keep the bond alive in spite of geographical distance. One of my friends has a teenaged granddaughter who lives in another city. They e-mail almost daily, and my friend helps this shy, introverted girl through the thorny social thickets. Most innies get a kick out of communicating with grandparents who live in another area. Here are some ways you as a parent can help long-distance family members stay involved:

• Try a "Circle Journey Kit." A grandfather jots his thoughts in a journal or letter and sends it to his grandchild. The grandchild continues the chain journal or letter by adding her comments, questions, or answers. Then she shoots it back to her grandfather. It's an interactive diary, a written conversation documenting their relationship over time.

• Give older relatives on fixed incomes a prepaid phone card.

• When relatives visit, cook or bake together. Write down the recipes and talk about or call the relatives when you make the dish again.

• Use snail mail. It still works, and everyone looks forward to getting mail.

• Send frequent e-mails, file the good ones to read again later, and take digital pictures and send them via e-mail.

Ellen and Dan talked with Dan's parents and asked them to release their expectations. Could they expand their view and see that all children are not created from one seed? Like flowers, children come in assorted shapes and types. Could they let go of expectations for their innie grandchild, who can't just change to become someone else? They described the scientific discoveries that explain why and how introverted children are hardwired. Once grandparents can see each and every grandchild as a separate seedling, it will help everyone grow.

Dan and Ellen tried to help his parents learn to read Zara. Is she wearing a glazed look suggesting that she's overstimulated? Is she getting cranky? Or withdrawing? Has her energy dropped? Have there been too many activities? Can they observe how she eases into new experiences and checks things out first? If they can begin to ask themselves these questions, they are learning to read her and are ready to relate.

Relating to their grandchildren means not merely talking but developing the ability to be flexible and adjust to children. If your grandchild is worn out, don't add more stimulation (even if there is a special game you've been waiting to show her all day). Push your mute button (everyone has one). Be sure to give her breaks. Don't expect to relate to innies in a group as well as you would privately. They will respond better if you subtly acknowledge them with a wave, a wink, or a nod. Later you can find a nook where the two of you can chat alone.

Standing Sentinel

"The person who has had a bull by the tail once has learned 60 or 70 times as much as the person who hasn't."—Mark Twain

The number-one job of parenting is protecting our children. We need to be sentinels, ever alert for what could harm our kids. Some of us weren't protected as children. Because we didn't learn those skills, we may not be very good at guarding our own children. Or we may leap over to the opposite pole and overprotect them. Introverted children, in particular, need middle-of-the-road sentries: a mixture of encouragement and security.

Innies at Large Family Gatherings

Big family parties at holiday times or to celebrate special events can be stressful for everyone, but especially so for innie kids, who may wilt at all the stimulation and attention. Here are a few tips to help make things go more smoothly:

• Before the party, explain to key family members that your child is introverted and may seem unfriendly, but they should know it's not personal—it's physiological.

• Since his energy level directly affects his ability to deal with social events, make sure your innie is rested and has eaten before the gathering.

• As they get older, encourage innies to wave, nod, or smile as they are easing into the gathering—they can talk later.

• Innies may talk more around fewer people, so let them seek out smaller groups. They're likely to be reserved in a crowd, even if they know everyone.

• Try to give your innie breathing space. Physical closeness can drain an innie's energy.

• Warn family members not to expect kisses and hugs until your innie is ready.

• Don't push innies to open gifts in front of the crowd. They may enjoy opening them with just a few people around.

One giant step we take as we move from youth into adulthood is when we speak up for our children within our very own families. It's called differentiation in the world of psychology. It's like taking a metaphorical bull by the tail and the horns. It's so difficult many people don't ever do it. It may involve facing one's fear of being gored. But we all need to stand up for our beliefs and psychologically separate ourselves from our families of origin in order to really be our adult selves. This is often achieved by stepping out and saying no to protect our children around our own families. Ironically, saying no in our families of origin often frees us up to appreciate and enjoy what we also value about them.

In many instances, family rules—both spoken and unspoken—don't fit for an introverted child. These include directives such as, "You must eat all your food; you must kiss Aunt Edna (whom you don't know all that well) good-bye; you must play with cousins whom you haven't seen in a year; you must open gifts in front of a large group and show how excited you are." You may be inclined to follow someone else's rules when it is fitting and causes no discomfort. But sometimes family rules can be harmful.

My client Milt was brought up in a clean-your-plate home. Milt was fine with that; as a child he swabbed his plate until it shined. However, his introverted daughter, Sylvie, turned out to be a picky eater. She was picky enough at home but was even pickier at large family gatherings—which brought her up against the clean-your-plate squad. One Thanksgiving, Milt's father got irritated with Sylvie's lackluster appetite. He told Sylvie that she couldn't leave the table until she had finished everything on her plate.

Milt saw that neither was going to back down. He took a big breath and grabbed that grandfather bull by the horns. He said, "We are glad to follow most rules you have in your home, but I'm afraid the clean-your-plate rule isn't good for Sylvie. She doesn't have to clean her plate." A deafening silence fell over the festive table. The bull sputtered and snorted; no one had challenged him on that before. Milt told Sylvie that she was excused from the table. Grandfather pawed the ground for a bit. He never directly acknowledged the incident, but he also never told Sylvie to finish everything on her plate again.

Sylvie felt protected by her father. She was surprised that her dad had stood up for her against her grandfather. And she was relieved she didn't have to eat all that greasy gravy and spicy stuffing. She also knew that she would still have to follow some rules at her grandparents' house that she might not like. For her part,

Milt's wife was impressed by her husband's assertiveness. She thought that it was good for Sylvie to see her father modeling how to stand up for his daughter, and that it might serve her well in later life. Milt felt more independent and adult because he survived in the family bullring.

Innies and Child Care

Just as family members can create strong, valuable bonds with innie kids, so can caregivers. A good caregiver can become a trusted friend, often offering a different perspective than the family provides. So please don't let just anyone take care of your innie. Introverted kids are especially sensitive to the adults around them; they need a good fit. It's worth the extra time and effort to find a safe, reliable, attentive, flexible person or day-care center to care for your child.

Ideally, innies under three should be taken care of by one consistent, kind, caring person who isn't angry, nervous, or impatient, in your own home, if at all possible. It's less stressful for your innie and less work for you. If you can't afford that, be sure the caregiver is taking care of only a few low-key kids.

I have numerous clients who have turned to lovely, even-tempered, middle-aged women who have raised their own flock—now flown from the nest. These women are usually flexible, and they enjoy picking up, delivering to lessons, doing errands, and playing with school-aged innies. You might share the expenses of this caregiver with the parents of another compatible innie. A college student learning child development (psychology, education, or another related discipline) or a preschool aide can also be a good babysitter for an innie.

It will be fruitful to discuss your child's temperament with your caregiver or the day-care center staff. Such a conversation can save much trial and error. You can specify that your child might not be highly sociable and that he may need time to recharge after particularly busy stretches. The more your caregiver knows about introversion, the better she will be able to understand your child. You can even give your caregiver a copy of the Temperament Quiz on page 16 to take. Appreciating the power of temperament will help a caregiver not just with your child but with all in her charge.

Conversation and Language Development

The first three years are crucial for language development. I believe it's essential that the caregiver speaks the child's primary language fluently. Although hiring a caregiver who speaks another language, such as Spanish, will help your child become bilingual, you don't want to sacrifice competence in the child's primary tongue. If your child's first language isn't that of the caregiver, please be sure that the sitter's accent isn't too thick, as this can interfere with an innie's language development. (Innies are dominant on the slower hearing pathway, and heavy accents make it difficult to decode what is being said.)

Explain to the caregiver that she needs to talk with your innie. I have seen many cases where caregivers don't talk very often to the children for whom they are responsible. As we've seen, innies need conversation.

Discipline

Discuss how you want to handle tricky situations like discipline. Notice how receptive the caregiver is to what you have to say about your child. You want someone who is attuned to your child's interests and concerns. Don't allow hitting, yelling, or shaming. Discuss in private the guidelines for gently setting limits if your child needs them.

Socialization Opportunities

Sign up your caregiver and toddler for a music, movement, or art class when your child is ready. But be sure your caregiver understands that the point of the class is to give her an opportunity to interact with your innie in a fun, enriching way, and to help the child take a few wobbly social steps. When I took a toddler class with my granddaughter, all the other adults in the class were caregivers. Most paid little attention to their respective charges. They were there for their own socializing. Toddlers need lots of adult supervision to learn to climb the social ropes.

Keep an Eye on Things

I am sorry to say that I also recommend hidden video cameras known as "nanny cams" that the caregiver doesn't know about— watch a bit of the film every day to see how she interacts with your child. The fact is that not everyone is cut out for taking long-term care of a young person, and you want to be sure that your caregiver has your child's best interests in mind. Taking care of even an easy infant or toddler can cause some adults, especially if the caregiver is tired or ill, to snap. Hidden cameras are good insurance because your child may not be old enough to tell you if he is harshly treated. Another way to keep tabs on things is to occasionally drop by unexpectedly or have a friend or relative visit unannounced.

Stay Connected

Assure your child that you are thinking of him, even though you can't be right there. Stay in touch with your child during the day. Phone him, and as he gets older, leave notes or send e-mails.

Transitions

Saying good-bye to you in the morning may be difficult for your innie. (Innies often have meltdowns during energy-draining transitions.) Give him ample warning before you're heading out and try to establish a routine he can count on. You might want to create a ritual (the familiar action eases the child's anxiety) for saying good-bye. A fun, short one for a young child goes like this: "Good-bye, high" (you each raise your hands and clap them together) and then, "Good bye, low" (clap your hands low together). For hellos, have your

Warning Signs

Always ask your child how the babysitting experience was. As he tells you, stay alert for any hints of trouble. Pay attention if your child complains about the caregiver. If she suddenly becomes moody around or unfriendly to her caregiver, *or* she doesn't want to go to day care, immediately investigate the child-care environment. If she complains of physical symptoms like tummy trouble, or her eating or sleeping habits change suddenly and nothing else has changed in her life, check out your caregiver.

caregiver alert your child a few minutes before you arrive. Let your child adjust to your arrival. He may not show how excited he is because he is feeling overwhelmed. Be assured he is glad to see you.

Have a Backup Plan

Make a list of two or three emergency caregivers for when your child is ill, your caregiver is sick, or some other type of unforeseen emergency arises. As your child gets old enough to understand, let her know you have a backup plan. Tell her who will step in if needed. It reduces her anxiety. Send your child's medical information and releases to at least two adults near her school or caregiver's home in case of an emergency or situation where you or your spouse can't reach your child immediately.

Evenings Out

When you go out at night, be sure that your child knows the sitter. If possible, have her visit while you are there several times before you leave them alone together. Prepare your innie for your outing, and let him know in advance that you'll be leaving him with relatives or a sitter—give him time to consider what he may need. Give him your phone number and leave him a bedtime note. As a special treat, you might let him sleep in your bed or make a tent with the sitter in the living room. Make parents' night out special for him, too. Remind him that you'll be back and that if there's any emergency, he can call you. Acknowledge that he may enjoy a break from you, too!

A childcare provider represents another adult with whom your innie can form a trusting, meaningful relationship, much like a grandparent or family friend. In the best cases, you feel secure that your child is well cared for, and your child gains confidence and learns more about the world.

The Heart of the Matter

- *Encourage innies to make friends under their own family tree.*
- *Innie and outie relatives expand your child's world.*
- *Warm and understanding caregivers are essential for innies.*

PART IV

Bringing Out What's Inside

"If you can find a path with no obstacles,

it probably doesn't lead anywhere."

—Frank Capra

CHAPTER 10

Innies in the Classroom

When You Know How Innies Learn Best, You Can Help Them Navigate the School Years

"Once we stretch our mind around a new idea, it never returns to its former shape."

—*Oliver Wendell Holmes*

Julianne's mother didn't understand what was happening. In kindergarten and first grade, Julianne loved school. Once in second grade, however, her daughter complained about going to school and her marks fell. Julianne kept coming home with sad faces instead of smiles stamped on her papers. She cried at bedtime, knowing she would have to go to school the next morning. "I hate to get those sad faces," she told her mom. Julianne's mother met with her daughter's teacher, Mrs. Chan, who told her that she thought Julianne should have been held back in first grade. Julianne's mom was shocked: How could she think that when Julianne had done *so well* in first grade? Mrs. Chan said she considered Julianne slow because she didn't participate in class discussions, didn't catch onto directions quickly, and frequently asked questions about assignments. The teacher also had Julianne stay in at recess because she took too long to do her work. Julianne's mother staggered out of the classroom, shaken.

Unfortunately, this is a real-life example of the collision between an introverted child and a teacher with fixed expectations. Mrs. Chan prided herself on launching the year with strictly new material. She valued speed, and she believed that directions should only be given once. If a child didn't hear something the first time, then she must not have been listening. Mrs. Chan was rather stern, and to top it off she had an accent that made her a bit difficult to understand. Julianne's previous teachers had been a better fit for her.

Julianne's mother and I tried to strategize. The school wouldn't move Julianne to another second-grade class, so her mother got Mrs. Chan to assign another classmate as a helpmate to Julianne. She could ask her helpmate questions about directions and assignments. The classroom aide assisting Mrs. Chan was also able to play a role, as she was warmer and more responsive to children's individual needs. Julianne's mother talked to Julianne about how her mind worked and why she needed more time to think things over. Julianne's mom kept encouraging her to do what she could and to realize that it was okay not to get everything right. The seven-year-old muddled through the school year. It was heartbreaking for her mother and me to watch from the sidelines. Even with help, Julianne was discouraged and hated going to school. She thought she was too slow at everything. She and her mom put stickers on the calendar to count off the days until S-Day: the day summer vacation started. By then, Julianne had tummy trouble and dark circles under her eyes.

During the summer Julianne perked up, but she grew anxious as third grade loomed closer. Her mom had requested a third-grade teacher she thought would be more compatible. The school, however, wouldn't guarantee she'd get that teacher. We all gave a big sigh of relief when Julianne lucked out and was assigned to the easygoing teacher who understood that all children's minds are not identical. After about six weeks in her new classroom, Julianne said to her mother, "I'm beginning to like school again."

Innies' Challenges and Advantages

School is full of hurdles for any child. But innies face particular difficulties in the classroom setting. First, just being out in the world and focusing externally burns their energy. They're often operating outside their comfort zone, which makes it harder to do their best. Typical classrooms consume gallons of fuel because they are noisy, full of visual distractions, and require close proximity to others. It's difficult to hear, especially if people speak quickly or have accents. And on top of all this, there's often little time or space to recharge.

Second, innies are pressured to process information, communicate, and finish work quickly. They are measured by the ability to work speedily, assume tasks before they feel ready, and take timed tests. In addition, they are often forced into situations that they struggle with, such as speaking before the class, assimilating others' standards and views, managing interruptions, shifting from topic to topic, and working in groups. Plus, innies may be overlooked in classrooms. Rowdy students often take up the teacher's attention.

Teachers, especially outies, often misunderstand innie behavior and qualities. Since it takes innies longer to access information, they may not respond to teachers' questions if they don't feel comfortable. If pressed for time or if they feel any other type of pressure, innies may not show enthusiasm. As a result, they may appear to lack interest or motivation—their real feelings don't show on the outside. And since their auditory track is slower, as I have said, they may not catch directions the first time and so may seem a beat behind. The introverted child, then, may be perceived as not very smart, not keeping up, lacking enthusiasm, too stubborn, too independent, not social enough in the classroom, or asking too many questions about directions or the materials.

Those are the potential problems. But most innies are eager to learn, and teachers often recognize innies' strengths and encourage them. This happened to me, and many innies have told me they've had similar experiences. Some teachers are drawn to innies because they like their ability to have more complex conversations. Teachers value their keen observations and insights. Innie students may even become teachers' pets because they are helpful, easy to handle in the classroom, and some even seek out their teachers. My grandson has loved, loved, *loved* his kindergarten, first- and third-grade teachers. My daughter's ears have almost fallen off hearing about Miss McDonald, her son's current favorite. Many innies find they are more interested in their teachers because they have more in common with them than with their classmates. Indeed, many innie children prefer conversing with adults, in general, rather than with their peers. Outie teachers often find innies fascinating when they get a glimpse of their inner world.

Many innies find school a flourishing garden of knowledge, despite the drain on their energy. They enjoy learning. In order to

It's What's Up Front That Counts

Remember, innies are hardwired to use a direct pathway to the executive area, in the front of the brain, which integrates and develops complex ideas and concepts. As innies grow and develop, their thoughts, emotions, and experiences become integrated. This blesses them with the ability to use complex mental functions. The front, or *bonnet*, of the brain also holds the keys to judgment, social and ethical behavior, creativity, and what may be our greatest gift, *mindsight:* the ability to know other people's minds and understand their intentions, the most sophisticated type of emotional intelligence.

help themselves enjoy school, some find inventive ways to cope with their overstimulation. Often they uncover less frenetic places at school to recharge. They might spend their lunch period in the library, if it's a quiet place. An innie I worked with went to the kindergarten class to read to a child for an hour. Another used to visit the school nurse and chat with her during his lunch break. I helped out in the quiet back office for one period in high school. When one of my daughters was in high school, she went to the local elementary school to develop arts-and-crafts projects for the teachers during a free block of time.

How Innies Learn

"I believe that everything in a child's development is connected—what has gone before, what is happening now, and what will happen in the future."—*Fred Rogers*

Whether a child is an innie or an outie greatly determines how she learns. Extroverts form their perceptions from *external* past events in the back, or *boot,* of the brain. Introverts base their experiences on *internal* thoughts and feelings. These are processed in the front, or *bonnet,* of the brain. Learning is a complex function that activates numerous parts of the brain in rapid succession. In a way, learning requires riding a roller coaster around and through various parts of the brain. Let's see how the process differs between innies and outies.

Innies attend to what interests them. They receive information from their bodies and brains on slower, more unconscious pathways. Their minds work associatively, drawing on long-term memory. Experiences are compared and contrasted with past, present, and in the front of the brain. More complex perceptions are constructed during overnight processing as the day's memories are integrated and stored when they are dreaming. At this point, thoughts will have coalesced, and they will be ready to form an idea or plan of action. Innies need time and encouragement to demonstrate their internal knowledge to others. To expand their knowledge, they need to test their ideas by applying them in the real world.

Outies focus on what catches their attention. Information from their senses enters the brain via fast, conscious pathways. The data is matched to old experiences—good and bad—to generate a rapid perception in the back of the brain. They may make a quick decision or take an action like speaking, writing, or changing an opinion based on this small amount of data. Information flows quickly in and out of short-term memory—it only holds about seven items at any one time—and may not stick. To expand their learning, outies need help to pause, reflect, and connect more associations in the front of the brain to develop more complex perceptions, plans, and actions.

Good teaching can be understood as the art of enhancing the brain and the brain's ability to learn. The brain is designed to learn; in turn, learning alters the brain. When a child's knowledge is expanded, neural connections are increased. First, the child builds a foundation of experiences at home and in the world. Then, new information is connected to those built-in experiences. The result is that a new piece of knowledge, with an entire new constellation of associations, becomes part of the child's mental repertoire.

An introverted child's strong suit is learning by association. It's an innie's natural inclination to forge links—to connect the dots. Teachers provide new information, which helps innies draw lines between the existing dots of data already in their brains. Now they are linked together. An outline of a fuller picture begins to emerge as the child situates new information within the context of his own personal experience.

When Mrs. Chan didn't review what was learned in first grade, Julianne was left without any dots to link up with the new material. No coherent picture formed for her. All she found was disconnected units of information. Connecting the dots means that the child sees associations (for instance, "Oh, if I learn math it will help me figure out how to count money" or "Learning science can teach me how to grow a sunflower"). Innies have lots of internal dots, a virtual treasure trove of potential hooks on which to hang new learning. But they need to take in information in a sequence to help connect these dots.

In the classroom, children learn best when new information is taught in an engaging, hands-on style that, literally, stimulates their brains. Lively stories, for example, connect all areas of the child's brain: emotion, cognition, meaning, and memory (past experiences). Rote learning tends not to generate knowledge or innovative thinking. Real learning appeals to all levels of the brain. It transforms learning from a simple mode of receiving and filing information in the brain to a more complex process: receiving information and then *creating* knowledge, by sending it along the introverted path to the executive areas of the brain.

What Learning Environment Brings Out the Best in Innies?

Introverted children require time and space, and need to set their own pace. Because innies turn inward for energy, safety, and satisfaction, they flourish in a well-ordered, quiet classroom where subjects are discussed in depth, one topic at a time. They demonstrate their attention by being still (not because they are necessarily expected to, but to conserve energy when they're listening keenly). They sit watching, often without expression (again, to conserve energy). Occasionally, they may look away or look down (to facilitate processing information). Noise and movement interrupts their ability to concentrate.

Innies thrive in an atmosphere that's accepting and patient. If innies are asked questions on the spot, the answer usually zooms right out of their heads. But this doesn't mean that the information isn't in there—it just needs to be lured out the right way. Without

Choosing a School

"The best thing you can give children, next to good habits, are good memories."—Sydney J. Harris

Innies need schools where the environment is calm, encouraging, flexible, and warm. I have worked with many adult innies who went to competitive, judgmental, shaming, rigid, and harsh schools. In that kind of atmosphere, innies may shut down, not learn, fall behind, and, sadly, think they aren't smart. They need a school environment where the staff enjoys children (unfortunately, this is often not the case) and where students are viewed as individuals. They need teachers who can adjust to different learning styles. What is most important is an environment where innies can use their gifts. They need a quiet, structured classroom where expectations are based on the individual child. Smaller is better. If teachers are open to learning about your child and allowing her the space and reflective time her brain needs, a good fit can be made.

Many parents don't have a choice of schools. If you do, try to find one that encourages individual strengths and doesn't put undue pressure

pressure, they can volunteer answers. And in an atmosphere of trust and space, they can surprise others with the complexity of their responses. In Jonathan's fourth-grade class, for example, they were studying the history of flight. Suddenly, he raised his hand, and the usually quiet child launched into a whole wellspring of knowledge. "Did you know that they built one hundred B-1B bombers? They are stealth bombers, and they fly very close to the ground so they can't be picked up on radar. They are very sleek, and their wings retract after they take off. But four crashed because they sucked birds into their engines. Now they fixed that problem and they are using them in the Iraq War." After a stunned silence, the teacher asked Jonathan more about the B-1Bs.

on the child. Homeschooling and charter schools can work well for innies if they are based on one-on-one, individually designed learning. However, homeschooled innies will need other group and social experiences to strengthen their extroverting muscles. Schools for children gifted in the arts and sciences are often very helpful for innies, as long as they aren't too competitive, rigid, or demanding.

The optimal learning environment for innies includes:

- A quiet, structured classroom with few surprises.
- Time and space to reflect, process, and prepare.
- Having the big picture presented first, and relating material to students' lives.
- Having a choice of whether to work in groups or alone; the option of having a pal to work with or ask questions of; individual, rather than group, credit on assignments.
- Having a designated "Learning Lair," a private area or one set off with screens, complete with earplugs and headphones.

Innies are private and need to have a sense of ownership over their space and belongings. When innies share space and supplies, they may feel intruded upon. In some school districts, students share desks. This depletes innies' energy and reduces their ability to concentrate. Ten-year-old Tony is typical in that he can't bear even to read with someone looking over his shoulder. When he senses somebody there he altogether loses the ability to think! I have worked with teachers who give innies their own place and space, and the children function much better.

Innies like clear instructions and information. Once they have a clear sense of the task at hand, they take off on their own. They are

Rewards Come to Those Who Wait

Psychologist Walter Mischel, Ph.D., conducted a longitudinal study at Columbia University with four-year-old preschoolers that measured their ability to wait and resist the temptation to have some candy. The children's waiting ability ranged from a few seconds to more than five minutes. These same children were studied again as teenagers. Those who tolerated longer waits as children had higher SAT scores as teens. They had more advanced social and cognitive abilities. And they were able to tolerate stress and frustration better than their peers. The researchers concluded that there is a vital link between a young child's ability to wait, and his later emotional and cognitive capacities. What many parents see as a disadvantage—innies' inhibition—is also the advantage of self-control; the built-in ability to wait. This ability gives introverted children a solid foundation they can use as adults to reach their academic and life goals.

especially self-motivated if they find a way to connect with a topic personally. Hayden's fifth-grade class is studying South America. Hayden is interested in mountain climbing. He wonders, "What is the highest peak in South America? And which peaks have been climbed?" His curiosity is such that during recess he goes to the library and looks up South American peaks in a reference book and on the Internet.

Innies enjoy polishing their ideas and impressions, letting them steep. If stumped, they prefer to do Internet research, watch a video, or read a book and perhaps discuss it with a trusted person. Before doing anything in public—even in front of one single person—they want to prepare and practice. In one school's annual Shakespeare production, Veronica, a twelve-year-old innie, did an amazing job in the role of King Lear. Even her mother was stunned.

She had no idea how completely Veronica had mastered the lines; she had done it entirely on her own.

Innies appreciate feedback and input from others only when they feel they fully understand the concept themselves. They like the stimulation of others' ideas, but the timing needs to be right. Too much input in the formulating stage can stall their process and ruin their ability to puzzle something through to its completion. Innies are sensitive to input that they feel disregards or minimizes the time and effort they have expended to arrive at their conclusions. If they feel that their ideas are appreciated, then they like to collaborate and expand or combine their ideas.

Classroom Pitfalls for Innies

Classrooms can be overstimulating. The traditional classroom setting is not designed to bring out the best in innies. Many classrooms are crowded and noisy—too much commotion, too much bright light, too much pressure, and, it seems, too much of everything. Innies may not get the chance to catch their breath and reflect, concentrate on what they're doing, or prepare before it's time to submit their work to scrutiny.

Teachers may misunderstand innies. Most elementary and secondary teachers are themselves extroverts; this makes sense since teachers need tons of energy to make it through even an ordinary school day. Most teachers don't understand innies. They equate "smart" with "fast." Studies show that teachers tend to ask a question and move on in a few seconds if a student doesn't provide the answer. Innies often feel like they are in a race where they can't keep up. Unfortunately, in such environments, only a tiny bit of an introverted child's talents and abilities is seen.

Teachers or classmates who don't understand innies may feel rejected by them. Some teachers will misinterpret an innie's behavior, thinking that a child is rebellious, unintelligent, apathetic, or won't or can't communicate. Some teachers may feel frustrated because they think they are failing to reach such a child. What's sad is the way that others construe an innie's tendency to draw inward as a negative—as a rejection. Actually, the child is most likely trying to process and integrate the material presented to him. An introverted child's outward behavior does not necessarily reflect what's going on in his mind.

Teachers may overlook innies. Innies are often model students —quiet, focused, and not disruptive, so they may receive less attention while the teacher deals with the rowdy kids.

Moving Through the School Years

"A sense of curiosity is nature's original school of education."—Smiley Blanton, M.D.

When we think of school, we tend to think of reading, writing, and 'rithmatic, maybe with a little science and history thrown in. But school is more than just academics. Your *whole* child goes to school. And many factors besides what's written on the blackboard affect how your child learns: emotional ups and downs, a sense of fitting in, having friends, energy levels, and relationships with teachers, to name a few. Here is a brief rundown of how your introverted child progresses through the educational system. Knowing what's up—and what's ahead—will help you advocate for her.

Preschool

For innies, preschool is about learning how to self-regulate while extroverting without parental help. Introverted kids are learning to handle themselves in unfamiliar territory, expanding their relationships outside the comfort zone of their immediate family, and discovering how to modulate their energy, emotions, and stimulation levels.

Introverted children usually start preschool around three. Starting out with a limited schedule, say, three mornings a week, provides consistency yet allows for plenty of quiet time at home. A small preschool usually works best with no more than ten to fourteen children per class, and at least two teachers. A well-structured, predictable program will allow your innie to settle in easily. It's helpful if there's a quiet corner or nook. A well-trained preschool staff understands individual temperaments and knows the developmental tasks children are mastering at each stage of growth; they are trained to work specifically with preschool children. You ought to be allowed to stay until your child is comfortable. A good teacher knows that some children need to ease into the class, slowly learning to manage the separation, and will allow you to stay until your child is comfortable. Usually innies need to ease into school transitions, especially if they have stressors, such as a new sibling. It may take a week for some children and several weeks for others. Even after a break, say, returning from an illness or vacation, they may need a bit of reentry help.

Bring your child to see the school before starting, perhaps visit the playground on the weekend, and discuss the upcoming adventure. Throughout the year, help your innie prepare for any upcoming transition, such as holidays and the end of school.

Keep talking with your innie during your daily chat time about what's happening at school. Is she concerned about anything? Ask your child about his day when he is rested, and encourage him to share something he is excited about with the rest of the family: "Hey, I heard the snake wrangler came today! Can you tell us about it?" Be sure to let him rest after school.

Keep communication lines open with the teachers. Encourage the teacher to invite others to play with your child if he frequently plays alone. If the teacher reports that your child doesn't speak up when another child takes his toys or knocks over his blocks, practice similar scenarios at home. Pick a time when your innie is rested and suggest playing blocks. You can make a move to knock over the blocks and suggest that he say, "Hey, don't do that!" Switch roles, and then model a way to shift the situation to cooperative play, inviting him to make a block bridge next to yours. Speak out loud about your own playground tussles. This helps innies learn that others also grapple with what to do in these situations.

Innies are sometimes frustrated with other kids who can't play longer and who behave impulsively. This presents a good opportunity to discuss how each child has her unique temperament and develops at her own pace. Discuss with your innie that she has strengths in this area, just as other kids who might be more impulsive right now have their own special talents.

Kindergarten

Five is a prime social year for all children, and most children are delightful at this age. Innies are learning to compare and contrast their inside world and the outside world, striving to make sense of the kids, the teacher, and what they are learning, and to put their own thoughts and ideas into action. They are taking in and integrating new experiences. All of this takes lots of fuel.

Innies who didn't make one or two special friends in preschool usually do so in kindergarten. Now that your innie is more acclimated to school, she is able to apply her observing skills to other children. She sees that some kids are fun to play with, and some are not. She is connecting a child's behavior with his or her intentions, and learning to handle conflicts.

Many innies, especially those with older siblings, are anxious to go to "big" school. Have your innie visit the school before the first day. Check out the whole school, including the bathrooms, the cafeteria, and the office. Point out children having fun in class. If a friend or older sibling attends the school, let your innie visit at a holiday party or other fun, casual time. Encourage her to say hello to the teacher during the visit.

The biggest challenge for innies is the increasing pressure to learn in an environment that isn't conducive to their hardwiring. Sometimes they want to go back to their old school. Help your child adapt by acknowledging her experience. "I know it's noisy and hard to think." Help her find solutions. Encourage her to brainstorm with you: "What do you think will help?" Innies come up with great ideas.

As she becomes more comfortable in class, suggest she take a small gift like a flower or card and give it to the teacher. (It's okay if she wants you to help her approach the teacher.) If your family goes on a vacation, bring back small tokens of the trip, such as pretty seashells, for your innie to give to the whole class. This models valuing her class and lets her express that she feels part of the group. Plan brief playdates with children she enjoys. Keep up daily chats with your innie so she can hash out thoughts and feelings about school. This also gives you a chance to interrupt any negative self-talk. Even at this age, innies tend to internalize things, and they easily blame themselves. For instance, you can say, "Are you thinking Nemo II [the classroom fish] died because you did something wrong?" "Yes, my job was to feed him, and I think I must have fed him too much." "Honey, I'm glad you told me because it wasn't your fault; Mrs. Clark told me he was a very old fish."

Elementary School

Entering elementary school is a big leap for innies. The added pressure and subject matter can overwhelm them. They need to be assured that it will get easier (and it will). Innies learn best if they can tie new information to an anchor of something they already know. They build off their foundation of previous lessons and experiences. Innies learn best when material is broken up into digestible, bite-sized pieces. They need lots of practice to learn the fundamentals in creative ways: flash cards, drawing pictures, singing, making up silly rhymes, or reviewing in the car. Help them develop strong phonetic and sight-reading skills, and good math fundamentals. Innies aren't as strong on short-term memory, which is used for math, so they need lots of practice adding, subtracting, and mastering multiplication tables. They may be slower to grasp these basics, since they are still learning to manage the stimulation of the classroom. But once they get on solid footing, stand back—especially around third grade—and watch them take off. Many innies begin to really love learning at this stage. Their key challenge is learning to speak up and show what they know.

Talk with your child about his learning preferences. Help him stay organized, so he doesn't waste energy on anxiety, which only reduces his learning ability. Many innies do better with colored bins and baskets to keep their work organized and in plain sight.

If the teacher mentions that your child doodles, daydreams, or withdraws from class activity, take note. This may mean he is trying to quiet his active brain so he can listen better, or they may be signs of disengaging. If he is disengaging, you may want to talk to him about what is happening: Is he uninterested in the material? Is he confused? Is he overwhelmed? Is he behind? Is the classroom too noisy? Keep up a dialogue with him to help him problem solve.

Middle School

During the middle school years, many innies struggle with feeling different. Your child will need help recognizing her strengths since she is no doubt becoming more aware that she isn't the American ideal. Encouraging her gifts and her personal interests will help her accept her differentness. The fact is that most kids are outies. Knowing this validates your introverted child's sense of being different and also frees her to be who she is. Feeling accepted by family and a few friends—plus finding interests that spark her fancy—goes a long way to balance the realization that she may not be the most outgoing or popular student in school.

Middle school consumes lots of energy for innies. They have to manage the increasing pressure of tests and handling several classes at once. This is another period of learning new basic skills—skills they will need for high school and college. One such skill is note taking. Innies' slower auditory pathway can make this difficult. One system that works well for innies is the three-column system: Fold a piece of paper into three sections. Show your child how to write main points in one column, more details about those points in the second column, and, after class, make any further comments that seem important in the third column. You can also help her prioritize assignments and break longer projects into shorter steps.

Feeling comfortable socially and emotionally is all entwined with learning—and never more than in the middle school years. Kids at this age may drift away a bit if parents don't make efforts to maintain a connection. Show an interest in what your child is learning at school. If she is studying famous painters, for instance, take her to a museum or take books out of the library that describe the painters' lives. Model friendly behaviors that are hard for your innie, such as joining a table full of strangers when you're at a community event. You can tell your innie, "Let's squeeze in with those folks." Then say, "Hi, this is my daughter Gretchen and I'm Lindsey. The food here is great, isn't it?"

During these school years, there are more after-school activities available to your child, such as Scouts, school enrichment classes like extra science courses, 4-H, sports, arts and crafts—and you can encourage her to take advantage of them. Suggest she try one new thing each semester.

Remember that it's important for your innie to know that you are in her corner. Also bear in mind that learning happens both in and out of school. The middle school years are especially difficult because, to some extent, *all* kids feel off-kilter during this period of adolescence. Keep reminding your child of her advantages and help her boost up her internal talk so she doesn't fall into self-criticism. She is still coming into her own.

High School

Many innies tell me they hated high school. It's loud, crowded, and bursting with group social pressure. Innies are often out of step because, at this stage, they are ready for a richer learning experience. The best tack is to find ways to fit in that suit an innie's strengths.

Learning the intrinsic value of marching to one's own drummer can make high school tolerable. Plus there's always the knowledge that college will be better.

In high school, innies are probably working harder than ever to balance their private time with socializing time, which takes their energy. Encourage them to take some downtime, though it may not seem convenient (or cool). Sleep is key; sleep researchers have proven that teenage brains need more sleep to grow.

An innie teenager may be sensitive about being seen as a nerd or a geek. Suggest that your child take some classes that aren't academic, like acting or photography, or get involved in extracurricular activities that will introduce him or her to a broader range of kids. Playing in the band, working on the school newspaper, or playing on sports teams may allow your innie to meet new kids, or to show himself in a new light to kids he already knows. Some innies like to debate, since it provides a structured way to discuss things they feel strongly about. Encourage volunteering outside of school to develop interests and a sense of responsibility. Or, if they're keen on exploring a particular career, help innie teens find an unpaid internship where they may be able to help out while gaining a glimpse of the field.

Sometimes innies get bored in high school. They may want to study only subjects they like. See if you can find a way to link school material with your innie's interests and experiences. Discuss these ideas with him, and see if he can reframe his experience at school. It's an important talent in life to not only know what interests us but to also know how to make a subject compelling. All through life it's necessary to engage in some things we don't find too fascinating. If the topic at hand is a particular era in history, are there biographies available, family roots investigations to be undertaken, or museums about the period your teen could visit to bring the dry facts to life?

Two other factors can impede an innie's performance in high school. One is the fear of standing out. Girls, especially, often undermine their own talents so as not to attract attention, or to avoid being teased for being smart. The second factor is rebellion. These reactions grow out of low self-esteem and, at times, anger at a parent or other authority figure. Your innie may also be scared about growing up, and even sabotage his school performance.

Remember, innies feel best when they are prepared. Know that he needs to practice organizational and time-management skills. These skills will give your innie teen confidence in his ability to live independently. Remain an ally as he wrangles his way though high school, even though at times he may reject your presence and help. He may still need your assistance to manage his schedule, plan his classes, and strategize how to approach his schoolwork. Walk that fine line between helping him to problem solve while encouraging his sense of responsibility.

The Forest and the Trees

"It is by logic that we prove, but by intuition that we discover."—Henri Poincaré

As discussed in Chapter 2, the right and left hemispheres of the brain often operate independently of each other. The right brain perceives the forest; the left brain sees and assesses each individual tree. But the two must work together to unite such functions as thoughts and feelings, and unconscious and conscious processing. Children who are right-brained dominant are in the minority. Most elementary and secondary schools are designed for left-brained extroverts, as this is the majority of our population. Most teachers are also left-brained extroverts—until you reach the college level.

Leading brain researcher Daniel Siegel, M.D., says, "Someone has got to stand up for the right hemisphere! Remember, the right-hemisphere brain processes are important for self-regulation, a sense of self, and empathetic connections to others." Like introverted children, right-brained children often have trouble in school. In fact, some brain experts think attention deficit disorder (ADD) is not a disability but rather that it reflects right-side dominance. I think that it may be possible that attention-deficit/hyperactivity disorder (ADHD) may be right-brained extroversion, and ADD may be right-brained introversion. In that sense, these conditions simply reflect different brain strengths rather than being actual disabilities.

Left-brain skills are used in learning the three Rs (reading, writing, and 'rithmetic) and the three Ls (linear thought, logic, and language). But this orientation has limitations, such as too great a focus on details, black-and-white thinking, resistance to new information, and not grasping the big picture. Right-brain abilities include recognizing patterns, noticing bodily and emotional sensations, comprehending the big picture, using and understanding symbolism, artistic creativity, and receptiveness to new information. However, the right hemisphere is limited in verbal language, has difficulty narrowing down, and is prone to becoming overwhelmed.

Knowing your child's brain dominance helps to bolster his strengths and may explain certain limitations. Below are strategies for right- and left-brained children.

Right-Brained Children Learn Best When You:

- Use visuals, metaphors, and music.
- Create unstructured time for class work and activities.
- Assist with time management and conflict resolution.
- Provide room for spontaneous reactions and emerging information.
- Allow flexibility to pursue alternative assignments or take creative approaches.
- Value the student's empathy and unique perspective.
- Connect material to other people and to the child's own life and experience.
- Respond with encouragement and use criticism sparingly and carefully.
- Recognize and acknowledge right-brain attributes like curiosity and creativity.

Left-Brained Children Learn Best When You:

- Create structure, clear expectations, and grading criteria.
- Use concrete cause-and-effect reasoning.
- Validate left-brain attributes, like being good with words and numbers.
- Provide opportunities for critical thinking and problem solving.
- Create opportunities for debates and oral reports.
- Expand students' ability to be flexible and to reflect before making decisions.
- Teach the value of differences between others and the benefits of group decision making.
- Offer chances to use investigative skills to create independent work.
- Minimize acknowledgement of flaws in people, things, and ideas.
- Reward success; minimize emphasis on failure.
- Balance competition with cooperation.

Education is not a one-size-fits-all enterprise. We're still learning about how different settings, teaching styles, and educational modalities work for different students. By understanding how innies experience school, you will be able to help your child get the most out of his education.

The Heart of the Matter

- *Innies usually attend schools designed for outies.*
- *Innies blossom when parents and teachers understand how they learn.*
- *Right- and left-brained innies have different learning strengths.*

CHAPTER 11

Support Your Introvert at School and on the Playing Field

Lend a Helping Hand with Teachers, Studying, Homework, Preparing for College, and the Sports Scene

"A child is not a vase to be filled but a fire to be lit."

—*Rabelais*

Innies are born learners; that is what they're hardwired for. They are quiet observers who enjoy working independently and are always reflecting. They need information that is stimulating to feed their brain pathways. If their parents and teachers understand the way they think, they will flourish in the classroom.

Unfortunately, because most traditional school environments aren't designed for introverted children, innies must expend a lot of energy to function in them. Often they don't get much encouragement, since

they may be unseen and misunderstood. It is incumbent on tempera-
ment-wise parents to ensure that their introverted children are taught
in an appropriate, meaningful way. This will mean taking an active role
in your child's schooling—which has positive benefits for students and
their families.

Don't Let Teachers Be Strangers

You may want to talk to your child's teacher (or teachers) about your
child's temperament and how he is "wired." If his teacher understands about his temperament, she or he is more likely to
accommodate your child's learning style. Try to form an alliance with
the teacher. Tell her about your child's needs and behaviors at home if
you think it will shed light on the school situation. Assure the teacher
that your child likes to learn—but at his own pace. You can describe
instances that demonstrate your child's interest in the schoolwork, such
as an animated conversation you and your child had on a given topic.
The teacher may be surprised, and encouraged. If there are particular
teaching methods your child finds difficult, such as quickly moving on
to a new topic, ask about these. Sometimes understanding the reason
behind what the teacher does will allow you to either prepare your
child better or find ways to work around the problem. Ask the teacher
what *you* can do to make school more productive for your child.

As you talk to the teacher, try to guess if she is an innie or an outie.
This will enable you to talk to her in her own language and thus help
you better convey your child's needs. (See "Be 'Bilingual': How to
Speak Both Innie and Outie" on page 247.) Does she have quiet
energy, organize few group activities, expect children to have creative
ideas, and keep a fairly structured classroom? She may be an innie.
Does your child's teacher have lots of energy, encourage lots of group
activities, expect classroom discussion, and maintain a lively atmosphere with lots going on? He may be an outie.

Think about temperament when you talk to piano teachers, coaches, and other educators. For instance, sports coaches are often outies who think all children have the same level of energy and motivation as they do!

Tips for Talking with Teachers:
- Develop a relationship with the teachers, principal, and staff at your child's school from the beginning.
- Help out in your child's classroom or find other ways to support the school. This shows the teacher and your child that the school is important to you.
- Remember that teaching is an enormously difficult job. Avoid blaming or criticizing the teacher. Consider sending a thank-you note or e-mail—or just say thanks—every now and then.
- Plan what you want to say about your innie and introversion. For instance: "Pat really likes you and enjoys the class. She has an active mind, and the classroom can be overstimulating for her. She has a lot to say when she has time to develop her thoughts. I think you will be surprised with the results. What have you found is successful with a student like Pat?"
- Be open to the teacher's view; you may not have the whole story.

Knowing that he has an ally at home who can advocate for him if necessary will help your innie deal with the ongoing challenges of school. It may be a matter of a teacher not understanding a student, as with Julianne, whose story begins the previous chapter. Or it may be that the student is always rushed and never given a chance to finish work. Or you may feel your child is being unfairly penalized for work habits that are related to temperament.

The point is that you can't assume the teacher is necessarily going to figure out the best way to reach your child. An extroverted parent may fall more easily into the advocating role. An innie parent may choose to send her extroverted spouse or to strengthen her own extroverting muscles. When you understand what your child is confronting at school, you can help him prepare and draw on the family brain trust to find creative solutions. Rather than feeling affronted by your suggestions, the teacher should thank you.

Innie-wise Study Secrets

Innies are wired to be good at studying, with their tenacity and ability to concentrate. Like all kids, however, they may need some help in creating good study habits. Study skills are greatly helped when the student appreciates his own learning style. Here are some study tips that build on innie strengths.

Memorizing

Innies primarily use their long-term associative memory. They remember better when they can link new learning to personal memory, and when they can engage their visual and auditory memory systems. They tend to be weaker in their short-term memory, which impacts word retrieval and math skills.

Here are some suggestions to help them maximize their memory power.

- Link new material to something she already knows (learn fractions through cooking, money with allowances, etc.).
- Create acronyms, word associations, and silly sayings. It's easier for innies to retrieve material when it's in an associative form.
- Tie new information to visual mental pictures. For instance, if your child is learning about Abe Lincoln, show her illustrations of Lincoln in various situations.
- Review, review, and (oh, yes) review.

Studying

I am always shocked when kids say they aren't smart because they need to study. This misperception is a reflection of our cultural

Turn Up Your Encouraging Word

Keep an eye out for how your innie talks to herself, and model positive internal self-talk. Important for anyone's self-esteem, this is vital for innies because their dominant pathway goes through the internal speech area of the brain. Here are steps you can teach your innie for switching negative self-talk to positive self-talk:

1. Notice what you're thinking: *"I am so lame."*

2. Attend to the feelings under the thought: *"I am disappointed and frustrated that I didn't get a higher grade."*

3. Turn up your encouraging word: *"It's okay to be disappointed. I worked hard on the paper. Maybe I need to learn something to improve my grade. There will always be another paper to work on."*

Some other encouraging words for a variety of situations:

"It's frustrating sometimes, but life isn't always fair."

"I don't like this, but I can cope."

"I'm doing the best I can."

"All humans have crummy things happen to them."

"I'm sad today. It will pass."

And my personal favorite: *"Humans are weird and so am I."*

assumptions about speed being better. Speed isn't necessarily better. Learning to study is vital for all kids, and it's crucial for innies, who need to learn in small steps that build from the simple to the complex.

• Watch to see if your child is avoiding studying as a way of reducing overstimulation. Innies usually enjoy studying and do their homework without prompting. However, they may try to avoid entering into their deep concentration zone if they anticipate interruption because it can be painful to leave the interesting book or topic to return to the outside world. Also, they have very

Help Your Innie at Home

You can prime your introverted child's learning power at home. Innies need lively conversations, artistic experiences, and an environment where questions are welcomed. They also need room to toy with ideas, dream, invent, and contemplate. Activities that correspond with their ideas and abilities will boost their "connecting dots" and stimulate their perceptions, ideas, and insights. You can equip your child with an understanding of how he learns best. Furthermore, encouragement from family members will build confidence and support his native tenacity.

Here are some ways to build your innie's love of learning and brainpower every day:

• Read aloud to your children, no matter how old they are, and play audio books in the car. Create reading nooks. Take books along for waits at the dentist's or doctor's office. Have your emergent reader read anything to you—even labels and receipts.

active minds, and learning something new can actually be too exciting. To avoid this discomfort—which they probably aren't even aware of—they may avoid studying to keep their brain from going into overdrive. It helps if you explain this strange phenomenon to your innie and teach her how to keep overstimulation at bay. She can learn to say, "Okay, brain, hold the flood of thoughts." This gives her a chance to step back.

• Suggest that you help her start by sitting with her or by breaking the work into manageable bits.

• Remind her that taking small steps beats trying to tackle too much at once.

• Highlight with different color markers and Post-its. Visual learners remember color better, so underlining any reading in color improves their retention and comprehension. Markers of any kind break the information into manageable segments.

- When you're reading aloud, stop a book near the end of the story and ask, "What is going to happen?" or "What do you want to happen?" This opens your child's mind to different possibilities and alternatives.
- Make dinner-as-a-family a special time to talk about current events and discuss what each family member is doing at school or work.
- Play "What If?" Each person writes up a "What If" card, such as "What if I lived on the moon?" or "What if we had a pet elephant?" Choose one and muse over the possibilities.
- Leave notes, like lunch-box messages or scavenger-hunt notes, that lead to a small surprise and encourage your child to leave notes for you. Innies of all ages like finding and leaving notes.

- Innies are visual and/or auditory learners. Have her listen to tapes or watch videos about study topics. Let her listen to music if it helps her to relax and concentrate.

Testing

Innies need to feel well prepared and relaxed in order to do their best on a test. Outies may think its fun to feel juiced and jolted, and it may actually improve their performance. But adrenaline and dopamine reduce an innie's ability to think and show what she knows, so it's best to stave off the rush.

- Be sure she is rested and has had enough water and protein.
- Teach her to calm down, take breaks, and breathe deeply.
- Teach her to use her internal voice to be encouraging.
- Tell her to remind herself that she will remember what she has learned.

- Have her scan the test, read directions carefully, and answer what she knows first. Once she finds the door into long-term memory, she will be okay.

Class Discussions

Innies tend to hang back during class discussions and may freeze when called on. The following tips will give your child enough confidence to raise her hand on her own.

- Have her break reading into sections and determine the main point in each section. This will help ready her to ask a question, make a comment, or answer a question.
- Have her prepare for class by selecting two main points, writing them down, and practicing saying them aloud.
- Have her come up with one question to ask about the material in class.

Group Dynamics

When working in groups, innies often end up doing most of the work because they enjoy exploring subjects in depth and care about doing a good job. If the others aren't hard workers, the innie gets the bulk of it. I have many innies who have learned to negotiate so that they prepare a certain amount of the project and an outie then presents it.

Minimize Homework Havoc

"Home computers are being called upon to perform many new functions including the consumption of homework formerly eaten by the dog."—Doug Larson

For homework to have value, your child has to be able to give it time and attention. Trying to cram a dozen math problems into the five minutes remaining before bedtime will only leave everybody frustrated—and the work incomplete or badly done. Together with your child, figure out the best time to do homework. Help him to assess his energy level and know his peaks and valleys. What is his easiest or hardest subject? Which should he do first? How should he prioritize? Does he want to reward himself by having dessert after he finishes his work? Don't overschedule your child so that homework ends up being rushed. Innies aren't at their best when pressured; they'll just get discouraged. Unless they are tired or struggling with the material, innies will usually readily do homework. Be flexible where possible and don't make a fetish of homework; be sure your innie has play and creative time.

When it comes to homework, your innie may:

- Want you nearby.
- Need a snack and some time alone first.
- Do well with several breaks. Start by doing his math homework, then pick up his sister at her music lesson. Then do his science homework. . . .
- Be able to work in the car on the way back from school or after-school activities.
- Prefer working after dinner or after a bath.
- Need to strategize on finding quiet spots, especially if in after-school care.

Providing Homework Help

You can encourage your innie to break projects into small steps spaced out over several days. For example, on Monday, read requirements and get any necessary supplies. Tuesday, research topic. Wednesday, write down main ideas. Thursday, try a draft. Friday, go over it with a parent and revise. Finish over the weekend and turn in on Monday. Here are some other ways to give an innie homework help:

- Set up a quiet space protected from interruption. Make readily available supplies and nutritious snacks.
- Discourage perfectionism. Point out that everybody, including you, makes mistakes.

- Remind your innie that he needs to sleep on what he's learning. By studying tonight, he will know it better tomorrow.
- If he's struggling, listen to his concerns and ask what he needs. Keep asking questions to help him clarify his thoughts and feelings. Don't think you know more than he does; he's the one in the classroom.
- Encourage him to use mental pictures to jog his memory.
- Help him find a personal connection with what he is learning. "This tells you about how cells work in the body. You are starting with this one type of cell. Is that right? Isn't it amazing that all these tiny cells work together to make one organ, and then they make a whole person?"
- Ask process questions to help him think through problems, but don't do his work for him. For example: "What do you think is the most important point? Why do you think your teacher wants you to know this? How do you think that happened?"
- Encourage helpful self-talk. "I can do this." "It will get done step-by-step." "I know more than I did yesterday."
- Help him connect the homework to his own life. If he is learning about money, ask him: "How many Baby Ruth candy bars [or his favorite] would eight quarters buy?"

Innies and Giftedness

"You know your child is gifted when they ask for a dictionary for their birthday."—Judy Galbraith

There is an incredible irony about introverted children. Teachers who don't understand their physiology may regard them as slow, dense, or not very smart—as we have seen. This can be a great loss to society. At least 70 percent of all gifted children are innies. When you understand their hardwiring, it's easy to see why.

Many outies have a comprehensive and wide-ranging intelligence. But fields such as science, computers, medicine, engineering, architecture, psychology, and higher education are dominated by introverts, due to their unusual ability to deeply concentrate on complex information. As Albert Einstein said, "My greatest strength is my ability to think about a problem for a long time."

One downside of innie giftedness is that such children can feel quite isolated, since it's hard for them to find their emotional and intellectual peers (even in their own family). They can also lose motivation if their talents are overlooked. Without complex interests to feed their brain, gifted innies may not know about their own intellectual power. This is how smart kids become involved with drugs, to fight the isolation and lack of stimulation. So it's vitally important to understand their talents, expose them to enriching experiences, and help them find other adults and kids to share their think tanks with.

Even when an innie's gifts are recognized, there still may be pitfalls. I have worked with introverted children assigned to what are called GATE classes, a program designed for "gifted and talented" children in California, where many end up feeling *less* intelligent. This is because the program puts pressure on students to learn specific material quickly, to prepare them to perform well on standardized tests.

The bibliography at the end of the book recommends titles about gifted children. Take a look at some of them; you may be surprised to discover that gifted kids sound just like your innie. You'll also find suggestions on how best to nurture his talents.

Surviving, Thriving, and Deriving a College Education

Many innies bloom in college. Start early to help your innie select a college and a major that is just right for him. Innies can also begin early to save money for their education. Such a daunting transition can be overwhelming for an innie, so it's best to help him consider all aspects of higher education in measured steps as he is growing up. Visit different college campuses on vacations and trips. I have taken my grandchildren to plays, planetariums, and lectures at our local universities. We explore the buildings, and I tell them stories about my college years. Ask friends and relatives to discuss their college experiences with your child. What did they like and what didn't they like? Why did they choose their college?

As your child gets closer to deciding on a college, keep the process an adventure of discovery. Help your innie use her compare-and-contrast brain to explore the options available to her. Keep the lines of communication open, and discuss all aspects of the upcoming college experience. An introverted teen will take longer to make decisions about college, so start early.

Some factors innies and their parents should consider when choosing a college are the size of the college, its atmosphere and philosophy, communal living, location, selecting a major, and the student population. Larger colleges can be overwhelming and may not offer the Hardiness Zone innies need. I have worked with several innies who chose to attend large, competitive universities, and they were miserable. After freshman year they transferred to smaller colleges where they found like-minded students, felt less overwhelmed, and had more personal contact with instructors. Location can be important because innies may want to come home more frequently at first. A small college town can be less stressful to an innie compared to a large metropolitan city.

Large, competitive institutions that require learning in enormous lecture halls or schools that have reputations for constant partying are generally not the best choices for innies. Smaller colleges often provide a calmer, quieter environment with more serious and dedicated students. Sometimes I'm surprised that parents feel that attending a junior college is less prestigious. But for many innies (and this was true for me) a more laid-back junior college can be a good entry point into academic life, and many junior colleges have excellent reputations. Living at home for the junior college portion can also serve as a good bridge for introverted coeds. They can transfer to a larger university when they have become more experienced in managing college.

Communal living, studying, and eating can be quite challenging for innies. It's important for them to have a compatible roommate since they will be squished together in a small room. They need to find private places to recharge and study. Staying on campus on weekends and even holidays when most students leave is a great way for innies to recharge. Today many colleges match roommates for all sorts of reasons including temperament. One study showed that pairing roommates with similar temperaments increased their satisfaction with school and decreased requests for roommate changes by 65 percent.

Studies show that innies take longer to decide on a major. My guess is that this suggests they haven't been exposed to enough experiences to know their own interests. Again, start early to help them learn what turns them on. Studies also show that in college, innies socialize and date less than outies do. So assure your innie that he doesn't need to be a social butterfly. Support your child's interest in furthering his education. Graduate school is the land of innies because of their love of learning and their interest in delving deeper into more specialized subject areas.

The Kids' Sports Scene

"Sports don't build character, they reveal it."
—Heywood Hale Broun

Many people equate "athletics" with competitive team sports. But there is a whole world of outdoor and indoor physical activities, and different children are drawn to different types. According to the American Academy of Pediatrics, children shouldn't play in organized sports until they are at least six or seven; it sends the wrong message—it puts the focus on highly structured team play and winning. There is often little appreciation for the child's developing body and individual skills. When sports are organized by adults, kids are expected to be team players much too early. Furthermore, participation in organized sports consumes a child's time for free play—which is a child's real job.

Introverted children often like individual sports, such as martial arts, hiking, skating, and kayaking. I worked with one teenager who told me he had reconciled himself to being a nerd. He decided to join the swim team so that he could earn a letter in a sport. This way he could balance some "jock-ness" with his "nerd-ness." Indeed, he felt more included socially, and he loved the challenge of improving his swim times.

In this era of parents coming to blows over a disputed goal in a child's game, it can be useful to step back and ask: What is the purpose of sports for children? Be careful not to confuse your interests with those of your child. Taking lessons and playing on teams should help children get some exercise, learn interpersonal and physical skills, gain the experience of team effort, and have the chance to discover what they enjoy. It's about practice, exploration, and fun; except in the rarest cases, sports will not become a glamorous lifelong career. Let your child try out a sport or a set of lessons to find out what he likes. It may not be the first thing he tries, or the same sport that you enjoyed as a child.

Many innies hate those times at school when kids are picked to be on teams—often they aren't chosen. Discussing this experience and helping them find a solution is a good idea. Maybe your child can practice the most popular games (kick ball, or four square, for instance) at home first so he will be better at them in school. Developing an individual sport can help innies build their strength and confidence. They may also feel less rejected if they are left off of school teams.

If your innie is on a team, you need to monitor your child's coaches. Many coaches are appropriate, but some are too harsh and focus on winning rather than sportsmanship. Parents need to intervene—this is not the point of children being in sports.

A young introverted child I know had taken gymnastics for several years. Mia had always loved it, but suddenly she wanted to quit. She cried and refused even to enter the gym. Her mom was stunned and asked me what she should do. I told Mia's mother to simply listen to what Mia said. Later, after Mia was calmer, she could try to find out the underlying problems. She could gather facts. I suggested that she talk to the other parents and the coaches and look for other signs of stress in Mia. Had there been any changes, such as a new coach? Was Mia being teased or bullied during lessons? Was there too much pressure? Was she being left out?

It turned out that Mia's class was moving into more sophisticated levels of skills. As Mia is an innie who tends to be a perfectionist, she was feeling afraid and discouraged. She didn't think she was doing well enough. She didn't know that her coach thought she was doing great. Her mother talked to the coach, and asked her to be more overtly encouraging to Mia. She also urged the coach to have Mia talk with some of the other girls on her team who were also nervous about learning the new skills, so that she no longer felt alone in her apprehension. Mia is still in gymnastics.

If your child wants to stop participating in a particular activity, try to find out what's going on. If, after gathering the facts, you think it's reasonable that he quit, ask him to pick one thing to stick with until the end of the season or session. And then drop the others. If it's still not clear what's going on, have him stay in for two more weeks and see how he feels then.

The Heart of the Matter

- *Explain your innie's temperament to her teachers.*
- *Help her study for how her brain works.*
- *Remember, proportionately more innies than outies go to college and graduate school.*

CHAPTER 12

Innie Social Savvy

What Friendship Means to Innies and What to Expect as They Travel Through Childhood

"Friendships multiply joys and divide griefs."—H .G. Bohn

The social arena is where innie and outie differences show up in bold relief. Extroverts enjoy meeting and talking to lots of different people and generally have a wide range of friends. Innies like other people, but tend to gravitate toward smaller groups and one-on-one situations. The common assumption is that introverts aren't social. Yet as we've seen, innies aren't necessarily shy, withdrawn, or quiet—especially in comfortable, familiar environments. The confusion stems from the notion that there is just *one* way to be social. Take a look at how we usually regard socializing, which is through an extroverted lens. The criteria include: Is someone popular? Does he have lots of friends? Does he enjoy parties and seek out group activities?

If we take a glimpse through introverted optics, however, we get a different picture: Does your innie have one or two really close friends? Does he value long-term friendships? Does he enjoy one-on-one conversations on topics that matter to him? Does he care about others' feelings? It becomes clear that the real story is that introverts and extroverts have opposing social skills and inclinations. Outies excel in the Western cultural ideals of being highly visible and out and about, and they are comfortable chatting with lots of people. Innies shine in the underrated and seemingly invisible up-close-and-personal intimacy skills.

Your introverted child can become poised, confident, and comfortable interacting with other kids and adults—introverted and extroverted alike. These capacities improve with practice and experience. Confident innies understand themselves and know that it's alright to withdraw when they need to recharge. They know what kinds of friendships and social experiences they value and enjoy. They have a few close friends, yet are friendly with other kids. They are calm in most social situations and believe that they are well liked. They have the ability to shift gears and "extrovert" when needed for social gatherings. However, they do so on their own terms.

Reward Systems

"The summit of happiness is reached when a person is ready to be what he is."—Erasmus

As I explained in Chapter 2, innies and outies rely on brain pathways that supply different rewards. Extroverted children are designed to be gregarious. Their brains are zapped with "hap hits" from kidding around, teasing, and playing in groups. They take pleasure in fast-paced chatter. They speak openly about most things and like jumping from subject to subject. Interruptions don't bother them. Physically, outie kids tend to like rough-and-tumble play more than innies do. They think of most kids as pals and have a large circle of friends.

Introverted children enjoy intimate conversations that may involve more complex topics. They like to kick back and chat, with time for pauses and reflection. They get mild but pleasurable "hap hits" when discussing something interesting. Their brains are made for lingering over thoughts and feelings and achieving a deeper understanding of a subject. They speak more slowly and lose their place if they are interrupted. They listen, ask questions, and consider the other person's ideas. In order to develop these inborn skills, innies need trusting relationships to help them practice the art of conversation. Innies are usually well liked, but they need to know another child well before considering him a friend.

Two Paths Diverge

Introverts' and extroverts' hardwiring result in distinct interpersonal needs and divergent social skills. Let's discuss three crucial ways innies' and outies' paths diverge: their views on friendship, their conversational styles, and their energy for socializing.

What Is a Friend?

Innies and outies see friendship differently. To introverted children, the term *friend* means a deeper-than-casual relationship. An example is Kathy, who at age eight has a best friend, Samantha. They love to pretend they are at school and take turns being the teacher and making up homework assignments. They can play for hours, inventing various dramas and scenarios. Kathy and Sam have been friends since they were three. Kathy knows what to expect when Sam comes over. They usually work out difficulties and make compromises easily. They don't have many arguments. But if Kathy's extroverted brother, Noah, bugs Sam—as he likes to do—Kathy jumps in to defend her friend. Interestingly, this is something she doesn't always do for herself. As Kathy gets older, she will want friends who can talk in depth about topics of interest to her. Already she realizes that friends are good to share and solve problems with.

Introverted children enjoy many types of friends. They can be older or younger; male or female; and of varied cultural backgrounds, religions, and temperaments. A 1999 study in the *British Journal of Social Psychology* found that extroverts rejected strangers who weren't like them more often than introverts did. Kathy, to take a prototypical innie, has a variety of companions. She sometimes drops in on an older neighbor, Miriam, who lives down the street. Miriam has been showing her how to knit. She also loves visits with her baby cousin, Zach. She gets a kick out of watching him learn about the world. Kathy's other best friend is Tom, an extroverted, action-packed guy. He is lively, fun, and makes spur-of-the-moment, exciting suggestions, like "Let's pretend we are the Spy Kids from the movie. We can use my spy gear to see what the kids in the neighborhood are up to." Kathy's mom notices that she is really tuckered out after Tom comes over, and so she keeps their playdates short. Innies often gravitate toward outies and they have lots of fun together. But innies need to have innie friends or they can end up feeling tired and pressured to be like outies.

Extroverts use the word *friend* as an innie would use *acquaintance*. Kim, for instance, likes to have her mom set up playdates with school chums and her other friends. But she is just as happy playing with kids she meets at the park or, for that matter, the many children she runs into wherever she goes. Friends of friends, cousins of cousins—anyone is fair game. Outies tend to like other outies; Kim's best friend is as lively and energetic as she is. They ride bikes, play ball, and skate. They have fun, but sometimes they argue about what to do. ("You got to choose last time!") As she gets older, Kim will also enjoy lengthy conversations but may not seek them out to the extent that innies do. Outies enjoy playing outdoors, playing board games, roughhousing, and being involved in numerous activities.

Conversational Styles

When you observe innies and outies in conversation, their differences become apparent. Innies are excellent conversationalists when they are comfortable with you. Paula, a four-year-old innie, looked me in the eye and asked if I had a cat. "Yes, I do," I told her. "What color is he? Or is he a she?" she continued, and paused to wait for my answer. I told her about Mocha, my chocolate-colored cat. I asked her, "Do *you* have a cat?" She reflected and answered, "Yes, he's a gray rag cat and he's four like me. He likes to sleep on my bed and on top of the refrigerator." She goes on to tell me all about his particular breed.

Paula's aim in conversation is to understand her own or someone else's inner world. She likes to chat in a relaxed atmosphere about something she likes. She listens, reflects, and remembers what I say. As she gets older, she will enjoy conversations that explore her own or other children's interests. She will value connecting and getting to know another person, finding commonalities (like a love of cats) and differences.

Extroverted Hallie, at nine, is often scolded for lying. She doesn't really understand why her mom gets angry. She was just talking. "Guess what? I am going to go camping with the Andersens," she had said to her mom. "Oh, really?" her mother replied, taken aback. "Well, they haven't actually asked me yet, but I think they will." "*If* they ask you, you let me know and *then* we can discuss it," her mom replies. Tomorrow Hallie may forget she even wanted to go camping.

Outies chat for the fun of it. They'll ask, "Did you know?" and talk about sports, clothes, whatever. They say what pops into their heads, hopping from subject to subject, casually interrupting each other without offense. When she was younger, Hallie once asked a woman why she was wearing such an ugly hat, and her mother cringed in embarrassment. But, Hallie protested, the hat *was* ugly! Extroverted children can and do jabber away about any subject— whether they know anything about it or not!

Expenditure of Energy

Give this some thought: *Everything an innie does in the outside world requires energy and gives little or no energy in return.* Add to this the fact that innies also have to expend extra fuel to keep their internal stimulation turned down so that they can shift to an external focus. Extroverts, on the other hand, go into the outside world and bask in its vitality. They are already focused externally so it doesn't require a shift. This difference has a huge impact on how innies and outies experience socializing and, in turn, how they are perceived.

At home our granddaughter Emily is a little whirlwind, constantly running around. One afternoon I took her to the children's play area in a mall. She seemed like a different child. For some fifteen minutes she sat beside me like a statue, her face perfectly still, merely watching all the action. She stared at the kids buzzing around the tree-house slide. "Tell me when you're ready to join the other children," I said. She watched them intently and finally turned to me and said, "Ready." As she played and explored, she glanced at me every now and then, silently checking my reaction for reassurance. I had taken her extroverted older sister, Katie, to the same play area many times. Katie would run right into the fray and hardly look back.

You can help your introverted child manage and make good use of his limited social energy. Teach him to store energy before social occasions. Limit the number of engagements he has, and don't stay long if he shows signs of dragging. Most innies are able to sit for fairly long periods, such as during a church service or a dinner out. They can play quietly for an extended period. Occasionally, an innie is more active and will get restless. But though they may seem content, they still need space, peace, and quiet in order to recharge their batteries.

Help your child notice what triggers energy drops, such as too many kids around, too much noise, hot weather, time pressure, conflict, or disappointment. He can learn to take a breather, stand in the shade away from the group, postpone dealing with a conflict until later, talk about what's bothering him, or take a brief walk.

Socializing Throughout Childhood—What to Expect

"Friends are relatives you make for yourself."
—*Eustache Deschamps*

Socializing is essential for any child's development; researchers say that the infant brain develops through relationships with primary caregivers. One's social sense begins in the family and expands to the outside world between one and two years of age. Even from a young age, innies—inveterate observers—like to scope out other children. As they grow, they practice and experiment with their burgeoning social skills in order to form friendships. Making friends is actually quite a challenging, sophisticated operation, involving many trials, dead ends, and outright rebuffs. Social aptitude takes a long time to build, with one skill block stacked on top of another. Innies will slowly begin to establish themselves outside the family. Within the relative safety of family life, they can practice give-and-take, sharing power, empathizing, being assertive, compromising, and handling rejection, and when they're ready, begin to take these skills on the road.

Here is a closer look at what is going on at different social stages.

Ages One to Three

Toddlers are beginning to test out independence. They are struggling with limits and wanting to explore the world in their own way. They are interested in other children, but they play next to each other rather than together. Innies usually stick closer to their parents for a longer time. Often they don't have as many tantrums as outies do at this age. But since they have their own mind already, they can become stubborn and pitch a fit if they feel determined to have or do something.

Build your child's social skills by organizing a play group, enrolling her in a class (like a tot music class), or taking her to a park.

Expose her to lots of different experiences. Go to gardens, ride a ferry, hop on a trolley, visit the zoo, and enjoy the aquarium and other toddler-friendly places. Just don't stay long, and avoid over-stimulation. Always let your child ease into new places or groups. These are practicing years.

Remember that toddlers need adults to smooth out wrinkles in their play. You can help her know when she needs a break or some calming. Encourage a bit of give-and-take with others. Remind her to use words, not grabbing, biting, or hitting. This is behavior you might see if she is tired, hungry, or otherwise overwrought. Encourage her not to be passive if another child takes her toys. The capacity to stand up for herself will help her feel safer and less vulnerable in social situations. Initiate a quiet activity as the playdate winds down, like reading a book or coloring, to ease into closure.

A big shift begins to occur by twenty to twenty-four months. Children's social interests grow in leaps and bounds during this time. They begin to copy one another. One child jumps off a box, and the others will jump off the box, too. Researchers see this as the beginnings of social interaction: back and forth; you do this, I do that. Introverted toddlers are usually more hesitant than extroverted children with new children, new situations, and groups. While they may be slow to take part, they do like to watch other children. Letting them observe is a good introduction to social settings. They may copy behaviors without actually joining in.

A few months ago I took a Half Notes music class with our innie granddaughter, Emily. There were about ten toddlers ranging from eighteen to twenty-four-months old. Emily loves music and dancing. My idea was to have fun with her while exposing her to a group of toddlers and helping her learn to tolerate groups. After a few classes, when we drove up, Emily would see the building and yell, "Babies!" She was eager to rush in, take off her shoes, and bang on the drums.

During the class she usually watched the other toddlers, hawk-like, from my lap or standing by the wall. She joined in some activities, but not as often as most of the other children. Occasionally, she would surprise everyone and be the only one to sing or speak up. Her participation ebbed and flowed, depending on her energy level, the size of the class, and how overwhelming the activity felt to her. If she had had a busy weekend before the Monday class, for example, she was usually more reserved. She generally joined in when the kids were taking out instruments or putting them back, and when they sang, "Clean up, clean up." But, like most innies, she became captivated by something unique—name tags! She loved to swipe another child's name tag and then slap it on the wall with a satisfied smile while swaying to the sounds of the music. It was soon apparent that she had started a fad as other toddlers followed her example.

Between the ages of two and three, children begin to show social preferences, often gravitating toward one child over others. Look for a glimmer of interest between your child and his playmates. Find children who enjoy similar play. Perhaps they like to play with building blocks, or they both like to pretend. Toddlers do well with other toddlers, playing in small, once-a-week play groups to begin learning social skills. Make playdates with their budding pals, and take their friendships seriously. Get two cups, two balls, or two small drums for them to play with, since at this stage imitation is more important to learn than sharing. Talk about your child's friend. "You're going to see Justin today. Do you want me to put away some of your favorite toys?" (Yes, it's good to have some no-share toys.) Innie and outie toddlers will need adult supervision to help them take turns and to guide their interactions.

Caveat: Don't overwhelm your innie with too many children or social occasions. Try to avoid long playdates or hectic transitions.

Ages Four and Five

Four and a half is usually the peak period of potty talk, bragging, exaggerating, and emotional unpredictability. Innies can surprise their parents with the sudden personality change. They may become quite silly, or their stubbornness may turn into defiance. At the same time, they are gaining a sense of emotional cause-and-effect: "If I hit my sister, she and my mom will be mad." This period of intensity calms down around age five, and children's relationships become more stable. They are learning to play one-on-one and in groups. While they still play with friends of the opposite sex, especially when role-playing and during imaginative play, they are beginning to show a preference for playing with children of the same sex.

Innies tend to thrive in this phase of amiable, cooperative play. A study that appeared in the *Elementary School Journal* in 2002 examined the word-for-word comments made by kids when they discussed differences of opinion. The researchers concluded that innies made more cooperative remarks and outies made more argumentative comments when kids were disagreeing.

Continue to help your innie ease into social situations. Establish regular playdates with familiar pals to provide consistent play experiences. It's nice to occasionally include other children—as long as your child knows beforehand that others will be joining. This gives you an opportunity to point out that other children play in different ways, and that he can practice slowly getting used to new children.

At this age, your child can use some help structuring playdates. Before the friend arrives, you can set a loose agenda. Have him select two or three games or other toys he wants to play with when the friend arrives. Tell him he and his friend will need to take turns with the selected toys. If a fight starts over a toy, use a kitchen timer: ten minutes of play each. If that doesn't work, remove the toy in a matter-of-fact way. If he wants to, let him put a few special toys in the closet—off-limits. He can't be expected to share everything yet. Support his friendships by including a companion on a brief family outing.

Casual groups start forming around age four. If you watch several kids running around as a group, you will notice more organized play at this time. They can stop, compromise, and fly off in another direction. The group won't cohere for too long, but it's fun while it lasts.

Innies can now begin to learn how to enter groups. It's usually a matter of physical joining—moving into the group's space. Teach your child to join into group play by nodding or smiling at a friendly-looking child, then copying what the group is doing. If, say, they are running around a slide, he can dart in and run with the pack. If the kids are jumping off a rock, he can jump, too. Encourage him to manage conflicts by learning to ask for what he wants.

Caveat: Don't invite too many children to play at once. Start with short get-togethers. Extend them for longer periods, as the children begin to play well together. The goal is to practice social skills in an enjoyable way.

Ages Six to Eight

When children reach this age, their personalities become more complex. While enthusiastic and cooperative, they are also demanding and difficult. They are practicing learning to calm down and pay attention to social cues. They are attempting to work out roles, and they begin to identify more with the same-sex parent. They can work out conflicts without adults, but remember, they still view the world through a combination of fantasy and reality.

School-age innies like other kids who are polite. However, it takes lots of energy to handle more dissimilar relationships. This is a period of trial and error for parents to try to help innies find their social rhythm. Sometimes children need encouragement to practice handling different people and situations. At other times parents need to back off and even suggest declining an invitation so the child can have some downtime.

Sign up your child for activities that tap into her strengths, such as art, dance, science, martial arts, or music. Find other quiet kids for your innie to play with. Innies usually have a best friend by five, the "social age." If your child doesn't have a special pal, ask her teacher if one of the other children would be a good fit. Arrange a short playdate, then a slightly longer one if the first works out well. Look for signs that the playdate is succeeding. Do they enjoy similar play and have similar energy levels? Do they look lively? Can they negotiate differences successfully?

Begin to help your innie assess friendships. Sometimes innies are attracted to outies but actually play better with innies. "You and Ana enjoy playing dress up and pretend games. But it takes longer for you and Stacy to find something to play. Why do you think that is?" Asking these types of questions in this way helps your child think about what kind of play she is up for, and what kind of friend she'd like to invite over.

Joining groups often remains a challenge for innies. Encourage your child to watch how kids act in both closed and open groups. In closed groups, children stand clumped together. Their bodies are tense, they don't look at others outside the group, and it's difficult to catch anyone's eye. In an open group, children are laughing and smiling. There are spaces between the members; they lean in toward each other and look relaxed. It is not difficult to catch someone's attention. With your encouragement, your innie can learn to watch, copy, and join in. You can remind her that it often takes more than one try. Many social tries don't work out the first time, but the next time might be successful.

Caveat: Don't limit your innie's friends to classmates, because she may enjoy younger or older children as well. It may help an innie feel more socially competent and comfortable with her peers to have playmates of different ages. This allows her to try out roles such as leader, follower, expert, and novice.

Ages Nine to Eleven

School-yard politics is now at its height. Peers take on a new importance. Children struggle more with difference, and with how others do or don't behave. You can help your innie understand social dynamics by encouraging him to reflect on his mixed feelings about other kids. For instance: "I like Michael when he plays by the rules, but I don't like it when he hogs the ball."

Remind your innie that it's okay to enjoy more alone time than many kids his age. And that it's okay to pick and choose which events to attend or not attend. Nor does he have to stay very long. Discuss what questions to think about when he's deciding whether or not to go. Has he had a lot of engagements lately? Has he been hanging around at home so much it's become habit? If he declines, might a friend feel hurt because this is an important event for him? Does he like the other kids who will be there? This is one of the most difficult aspects of parenting an innie. There needs to be an ongoing dialogue about the pros and cons of going out and staying in. He has to keep assessing: How tired am I? Do I like the kids and the activity? Will I disappoint a good friend if I don't go?

It's particularly important to innies now to feel a sense of belonging and acceptance. By taking a one-day-at-a-time approach, your child can practice his skills to increase his network of friends. One day suggest that he try flashing a smile at a stranger, passing a note of encouragement to a friend, saying hi to a new person, congratulating a friend who made a good play during sports, or saving someone a seat. Ask him how it went, and tell him you are proud of him.

Groups are always a challenge for innies, so help your child understand group patterns. Extroverted groups like chitchatting and light topics, and kids may come and go every five to fifteen minutes. These groups are always shifting and changing. Kids begin to feel antsy and want to move on, or the conversation winds down—so don't take it personally if someone leaves as you arrive. A good choice is a group where kids look like they are having fun, there isn't much arguing, and everyone is chatting. From a distance of about four to five feet, your child can smile and gauge the other kids' responses. Do they seem welcoming to a new member? If your child joins the group, she can smile, nod, laugh at jokes, and comment on the topic after a few minutes. She can try to speak in party talk—short, snappy, and light. "I know what you mean"; "That happened to me, too."

Tweens and Teens

These are the years of heightened pack behavior. They can be pretty brutal. There is a lot of group interaction and pressure to be like the crowd. Friendships may change overnight. It can be painful for any tween or teen, but innies especially can be hurt and become discouraged. They may not realize that even the most popular kids feel pain about not being liked during these years. Innies need help to understand the pack mentality; otherwise they may withdraw. Encourage your innie to maintain friendly one-on-one relationships with lots of kids. One or two good friends outside the pack will ease the rough patches.

Teenage innies often find a role model they admire outside the family, like a teacher, family friend, or even someone they have read about. It is important for growing innies to draw on a variety of resources to help build and sustain self-awareness and self-esteem.

Here is a teenaged innie talking about her social life:

> Talking takes tons of energy since I feel I have to work to capture the other kid's attention. If I actually figure out what I want to say and I gear up to spit it out—I am often ignored. I get discouraged. Quite often other kids or even adults keep right on talking like I didn't say anything. Later someone else says the exact same thing and everyone responds. I wonder, What did I do wrong? Then on my way home or the next day I think of a great comeback to a smart-aleck remark or an answer to a question I was asked in class. Where was that when I needed it? I'm not sure if it's my memory or if I am just empty-headed.
>
> My friend John said I was "standoffish." I don't understand why he thinks that. I guess I am quiet sometimes. Out in the world, sometimes not one word comes into my mind. I like my privacy. I know I keep my face straight and I look at my shoes when I'm trying to gather my thoughts to speak. But I really like other kids. I like to talk about stuff. I wish they didn't think I was so "mysterious." I don't think I am at all!

This offers a sense of how the social world looks to an innie. She is quite engaged with her friends, but sometimes struggles to keep her poise and is confounded by some people's vision of her as aloof.

Your child might feel independent in many ways but still need you to help her sift and sort out friends' behavior and attitudes. Encourage, help her practice social skills, and don't criticize. It is helpful to explain to older innies that there are different types of relating and that kids have different goals for their friendships. This keeps them from making a catastrophe out of a bump in the road with any one friend.

Many innies have good intentions, and they believe that all other kids share these goals. A good friend isn't nice one day and nasty the next. A good friend cares about you and can tolerate and discuss differences. When children have good will and they want to maintain a friendship, they can work out issues. Teach your innie how to articulate her desires and encourage her to speak up and tell others. Promote her ability to listen to what a friend wants and to negotiate. She can use her innate listening skills, reflect on what a friend says, and work toward a solution. It is very important to begin to develop these skills now, so that when your innie starts dating, she can recognize teens with better intentions.

Teach your innie to trust her feelings. If she is feeling protective or unclear, there must be a reason. If she feels shut down or not listened to, then the friend may be going through the motions of trying to work things out but isn't really committed. Talk about the importance of acknowledging feelings. When she is upset, show her how to calm down and shift into a problem-solving mode. Innies usually find their own solutions once their feelings are acknowledged. Then you can help clarify the problem and understand what your child wants to do. Comments that are neutral but make her thoughts and feelings clearer are most helpful: "Sounds like you might want Andi to come with you." "Are you worried she is already going with someone else? Is that right?" "If she has a date already, who else could you ask?"

One particularly destructive social motivation is revenge. During the junior high years, this behavior starts to rear its ugly head. The intent is to hurt the other person. The battle becomes more important than what prompted the fight in the first place. Kids who feel unsafe and frightened of others may see the world as a war zone. They try to feel okay by getting back at others instead of working through conflicts to find a middle way. Teach your child to detect and stay away from kids who are looking for a sparring partner.

Group interactions and configurations get more elaborate during adolescence, but the same rules hold. If your innie feels like an outsider but is willing to try to join in, it's best to pick an open group, as described above. Remember that talkative kids need listeners. They will appreciate someone else's interest. Remember also that social groups don't hang together very long. They may break up into smaller conversational clusters. Another bit of advice to pass along to your innie: When entering a new group, avoid disagreeing, making one-up statements, changing the topic, or asking personal questions.

Caveat: Don't pressure your tween or teen about making friends at school or attending every social event. A quiet child already feels social pressure and usually wishes he weren't so quiet. Frequent comments about friendships will just make him feel more flawed. There are times he will wish he were more extroverted. Sometimes it is hard for innies to tear themselves away from friends, but they know their energy is waning. At other times they may feel social pressure to stay with the group for fear of feeling like an outsider. Assure him that he'll have plenty of times to reconnect with friends.

Innies forge relationships based on shared interests and compatibility. You can encourage your child in the social arena by placing a value on meaningful friendship, as opposed to the light banter that many place at the core of social success.

The Heart of the Matter

- *Innies and outies have different social talents.*
- *Innies are skilled with intimacy, maintain long-term relationships, and are fulfilled by deeper conversations.*
- *Teach innies that socializing has patterns that they can learn.*

CHAPTER 13

Encouraging Your Introvert to Flex His Social Muscles

Practice Helps Strengthen Poise and Confidence, Even in Sticky Situations

"A good friend likes your name so they can write it in bubble letters."
—*Emily Barnett, age six*

While many parents see the social arena as beyond their control, be assured that you can have a strong, positive influence on your introverted child's social abilities. After all, it is through her daily experiences with you that she learns how to interact with others. One important way for you to help her build social muscle is by valuing and recognizing her social gifts and understanding her social challenges. And through your own example, you can teach social skills and increase her confidence in handling all types of social situations. Over time she will begin to "own" these strengths.

Transition Training

"One does not make friends. One recognizes them."
—*Garth Hendricks*

When it comes to innies taking on the social world, transition time is a biggie. Introverted children need time to think about upcoming events in order for them to properly adjust. As I discussed in Chapter 2, innies use the brain pathway that preplans a course of action. Then they evaluate the action taken, assessing what just happened in the context of imagined future action. You can help smooth the way by preparing your innie for transitions into social events. He will need to ponder the upcoming encounter, store energy, and gear up to shift to an external focus. The more he knows about what lies ahead, the less of a fuel drain it is. If you don't prepare him, he may devote energy to anticipating how the future will be and get anxious. He may also build up expectations, only to feel disappointed if it doesn't turn out that way: "Ben, are you all right? You look a bit sad." "I thought Noah was going to go swimming with me. I didn't know he had soccer practice." If you know what your innie is expecting, you can clarify misunderstandings and minimize any disappointment. "That is too bad. Let's find out Noah's schedule so we have a better idea about when he's available to come swimming with you." If you don't ask, you won't know what he's thinking.

Always tell your child about upcoming events a day or two in advance. "Maria, guess what? In two days Nana and Papa are coming to visit." An innie responds to changes in routine, such as having visitors, in various ways, depending on her level of energy, how comfortable she is with the people involved, and what other transitions are happening at the same time. Visitors bring lots of hustle and bustle. It takes a good deal of fuel to adapt to the excitement of a visit even from people she likes, with the added energy drain of more bodies in the house.

Verbalizing the schedule reduces an innie's anxiety about the unknown. "Let's put stickers on the calendar to mark the days till they come and the days they will be here." When you've done that, you can suggest making a list of what you need to buy for their visit, or do something like make chocolate chip cookies for them. Have your innie draw a picture of what she'd like to do with the guests. Innies often see pictures in their heads. If you help them shift the pictures to a new experience before it happens, they can cope better. ("Do you remember what we did during their last visit? We went to the children's museum. Your picture looks like you'd like to visit the zoo this time.") Occasionally, ask about the upcoming visit. One innie told me, "I like it when Nana and Papa visit, but I hate not being able to sleep in my own bed." Knowing this, you can avoid a meltdown by changing the sleeping arrangements.

Set up a private signal so your innie can give you the thumbs-up when he needs a break. Sometimes the need for a break is sudden—his energy drops like an elevator plummeting to the bottom floor. Providing an exit route is a good way to steer clear of tantrums or surliness.

You can do more than simply alert your child to upcoming social situations. Better to actually give her a way to get a firm grip on the event in advance. Let's say you're coming up on a big family wedding. Tell your innie something about all the major players and your relationship to them. Show photographs, if you have any. "See this young girl here? That's my cousin Anne, who's the bride. She and I used to sneak downstairs and eat ice cream." It's helpful for innies to have a mental picture beforehand, and it's even easier for them to ask questions about strangers once they have some tangible information about them. Innies will spend less energy and be less anxious if they are in-the-know about the cast of characters.

If the event involves other kids, a good way to help younger children break the ice is to bring some simple toys to hand out. A few Mexican jumping beans, stretchy lizards, or small gliders quickly get kids playing and ease awkward moments. A similar strategy for informal situations is bringing what I call "honey toys"—those that attract others kids like bees to honey. Help your innie make friends more easily by having other children come to him. When I take my grandchildren to our community pool, I blow long-lasting bubbles out over the water. In no time at all, all the kids are having fun trying to shoot the glistening bubbles floating above them. I also have a plastic treasure box full of "jewels" for kids to dive for on the bottom of the pool. In one instance Christopher (then six), who doesn't usually join in with new kids so readily, began playing almost immediately with a little girl who liked treasure, too. In no time, they had become pirates of the Caribbean, Jack Sparrow and his matey. They splashed and dove for hours.

Hindsight Is 20/20

Looking back on an event can be as productive as preplanning for it. Debrief a day or so after a significant social outing; talk with your child when she's relaxed to help her sort out her feelings and thoughts about it. Without this opportunity, she may draw mistaken negative conclusions, won't learn from her experiences, and might avoid social events in the future. An innie's feedback system can turn into a *backlash* system when it joins forces with her internal judge. If the judge/critic mouths off too much, your child can become discouraged. This will inhibit her from enjoying her out-and-about experiences. During your daily chat with your innie, ask, "Now that you've had some time to think about it, how did the sleepover go?" "Well," Abby said, "I think maybe I talked too much." (This is a common concern for innies, when they finally talk.) "Really. Did your friends lose interest in what you said?" "No, I don't think so, but I felt a little funny talking so much. I felt uncomfortable when they were all staring at me." You can then correct her perception. "It seems to me that if the other girls were looking at you, they were showing interest in what you were saying."

Icebreakers

Even for adults, one of the hardest aspects of socializing is starting a conversation. Teach your child about opening questions. These are easy-to-answer questions that convey the message "I'd like to know you better." They tend to encourage more yes than no answers; "no" tends to close down a conversation. Playing close to the moment—asking about the situation you are in—is usually the best approach (as in, "Is the water warm enough?"). The next best is asking a child his opinion. ("Do you like the swings or the tire better?" "Why did you decide to take karate?" "What did the teacher say yesterday about that movie? I was absent.") It's also good to make a comment about something you have in common. ("Hey, I have that same *Star Wars* shirt. Where did you get yours?")

Especially in situations where they feel scared, exposed, or nervous, innies tend to focus on the negative. It's part of their auditory learning system, which signals them to tag and store negative experiences. Since they also have delayed emotional reactions, they may misread other kids' responses in moments when they are nervous or overstimulated. You can help your child reevaluate the situation when he is calm, so he can have a more accurate picture of the actual response he received. I've done debriefings with innies that begin with "Everything went wrong," and finish with something like, "I guess it wasn't that bad, I did win first prize!" And this is no exaggeration.

Other Ways to Help

One of the most important things you can do to help foster your innie's social skills is to demonstrate interest in other people. Be friendly with everyone you encounter, and don't exclude outsiders.

Practice remembering your child's friends' names, and ask questions about them. Talk positively about your own friends. Give appropriate and authentic compliments. Model good social skills when your child's friends visit. Encourage your innie to be a host. For example, you can come up with a few possible activities to do and prepare snacks together before the guest arrives. Discuss Plan B: What they can do if the guest doesn't want to do the planned activities or boredom sets in. Following are other ways you can help your innie in the social arena.

Steer Him Away from Internalizing

Innies tend to internalize conflicts and to take things personally. On the one hand, this represents an advantage; innies tend not to blame others for their shortcomings and can thus use their experiences to grow and change. Also, this means that they know what they care about and what sparks their interest. However, living so much in their heads and having painful things happen to them may leave innies feeling like these unpleasant things only happen to them. ("I gave the answer and the teacher ignored me." "I couldn't think of anything to say." "I wasn't invited.") Most innies I work with think they are the only kids having problems. This is an impression you can correct.

Talk with your child about what aspects of social life he can control and what he can't. For one, he can't control other people's behavior. However, he can learn to identify some common social patterns and reactions. Help your innie turn down the volume on his internal critic so that he doesn't blame himself for normal childhood social rejections. It's vitally important to tell innies that they can make choices about their own behavior and choices about who to trust. They can learn what kind of friends they need and how to pick them. Assure your child that he is a good friend. Some kids will want other types of friends, but this is not your child's fault. And those kids may come around, too.

What your child *can* choose is when and how much she wants to socialize. Innies don't generally feel as much social pressure or the need to be included in everything that outies do. It's more a matter of managing their energy. Olivia invited her pal Ashley to her house on Saturday for a playdate, and that evening she had a piano recital. On Sunday, Sarah invited Olivia to her house for lunch and to go see the new *Star Wars* movie with their family. Olivia didn't want to go, and her mom asked why. Olivia said that Sarah's family was too big and when they went out she worried that she couldn't leave if she got tired. Her mom helped her compromise; she would have lunch with them but skip the movie.

Shaking the Homebody Syndrome

"Come on, Ryan. Let's go! Ryan . . . *Ryan*. Come ON!" Ryan's mom was getting exasperated. "I don't want to," Ryan, eleven, said, looking at his mother as if he had lost his last friend. "I have one more coin book to check out." Most innies are homebodies. Home is their refuge. It's familiar. It stabilizes their energy so that they can delve deep into their interests. Surroundings affect innies a lot—their system doesn't work as well in highly stimulating places. Since leaving home can feel like a wrenching shift, it helps to give innies a heads-up: "Ryan, in fifteen minutes we'll be leaving." From time to time when appropriate, let your innie stay home with a sitter or a relative, or alone, if he's old enough.

Getting motivated to leave home is hard for introverts, and this greatly affects their social lives. Simply put, there are times when your innie will have to tear herself away from the house, despite herself. This can be a point of negotiation and compromise. "You stayed home this morning, so this afternoon I want you to go with me to Uncle John's. I know you don't want to, but I bet you'll have fun with your cousin Libby." Notice how the outing goes. Resist the temptation to say, "I told you so," but you can reflect out loud after the event. "It's hard to decide sometimes, isn't it? You felt like staying home, but when you went you had fun." The experience can help motivate your child next time she resists an outing.

As your child gets older, help her assess how much she has been out vs. how much she has been cocooning. Too many engagements can lead to a social hangover. But if it's been mostly home time, even an innie can accept the fact that it's time to go out. Everyone gets stale after too much at-home time—though an innie might need to be reminded of this.

Teach Him How to Choose Friends

Innies can observe qualities they like and find pals that fit them. They may want a variety of friends. And, at various ages, they may change the style of friends they want. Give him your impressions of his friends, and ask for his. "I see you and Casey enjoy pretending together. She's good at making up imaginary lands." "Boy, you have good talks with Kevin about spaceships. He remembers a lot about what you tell him. Have you noticed that?" This type of discussion can help your child evaluate his friends and lays the groundwork for finding good fits in future relationships.

Innies do best with an innie friend or two. A good friend for an innie is a child who has a similar pace and with whom she can have good conversations. When she gets older, an outie friend is great for drawing her out and encouraging her adventurous spirit. However, with an outie friend, an innie does need to watch her energy level and be ready to say that she wants to call it quits. Surrounding herself with too many outie friends is unlikely to satisfy an innie; their attention span is short, they may not enjoy lengthy conversations, and they tend to argue more.

Building Bridges

I was driving a friend's eight-year-old son, Zane, home from school and needed to stop to drop off a gift at another friend's house. I explained to Zane that we wouldn't stop for long but would say hello for a few minutes. He said, "I'm not comfortable meeting new people. So I may not be very friendly." I assured him that this was okay; I knew this about him already. He then surprised me by being quite gregarious with my friend, asking lots of questions about her dogs, and showing great interest in the things in her house.

I thought about this later and realized that Zane's speaking up about his discomfort had the paradoxical effect of taking the pressure off—and thus relieving the discomfort. This provided Zane with the psychological space he needed to help him ease in. He presented his concern, and I accepted it. His statement to me served as a kind of bridge between his reluctance to meet someone and the actuality of the interaction.

Meeting strangers can be challenging for innies. Here are several ways that you can create a bridge:

- Hold your child (or hold his hand, or give him an affectionate nudge—depending on his age) and accept that he is anxious. Give him reassurance.
- Talk to strangers in a friendly way as you maintain contact with your child.
- Tell the person, "It takes Tim a while to warm up to anyone new."
- Never push him to be friendly before he's ready.
- Limit, if possible, the number of new people he meets at one time.
- Expose your child to the mail carrier, store clerks, neighbors, and acquaintances.
- Make meetings with new people brief, upbeat, and friendly.
- Don't step in too soon or interrupt him. Balance speaking up for him and giving him the space to pipe up for himself. Give him an opening: "You like that TV show, too, don't you?"

Appreciate Their Social Aptitude

Most innies are natural listeners. This is the number-one talent required for establishing friendships. This is also why innies often grow up to work in careers where strong relational skills are required. Let your innie know that she has good "earing." Tell her that you like the way she listens to you. Acknowledge what she hears and remembers: "I see you remembered that Jack is allergic to strawberries." Compliment her ability to tune in: "You're a good friend," or "I could tell you had your ears turned up to high, you were listening so attentively. I like that about you." Acknowledge her questions; innies are often very insightful.

Whether your innie is right- or left-brained will likely show up in conversations. A child who is more right-brained will notice feelings more and be sensitive to others' feelings. "You know what happened to my friend Amber's parakeet?" Carrie asks me. "He died from some germ he already had when they brought him home from the pet store. Amber thought maybe she did something wrong, but the pet store man said she didn't. He gave her another one, but she misses Al—that's what she called him. I told her I felt the same way when my hamster died."

Right-brained innies may have a high emotional quotient, or "EQ." They can imagine themselves in another child's shoes. This is called having empathy. From that vantage point, standing in his friend's sneakers, such an innie will be able to reflect back to the other child his feelings and thoughts. His friends will feel heard and accepted. Nothing is more powerful to friendship than knowing that someone understands your point of view.

If your innie isn't such a good listener or doesn't have as much empathy, she may be left-brained. She may like to discuss facts and such. You can help her learn to improve her emotional skills. Teach her how to reflect back, without merely parroting, to her friends what she is hearing. Teach her to listen for emotion and for the main point someone is making. You can indicate how to read people when you two are alone. "What do you think Ashley was feeling?" "She looked sad to me." "Me, too. Why do you think she might have been sad?" "I think her dog was sick."

Innies have built-in hardwiring to use the most advanced emotional system in the right front lobe of the brain. It's the home of mindsight and emotional intelligence. The ability to surmise what others are feeling and being able to intuit intentions are the central pillars of people skills. But innies' emotional wiring won't be turned on unless they have practice knowing their own emotions and feelings. Parents can help them hone this talent by playing games that tune up their emotional antenna like "Guess That Feeling" and "Guess That Point." "See if you can guess what I'm feeling when I tell you about my day and what is the most important point *to me* about what I'm telling you." Take turns. Let her practice reflecting what you were feeling and what was important about your day. Then you do the same thing with her. This will give her what we, in the therapy trade, call a "felt experience" of being seen and heard.

You can also demonstrate responding to thoughts and feelings by doing this in the moment with family members and friends. Andrew's friend, Ben, his eyes shining, was speed-talking in a loud voice about his new Game Boy. His words were tumbling out like a gushing waterfall. His mom said, "Boy, can't you tell by the way Ben's eyes are gleaming and how fast he's talking about that new Game Boy that he is soooo excited about that thing? Am I right, Ben?" "Yes, I am soooooooo excited," Ben says as he spins around the table. They all laugh, and Andrew and Ben run off to play. An added benefit here is that Ben will probably calm down a bit because he was heard.

Explain to your child that temperament affects how children act and speak. She can then learn to convert and adapt to each dialect, becoming, in effect, "bilingual." It is important for innies to understand extroverts, since they are the majority group. Beyond this, it is empowering. By learning the other language, innies can learn how outies think—and thus how to interact with them. As for outies, they can learn that some children are different from them. Becoming bilingual will widen their view of others. They can also gain the advantages they might have overlooked in innies. Help your child learn the language of innies and outies:

Be "Bilingual"—How to Speak Both Innie and Outie
When you're talking with an innie, try the following:
- Speak slower and and more softly and allow pauses.
- Tolerate silences.
- Use more complex sentences.

- Don't crowd them.
- Don't overwhelm them with emotion.

When you're chatting with an outie, you might want to:
- Speak faster.
- Use shorter sentences.
- Lean forward.
- Speak louder.
- Show expression.

When you're listening to innies, your best bets are to:
- Pay attention.
- Don't interrupt.
- Reflect back what you hear.
- Realize that what's being said has been thought out.
- If you need to, ask for clarification, then wait for his response.

When you're listening to outies, you'll do best if you:
- Offer immediate feedback.
- Nod, smile, and laugh.
- Realize that interrupting is okay.
- Give compliments.
- Don't take what they say as their final word on the subject.

Getting the Most from Parties

"Everyone with any sense and experience in life would rather take his fellow one by one than in a crowd."—P. J. O'Rourke

A few years ago I brought our granddaughter Katie to a fourth-year birthday party at Chuck E. Cheese. We looked around for the birthday girl. She was nowhere in sight. We finally located the

Follow Your Innie's Dreams

Supporting a child's interests makes all the difference in his social confidence. Jed has always been fascinated by movies and moviemaking. At age five, Jed wrote to the director of the latest *Harry Potter* movie and told him that he wanted to be a director when he grows up. His mom, with a fledgling Steven Spielberg on her hands, devised a great seventh birthday party for him. She made pirate costumes for every guest. Jed wrote a script for a play, and all the kids took part. Jed's parents videotaped the play, made copies, and gave them as the goodie bag gift when the kids left. For his gift, they gave Jed an inexpensive video camera. Jed reminded me of Peter, the introverted child in the film *Finding Neverland*, who wrote a theater script for his three brothers to take part in. J. M. Barrie was so impressed with Peter that he used him as the namesake—and model—for Peter Pan.

Now, this might involve more work than the typical parent wants—or is able to—devote to a birthday party. But the point is that Jed's mother acknowledged her son's avocation and showed him how, through his *interests*, he can connect to others.

mother standing by a table talking to the big, fluffy-costumed Chuck E. Cheese. "Where's Brianna?" Katie yelled above the din. The mother said, "She's under the table, and she won't come out." Oh no, I thought, another birthday party disaster.

Children's birthday parties have become big deals and very stressful. Some are overly fancy, crowded with kids and adults, and seem to go on forever. Help your innie prepare for a birthday party. When the invitation arrives, talk about it. If there are several parties in a row, let her skip one or two she doesn't feel strongly about. If she plans to go, put a sticker on the calendar for the date. When you call to RSVP, ask how many children will be there and what activities are

The Myth of Popularity

Many parents express concern that their introverted child has only one or two friends. Shouldn't she have more friends? they wonder. Shouldn't she be more *popular*?

Researchers have determined that many of our preconceived notions about popularity are incorrect. Interestingly, studies have found that being liked and being popular are two completely different things. In several replicated studies, children were asked who was popular and whom they liked. The researchers *were not* surprised to find that kids could identify the popular kids. But they *were* surprised to find that the popular kids weren't always well liked. Often the popular kids were actually feared and resented because they appeared to want power over others, not friendship. They were considered mean, bossy, and leaders of exclusive cliques. This supports other research about how often the most popular kids in high school don't fulfill their potential later in life. Power wanes as friendship skills gain. As kids enter adulthood, they need more than flashy

planned. Then pass along the information to your child so she can mentally prepare. Have your child help you choose and wrap the gift and let her make the card. This will help her feel more involved. Incidentally, many innies are insightful about choosing gifts and usually enjoy wrapping them.

Discuss the party earlier in the day. "It's almost party time. How are you feeling?" you can ask. "Is there anything you are worried about?" "I'm excited, but I hope there aren't too many kids," Reese says. "Well," you can say, "if it feels crowded don't forget to take a breather." Be sure your child is rested and has eaten before going. Remind him that intense bodily discomforts, like butterflies in the stomach or upper-body tension, will dissipate as he becomes more comfortable. Don't push him to interact before he feels ready. Let him ease into the party by watching with you from the sidelines. It power moves to get along with others—they need real people skills such as the ability to listen, empathize, and respect others' viewpoints.

Another study examined a different myth: If you want to be well liked, you need to be a social butterfly. But studies show that kids who are liked actually devote *less* time to socializing than many other kids do. Rather than "getting out there," the main trait that children valued in other kids was kindness.

Knowing how to strike up and maintain friendships and knowing how to work and play well with others are important. But that doesn't mean being the most noticed or the most invited. Don't overrate popularity. Encourage a few friends and a few activities—quality, not quantity, is the name of the game. Many parents invest in sports, academics, and other types of lessons. Without downplaying the value of these, don't forget to practice at home what will help your innie the most—strong, basic relationship skills.

might help to arrive a few minutes early to say hello to the host child and get acclimated before the other guests show up. Remind him to take breaks away from the hubbub, perhaps helping in the kitchen, stepping into a quiet, unused room, or sitting on the front porch for a while. If it's a long party, he may not want to stay for the whole time.

If you stay through the party, you can help simply by being open and friendly. If you chat with some of the kids, your child may join in after a while. Remind her that when she feels ready, she can wave, nod, or say hi. As she gets older she can learn to smile at a friendly-looking child and practice an opening question.

When your very young innie is having a birthday party, keep it small and simple, short and sweet. Let him select the theme and have a say about the food, and encourage him to help prepare for the party. He may, in fact, enjoy the preparations the most. Seven-year-old Todd's mom and dad planned his birthday party with both innies and outies in mind. They had a Spider-Man bouncer set up in the backyard. They also put out toy dinosaurs and Lego construction pieces in the living room. Any of the boys who needed a breather could get away from all the bouncing and bobbing. Boys flowed in and out throughout the party. Two introverted boys played alone with the dinosaurs for a while. One was the birthday boy himself.

As innies get older, they may prefer taking a friend or two to a movie or other special outing like a trip to the beach or skiing. By the age of eight or nine, your child may want to tackle a sleepover with a few friends. You might consider staggering birthday celebrations by separating family parties and friend parties. Usually, in our family, we have small parties. One celebration is for one set of grandparents and a few friends. Another party, a week later, is for the other side of the family and several other friends. We are quite flexible about the dates on which we celebrate birthdays and other occasions.

Innies' Guide to Dating

Introverts are private kids who feel exposed easily. Their pace for dating is usually slower than for outies, in part because they are less influenced by peer pressure. This is especially true of male innies. Studies show that even in college innies date less then outies. But, even if delayed in dating, innies are thinking about it—and they may have a secret crush. Don't tease or embarrass your child about liking someone or if you notice that another child of the opposite sex seems to like her. Keep a positive attitude. "When you are ready I'm sure you'll enjoy dating." "What do you think would make the best date?" Innies with self-confidence will feel better about easing into dating. Keep a respectful dialogue going. Answer questions about dating and sex, and talk about your own experiences. I have worked with many

Potential Parent/Teen Dynamic

Since many innies are fun to talk with and seem like they are adults, they become a parent's primary chatting companion. That parent can undermine the innie's move toward dating because, without even realizing it, he or she doesn't want to lose their conversation pal. Be on the lookout for this.

innies whose parents were very popular in high school. The parents probably think they are encouraging their innie by setting high expectations. But usually their innie child feels demoralized by his or her parents bragging about how easy dating was.

Teens don't always want to share their experiences with parents, but it's lovely when they do. My younger innie daughter always had male friends growing up, but she didn't seem interested in dating until she was around sixteen. One day, she asked me to drive her to the mall (she didn't drive until she was eighteen). She wanted me to see the quiet boy she liked. They hadn't talked much, but they had a letter-writing relationship going. We walked past the Orange Julius stand and she said, "He's working behind the counter and is the one who's a head taller than me, in the brown shirt and orange cap. But don't look in. I don't want him to see us." After we passed the place and I had eyestrain from trying to look without looking, she kept asking me, "Did you see him? Did you see him?" I said, "I think so, but there were about five boys that fit your description—they all had on the Orange Julius uniform! But I *think* I saw him, and he looks very nice. I'm sure he's a good choice." Soon after, they had a nervous first date, and now they have been married for fifteen years. He *was* a good choice.

Perhaps the most challenging aspects of dating, even for outies, is getting up the nerve to ask someone for a date. Your innie can practice, practice, and practice asking someone to a dance or to go out for a soda. Encourage your son to invite a girl to see a video at your house, for he will most likely be more comfortable on his own turf. You can promise to disappear. You can also help him brainstorm and plan other dating arrangements that would help him feel at ease. Be sure that he activates his internal self-talking cheerleader, not the critical judge. Remind him that everyone gets turned down. You can also remind date-wary innies that although they might not be good at small talk, they are good conversationalists. They possess the qualities that make good long-lasting relationships. Pat yourself on the back if your innie discusses the issue of being gay. They trust you a lot. It's hard to talk about. See if you can help them sort out their feelings. Is this just a crush on a friend of the same sex? Or have they had these feelings for a long

Pet Pal

Pets can be comforting and important friends for your child. Animals teach about giving and receiving love. They teach patience, responsibility, and they demonstate how to play and enjoy life. Research shows that petting animals reduces stress, anxiety, and illness. They also teach valuable lessons about loss. Innies often enjoy the responsibility of raising dogs, cats, birds, rats, mice, hamsters, or fish. And certainly dogs and cats make satisfying companions and can be important for innies through adulthood.

Today's parents are already so busy that many see pets as an added responsibility and expense. As a result, many do not buy pets for their children as often as in the past. But innies *need* to have a pet; they have love to give. Pets give a child confidence; having a pet teaches about trust. Choose a pet that is a good relational counterpart—not too aloof, rambunctious, temperamental, or nervous. You will be rewarded when you see your innie playing with and caring for his pet. You will be amazed by how nurturing your innie child will be with his pet.

time? Ten percent of all teens are hardwired to be gay. It can be isolating to be a gay teen so help them find some other gay teens. Encourage them to chill at your house. You may have strong feelings about your teen being gay and it may help you to join a group for parents of gay teens.

Introverted teens see dating as serious business and don't like superficial relating. Because relationships are so important to them, breakups can be devastating to an innie. Respect your child's feelings and acknowledge how painful it is to lose a girl- or boyfriend. Gently remind her that it gets better and that she will have other relationships. Watch for prolonged depression. If the brooding lasts more than a month or two, have her talk with a professional psychotherapist. Another problem I have seen with innies, both male and female, is *avoiding* a breakup that ought to take place because their boy- or girlfriend is their central relationship. Encourage your innie to maintain other relationships while dating.

There are many aspects of socializing and many ways to socialize. By staying tuned in to your child's social interests and apprehensions, you can help him take pleasure in friendships and enhance his comfort in groups.

The Heart of the Matter

- *Teach good social skills in daily interactions at home.*
- *Point out the strengths of innie and outie social patterns.*
- *Help innies prepare for transitions, parties, and dating.*

CHAPTER 14

Thorny Social Patches

Help Your Innie Manage Conflict, Bullies, and Other Challenges

"Some people are always grumbling that roses have thorns; I am thankful that thorns have roses."—Ambrose Karr

Friendship enriches our lives immensely, but no relationship is without its thorny patches. Differences crop up and, while stressful, they can actually help relationships grow. But when differences aren't handled effectively they can escalate into conflicts. Often this happens because of stress, misunderstandings, unmet expectations, unaddressed feelings, incompatible needs, or a failure to come up with solutions. Resolving differences and conflicts helps introverted kids learn how to manage in the world. They learn to appreciate and manage differences, which expands their ability to cooperate with others.

Introverts and extroverts have different physiological reactions to conflict. When an outie faces a conflict, her side of the nervous system says *battle*. She wants to argue or take action immediately. She interprets silence on her adversary's part as agreement. Outies get jolts of adrenaline and dopamine from conflicts, so some extroverted children actually instigate arguments in order to feel alive.

Under fire, an innie's nervous system says *pull back*. He wants to reflect on a disagreement before he talks about it. He may be silent because he isn't ready to disclose his opinion. Studies show that conflicts consume lots of energy for innies and require substantial recuperation time. It's easy to see why innies and outies have some challenges when there are conflicts.

It is very important to validate reality for your child. Some kids aren't nice. Peace-loving innies think all other kids seek harmony, too. Even as adults, they often have trouble realizing that some people have aggressive motivations. The fact is that life among peers is not always so idyllic, and not everyone plays fair. Some kids are good friends, others less so. Also, friendships are anything but static. They change over the years, and sometimes (especially in childhood) over weeks and days. Occasionally, a friend will pull away or even overtly snub you. Sometimes friendships just fizzle out.

Everyone faces rejection at one time or another. Relating with people always involves risk, and some risks turn out okay, some don't. It's helpful for innies to realize that rejection is a normal and frequent social experience. Rejection has its beneficial side; it motivates people to make a good impression and strive to improve their relationships and careers. Some innies (more often right-brained innies) may be particularly sensitive to rejection. They may bend over backward to avoid rejecting others, even when not being friends with that person is the right thing to do. Some—not all—left-brained innies may not be concerned about rejection to the point where they may appear arrogant or detached. Outies tend to be acutely sensitive to rejection but may not be mindful of how their reactions affect others. Share some of the rejections you've experienced with your child. This shows your innie that rejection is something you can survive, and so can she.

It is crucial to explain to an innie that if a child calls her a name or teases her, it isn't her fault. Since innies tend to internalize and personalize what happens to them, their first inclination is to think, "I must have done something." "Maybe I wasn't nice enough, and now they are teasing me." "They see something bad in me so they are treating me badly." Most innies care deeply about their primary relationships with friends and family, and so rejection, teasing, and name-calling really stings. You can say, "Some kids have short fuses, and they just act that way. It's crummy." Or, "I know you feel hurt, but it passes, and you are still okay." No one is born knowing how to behave with everyone. We all make social goofs as we are learning the ropes. In fact, that's exactly how we all learn.

An unfortunate reality is that innies live in an extroverted culture. As I have mentioned before, extroverts tend to prefer other extroverts. Other outies fuel their system. Innies usually don't give them enough high-octane interactions. Without knowing exactly why, outies may feel irritated by how innies behave and therefore avoid or reject them. On the other hand, outies feel rejected when an innie withdraws or if they feel the innie is withholding on purpose. They may not take the time to get to know an innie. This dynamic puts yet another hurdle on the innie's social path.

Dealing with Discord

"A friend is someone who isn't bossy."
—Chloe Cravens, age seven

Social bonds are fragile. Caring about relationships is the single strongest thread that secures those bonds, which is why many innies are well liked. They care. Part of their caring nature is an inherent tendency to be adaptable. Sometimes innies are seen as passive because they would "rather switch than fight." Your introverted child may need help to know that there are times to be flexible and times to stand firm—and how to tell the difference.

Even at very young ages, innies generally react differently than extroverted kids to toy snatchings and other aggressive moves. You can remind your child that it's okay for him to protect himself and his belongings. For example, an aggressive classmate gave one young introvert, Jared, a hearty shove. Jared's dad had previously coached him about such situations and told him that he should say, "Leave me alone!" in a loud voice. Jared knew the teacher would hear him and step in if needed, so he spoke up for himself. The other child stopped bumping him.

Innies need to learn that being nice doesn't work with all kids or in all situations. Different children have different intentions and motivations. Some kids want to be good friends, some like to be playmates, some want pals, and there are a few kids who want a gang so they can feel powerful.

Play typically turns aggressive when adults aren't near or those present aren't paying attention. It can be a fine line between boys' rough-and-tumble play and a sudden crossover to belligerent hitting and overpowering. A group of girls may be having fun talking one moment, and before you know it one girl has been excluded from the group. Help your child read the feeling she has when the play turns hostile. A sour note of discord can be struck quickly and without explanation. The feeling says its time to move on to play with another child or join another group.

Remind innies that even in one-on-one situations, conflicts are part of life. Finding solutions can actually be fun, like solving a mystery. The first step in handling disagreements is listening to what the other child is upset about. "Oh, you want to be Captain Hook?" Many innies can be too compliant and say, "Okay you can be Captain Hook." This is fine occasionally, but acquiescing *all the time* can set up a child to be bullied. The best way to build your innie's confident assertiveness during disputes is to model good conflict resolution in your family. Research shows that kids who are socially confident can accommodate both their own and the other child's concerns and be able to explain their reasoning. To wit: "Let me

Tried-and-True Conflict Clobbering

Teach your innie these simple steps to defuse a more aggressive child:

DO:

1. Validate the other child's concerns by empathizing with what's bothering him.

2. Try to step into the other child's shoes: *"Oh, you wanted to see my Yu-Gi-Oh! cards."*

3. Offer a compromise to defuse the tension: *"I'll let you see my cards. Just ask me instead of grabbing them out of my hand."*

4. Know that it's not merely okay but a good idea to discuss an argument later after both kids have cooled down. *"You were pretty mad the other day. Want to talk about it now?"*

DON'T:

1. Try to reason with an aggressive kid, especially when he's angry.

2. Contradict him or try to talk him out of his viewpoint.

3. Minimize his concerns or make fun of him.

finish sending this traitorous sailor down the gangplank. Then you can be Captain Hook. But you can make the sound of the clock in the alligator's tummy while you wait, if you want."

Discuss the conflicts your child has at school. "Megan doesn't want Jade to be in the talent show with us anymore. I don't feel good about leaving her out." Acknowledge your child's feelings. Talk about how to settle the conflict so that everyone involved gets some of what they want. Help her practice what to say, reminding her to explain her thoughts to the other kids. This is the step innies often leave out.

Uptight and Stressed

"Insanity is doing the same thing over and over and expecting a different result."—Rita Mae Brown

Lots of situations, including conflicts and disagreements in the social arena, leave kids feeling stressed. Innies and outies have different responses to stress. Heed these markers to see if your child needs some help working through a conflict or other kind of struggle.

If your innie is stressed, you may notice that she:
• Withdraws or avoids problems
• Stops talking
• Resists or becomes passive
• Feels overwhelmed and stalled
• Becomes rigid
• Becomes irritable
• Blames herself a lot
• Becomes physically exhausted and has increased muscle tension

If your outie is stressed, you may notice that he:
• Blames others or the situation
• Wants to talk it out *now*
• Becomes obsessive and compulsive about work
• Won't stop and reflect
• Becomes ill and has body complaints
• Becomes defensive and angry
• Becomes anxious and worried

Help both innies and outies regain their equilibrium when they are stressed by talking it out. When you see signs like anger, moping, acting in an obsessive way, or refusing to talk, and they have lost their sense of humor, ask if something is causing stress. This helps;

now at least he knows he is uptight. Acknowledging upset feelings is the fastest way to help kids reduce stress—now outies can mute the *battle* mode, and innies can *come out* from their retreat. After your child has regained his balance, discuss what caused the stress. See if he can learn to notice that stressed feeling before it gets him down and when he can do something about the situation. You can also use the tips below to help him wind down.

Helping Your Innie Handle Stress

- Give her time to think about the conflict or issue.
- Help her be aware that her feeling upset and fatigued stems from an unresolved conflict.
- Give her room to safely talk about her thoughts and feelings. She may prefer to write about them.
- Be patient. It may take her time to express her thoughts.
- Help her relax. Her body and her speech may be more constricted.

Helping Your Outie Handle Stress

- Let him talk about the conflict or issue.
- Know that he may see several conflicts or issues. He will sort out the most important ones as he talks.
- Be available to listen—he will want to discuss it right now.
- Don't be surprised if his thoughts change as he talks. Don't consider anything he says to be the final word on the subject.
- Give him space to move around. It helps him think.

Detecting People Patterns

It's important to start teaching introverted children early that people come in different stripes and to help them learn to recognize some of those variations. Innies can learn to be detectives and use their observational skills and their persistence to understand various patterns of human behavior. This will strengthen their social muscle. Help your innie think about what it's like to be with a playmate. Is this child fun? Is she trustworthy? Can she share most of the time? Does she cooperate? Does she keep private information private? Does she make your child feel good about herself? After playing with her, does your child feel tired but happy or really, really drained?

Maintain an ongoing discussion about how children and adults behave. Often adults feel that they shouldn't discuss how people act because it's critical or gossipy. So they act as if everyone were the same or as if all behavior were acceptable. However, introverted children do pick up nuances in people's social behavior. They need their reality validated in order to make sense of people. Listen, validate, and discuss what they notice from unspoken communications such as facial expressions, emotional vibes, and body language. It will enhance their ability to appraise people.

Reflect aloud about your friends' and family members' reactions: "Aunt Edna must be upset about something today. She is unusually snappy." And then say how you respond: "I usually enjoy visiting her, but I didn't think I should stay too long today." Give your innie permission to discuss his experience: "Ashley is so lively, but it seems like it might be exhausting to talk with her. It seems hard for her to listen, she talks kind of loudly, and she interrupts every two minutes. Does it bother you?" Respect your child's reaction if it's different from yours. You don't want to influence her opinions, but you do want to help her learn to notice what she likes and doesn't like about how kids act.

It can also be helpful to let innies know how other kids are reacting to their temperamental style: "Since you didn't answer right away, I don't think Brad knew you were thinking about an answer to his question. How do you think you could let him know you are still with him?" Innies tend to dwell inside their own heads. Playing people-detective lifts them out of their minds and into a comfortable observation mode.

Bully Busting

"He that respects himself is safe from others,
he wears a coat of armor that none can pierce."
—Henry Wadsworth Longfellow

Bullies are, without a doubt, the bane of the social world of childhood. Alas, they're everywhere, and not always where you would expect. They may be the stereotypical big, mean kids with short tempers and quick fists, or they may be quiet loners. They can be fat or thin, female or male, smart or not-so-smart. Every one of us has been bullied at one time or another. In third grade, I was small for my age, and a girl named Audrey—note that I remember her name—used to rush up behind me, grab me around the waist, and lift me off the ground. In an attempt to humiliate me, she'd yell out to the kids on the playground, "Look how strong I am!" One time I kicked and screamed and flailed around until she put me down. She had expected me to be a pushover, but I resisted more than she had anticipated. That detracted from her show of strength. She never tried to make me into a human barbell again.

Your child needs to feel safe at home and at school and en route between the two. Introverted children can easily become targets for bullies, since they're more likely to be on their own rather than in a group. In the past, we told children to ignore bullies or to just be nice to them. This is not a good way to handle bullies. It doesn't work. Your introverted child will need help to be bully-wise. Don't sit back—take action if your child is being bullied.

As a parent, you can do several things to help. First, be a good role model. Children who see violence and aggression at home can become a bully or the victim of one. Never verbally abuse or use sarcasm with your child. Second, explain to your child that she can't solve bullying on her own—the number-one deterrent is adult authority. If your child feels threatened by a bully, tell her to ask for

Signs That Your Child Is Being Bullied

*"One of my problems is that I internalize
everything. I can't express anger.
I grow a tumor instead."*—Woody Allen

Many kids don't tell their parents that they are being bullied. They view it as embarrassing, even (and here's that innie critic working overtime) shameful. And they often blame themselves: "I think I said something wrong, I'm not sure what, and then Jimmy and his pals bugged me and took my lunch money. I guess I'd better keep my mouth shut." These are clues that your innie may be dealing with a bully:

• Being depressed or uncharacteristically irritable

• Having problems in school

• Missing belongings, or coming home with torn clothes

• Not eating lunch (lunch money may have been stolen)

• Having nightmares and wetting the bed

• Coming home with unexplained bruises

• Having frequent illnesses

help from teachers, coaches, aides, or other parents. Third, step in and tell bullies to stop, if you see one in action.

One great concept is an antibullying program called the McGruff Safe Houses. Individuals and stores sign up and let kids stop in if they are bothered traveling to and from home. If there isn't a program like this in your area, consider starting one at your school. Staff and teacher training are also important because many teachers don't know the profile for bullying behavior. Schools need to send a message to students to show respect for everyone and support the children who are being bullied. Students need to be encouraged to speak up for kids who are bullied. Ideally schools would establish clear behavioral expectations and consequences for bullying. Books on bully-busting are listed in the Selected Reading on page 283.

Bullies deplete self-esteem the way vampires suck blood. They feel better about themselves by making others feel bad about themselves. Their tactics are varied. They may hit, punch, kick, tease, push, pull, pester, brag, taunt, harass, play mind games, frighten, heckle, insult, annoy, gossip, hurt, threaten, torment, start insulting rumors, ridicule, trip, pinch, act violent, and/or intimidate. Bullies have short fuses. They interpret others' behavior as hostile and personal when it isn't.

There is scientific evidence today that some children are hardwired to be bullies. They have a high level of aggression and a low level of fear. If children with this particular wiring are treated harshly, they may become bullies. Contrary to popular opinion, bullies are not friendless—in fact, they are often popular leaders. Other kids find them exciting, fun, and full of great ideas. They usually hold power over groups, often the "cool" group, which increases their influence and makes them even harder to deal with. Nonetheless, there are strategies that your innie can use to avoid being victimized.

Bully-proof Your Innie

- Teach your child how to spot a bully. Telltale clues: Bullies try to intimidate by standing close, talk in a loud, in-your-face manner, tease, may be nice one day and mean the next.
- Explain that you understand that some kids are bullies, and that she doesn't need to be friends with everyone.
- Explain that absolutely no bullying should be tolerated. *Always* tell an adult.
- Be sure your child has one or two friends—bullies sniff out loners.
- Explain to your child that bullies may feel jealous if you do well at something. Your success means that a bully feels like a loser.
- Teach your child how good friends behave and that bullies are looking to be top dog, not friends.

Innies On-Screen

Films can depict kids' social struggles and successes in powerful, comprehensible ways. Watching movies that show children a bit older can give your innie a sneak preview into what's around the corner socially. I recently watched the film *Stand By Me*, an authentic depiction of four preteen boys' growing pains, with my eight-year-old grandson. The boys all have difficult family lives. The main character is Gordie, an innie, who is an intelligent, bookish observer. He offers good solutions and practical suggestions to the group. Gordie and Chris, an outie who is kind of tough but a good leader, take turns leading the group through an adventure, settling disputes, and keeping the group together despite dangerous situations and despicable bullies.

Another good film for older kids (it has some sad parts) is *My Dog Skip*. Willie Morris, a friendless innie with a dad who doesn't understand him and a mom who does, gets a dog for his birthday. Skip the dog shows Willie how to make friends, even with some bullies. Another film, *My Girl*, is a touching story about a girl, Vada, and a boy, Thomas J., who are innie pals. Even without words they understand each other. Vada is an unusual girl who has had too many losses. She is open about her feelings, such as being in love with her writing teacher. She strives to work through her feelings in her own unique way. Once again, there are sad parts.

- Teach your child to let the bully's cruel words, looks, or gestures roll off her back and not undermine her self-esteem. Remind her that bullying behavior is immature, and suggest she picture bullies as big babies wearing diapers. Innies don't have to have their feelings hurt. Tell her: Bullies want you to feel bad, so don't give them the satisfaction. She can practice her internal voice: "You can't hurt my feelings. I won't feel little just so you can feel big." Kids appear stronger when their internal voice is an ally.

Digging to China is a great film about an innie, Harriet, who is living a chaotic life with her alcoholic mother and teenage sister in a broken-down motel. Harriet is precocious and brimming with creativity but lacks playmates. She befriends a sweet, mentally retarded boy, Ricky, and the adults misconstrue their relationship.

Once you start looking, you will see that many central film characters are innies. As is the case with children's literature, the narratives are usually written by introverted writers. Common innie challenges and resolutions may be depicted in films, so they can provide good role models for innies. Films also bring innies into the inner worlds of other children and adults. Those who are visual learners are particularly able to take in new ideas from movies.

It's good to discuss films with your child, perhaps a few days later. This is especially true of films, like those above, that address painful topics like relationship problems, loss, differentness, and cruelty. My grandson has already had his share of teasing and bullying. We have had interesting chats about bullies, why some kids are leaders, how kids relate in groups, and what makes a good friend. After seeing *Stand By Me* he said, "They are friends because they stick up for each other. If they have a fight, they make up."

- Tell your child to avoid groups of bullies.
- Teach her to walk to a police station, post office, library, or other place where there are safe adults if a bully is bothering her.
- Have your child take a karate or other type of self-defense class to gain the confidence they instill. Innies who stand tall, look self-assured, look aggressive kids in the eye, and walk with confidence are less of a target for bullies.
- Practice dealing with bullies at home with role playing. Teach your child to look a bully in the eye and say firmly, "Stop that!" or

Electronic Bullying

Internet bullying is on the rise and afflicts a surprising number of kids, particularly teens. I worked with a young girl, Tiffany, a sixth grader at a private school, who was being bullied over the Internet. When she and her friend Nic had a fight, he vented his resentment toward Tiffany by creating a Web site about her, complete with pictures and rumors about her wild behavior, among other cruel statements. He sent e-mails about the Web site to everyone he knew at school. Tiffany felt ashamed, because she thought the fight with Nic was her fault. She finally told her mother when kids at school started avoiding her because they believed what the Web site said. Her mom talked to Nic's parents, and they wouldn't do anything about the Web site. Tiffany became so distraught that her mom brought her to see me.

Unfortunately, online harassment is becoming more common, but you can do something about it. Take it seriously and report it to your Internet service provider and to your local police; the police are being trained in how to respond to it.

"Don't do that. I'll report you if you don't leave me alone." Tell her not to be afraid to yell. Remember, when in doubt, shout.

- Tell your school principal if your child is being bullied. Many schools have instituted antibully programs.
- Tell your child that it's good to bring bullying out into the open. It lessens a bully's power.
- Tell your child that it's okay to be scared and upset but to try not to cry in front of the bully (that's what he wants). Better to stay calm and walk away.
- Give the kids on your child's route a healthy treat when they are walking home or they get off the bus, and chat with them in a friendly way. Bullies are less likely to torment a child whose parent has been nice to them.

The Silver Lining

*"A blunder at the right moment is better than
cleverness at the wrong time."—Carolyn Wells*

Differences and conflicts are unavoidable. However, every clashing of minds presents an opportunity to learn something new. Learning to find ways to manage conflict without avoiding it helps innies develop into more capable and confident adults. It is extremely rewarding to teach innies the life skills to handle rough patches—especially when you see them realize they can come up with creative solutions to complex social problems. Innies will learn that some conflicts are worth the outlay of energy—the roses are worth the thorns.

The Heart of the Matter

- *Wherever there are people, there are conflicts.*
- *Conflicts are opportunities to improve relationships.*
- *Innies can learn to be prepared to use energy for conflicts and bully busting.*

Reflections as We Disembark

"The world may be a different place because I was important in the life of a child."

—Forest E. Witcraft

Each child's temperament presents gifts that are difficult or easy for parents to nurture. An extroverted child's gifts can be closer to the surface—with a bit of sunlight, water, and a smidgen of fertilizer they bloom. The biggest challenge for parenting an outie is the need for accurate and consistent pruning. Introverted children, on the other hand, are just the opposite. Their gifts may be harder to see. Parents need to learn how to bring them into the light. Innies need "just right" nurturing to mature and flourish. And it's best to go easy on the pruning.

You may have been surprised to learn through the course of this book that there is far more to temperament than meets the eye. Parenting an introverted child may pose particular challenges, since parents must first face the biases they may have absorbed from growing up in an extroverted culture. It is not easy to parent a child who doesn't fit the mold. Innies in particular require time, understanding, and patience. The preceding chapters have given you the tools you need to help your introverted child in all areas of his life. Most important, I have offered strategies for building on your innie's strengths and developing his self-esteem. Temperament is lifelong; it is not an attribute one can change or outgrow. Therefore, helping your innie to accept his own temperament and learn to negotiate the social and energetic demands of the outside world will help his future look bright.

Your Innie Needs YOU

"To the world you may be just one person
but to one person you are the world."
—*Mac Anderson and Lance Wubbels*

In today's hectic and impersonal world you may feel insignificant at times. If you are lucky and have an introverted child, remember that, to her at least, you are the world. While true of all children, it's doubly so with innies—because although they may not show it, they rely heavily on emotional relationships in their family. They need you. Introverted kids must have meaningful relationships in order to develop their gifts. A good relationship with you is the key to uncovering their hidden strengths.

Never forget: You are very important to your innie.

What Does Your Innie *Really* Require from You?

It's easier to parent with confidence if you are clear about what your innie needs. Knowing where to focus and direct your parenting efforts saves energy and increases your sense of satisfaction. It also provides a solid base from which to make daily decisions. Your love

Parent Trap

Whether you are an innie or an outie, it takes a lot of energy to parent. Let me remind you to keep your own energy reserves full. It isn't selfish to take time out for yourself. In fact, without recharging his or her battery pack once in a while, no parent can function well.

Plan to take care of yourself in the following ways:

- Keep your body healthy.
- Learn some form of physical and mental relaxation.
- Make sure you're not depriving yourself of adult company.
- Clear your mind. Try ten minutes of resting in a dark room, meditating, reading a good novel or other book you enjoy, soaking in a warm bath, or listening to soothing music.
- Stay organized. I know this is not always easy, but clutter saps energy.
- Keep the romantic fires burning in your life.

and support are what your child needs in the most global sense. Here we take a closer look at ten ways to ensure that your innie thrives.

1. Time
To a child, love is spelled T-I-M-E. Time with your innie is the raw material that builds a strong bond between you. Time can't be catch-as-catch-can. You have to consciously plan to make time to be together. Carving out time with your innie maintains the link your introverted child needs. Of course, there are thousands of demands that pull you in numerous directions. Like most parents, you no doubt wish the days were longer. But if you lose precious moments with your innie, they can never be recovered. Make time with your innie a priority, both for his sake and so that you don't miss knowing a remarkable child.

2. Trust

It can be frightening to think that you influence your child merely by being yourself. But you do. You are your child's primary role model. If you aren't honest, don't expect that your child will be. If you break the promises you make to your child, expect that she will learn to do the same. I have worked with so many parents who have no compunction about being deceitful but complain vigorously when their children lie—without making any connection between the two. Introverted children count on what you say more than outies do. They not only detect lies, but they remember promises, so it's vitally important to be honest with them. Lying erodes relationships and makes trust impossible.

3. Stability

Innies need constancy. Daily life requires less energy when your innie enjoys a predictable and stable environment. His world will be as safe and as stable as you make it. If you are unpredictable, his life becomes chaotic. If he has to worry about your mood or your whereabouts, he won't have the energy or attention to devote to his main job—growing up. Providing stability enables him to build a solid foundation.

4. Confidence in Her Potential

Become a student of your introverted child's world. Learn to watch, listen, and take notice. Can you tell when she feels upset or depleted? Do you know if she is giving a report next week? Or what she does and doesn't like? Help your innie discover her interests and talents. Innies have lots of potential—help your child tap into hers through your intimate knowledge of her.

5. A Slow Pace

For your innie's sake, if not your own, *slow down*. Innies can't think or talk unless they feel they can enter a pressure-free zone. They need a slow, patient pace as much as possible. Living in a rushed and tense atmosphere sucks the oxygen right out of them.

Don't let your life be ruled by stress. When you slow down, you will notice that your innie will bring more of his world to you.

6. Perseverance

Innies are hardwired to be persistent. You can model this valuable trait for your child by demonstrating stick-to-it-iveness. "Boy, I was so frustrated with my boss. I felt like throwing in the towel. Two days later we both cooled off and we talked. She saw my point of view. I'm glad I thought of another way to approach her." Point out and praise your child's resolve: "I liked the way you asked three times for a turn on the swing. And he finally gave you a turn."

7. Courage in the Face of Adversity

Help your innie realize that hardship is part of life. And help her face the music when she makes poor choices. Keep a balance. Don't shield her from the consequences of her actions, but don't let her be crushed or treated harshly. Discuss the roadblocks you've faced, and how you managed to hop over, dig under, or take a detour around them. Innies make good use of "me, too" stories, if they are told with a "we're in this together" attitude. If you rebound well from your problems, your innie will, too.

8. Acceptance of Mistakes

I'm sure you have noticed that no one is perfect. Your example of admitting mistakes and apologizing for them is a tremendous legacy to give any child. But innies in particular take things to heart and often blame themselves for whatever goes wrong. Thus it is vitally important to reassure your child when he is not to blame. Acknowledging your errors, failures, and disappointments teaches your innie that everyone makes mistakes. That's how we learn.

9. Encouragement

An innie needs to feel that you are in her corner—not just when things are going well, but all the time. Know what goal she prizes and help her achieve it. Show concern for her struggles, and support her achievements. Help her recognize options and make priorities. Satisfaction in life must be earned. So help her find what it is that sparks her mind and encourage relationships that aid her growth. Keep your eye on the goal of raising her to be a mature adult.

10. Delight

It always saddens me to see parents who don't enjoy their children. Of course at times we all tire of everyone in our lives. But it seems to me that nothing in life compares to the joy of holding your child's hand, watching him sleep, or looking into his eyes and seeing a unique person separate from you. All kids are marvelous creatures. Since innies are so attuned to their perceptions they can come up with startling insights, humorous perspectives, and creative solutions. Innies love it if you let your hair down. Play with them and let them show you the wonders that all too often pass you by. Even if you are tired, don't shrug your innie aside when he asks you to listen, look, or share. Real life is lived moment to moment, so don't let those vital minutes slip away.

I'd Like to Hear from You

"Make the most of your child's uniqueness."
—*LaVonne Neff*

I hope that you understand your innie, and maybe yourself and other family members, a little better after reading this book. I would like to hear from you. You can contact me on my Web site MartiLaney@theintrovertadvantage.com or by mail at P. O. Box 6565, Portland, Oregon 97228-6565. I welcome hearing about your experiences with your innie. Treasure your innie. He or she is a gift.

Appendix

Syndromes and Disorders that Are Sometimes Confused with Introversion

Introversion—and particularly introversion in children—remains misunderstood, even by professionals. For this reason, a child who is introverted may get tagged with other childhood problems and diagnoses. Knowing what these are can help you better determine how to help your child, as well as avoid being waylaid by false diagnoses.

Here are some syndromes and disorders that can be confused with introversion—and why they differ.

Sensory Integration Dysfunction. Children with this newly recognized problem may have intense aversions to loud sounds, being touched, the feel of certain clothes, messy hands, and eating certain foods. Or they may have the opposite reaction and *crave* touch, noise, and strong sensation. Sensory integration dysfunction can affect both innies and outies. It is associated with premature birth and seems to have a genetic component. Introverted children can be highly attuned to their sensory experience but not with the same painful level of intensity.

High Sensitivity. Every child has a comfort zone, much like Goldilocks with her "not too much and not too little" preference. The highly sensitive child has very narrow margins of comfort—things have to be *just right* or they are not okay at all. This condition, which affects 15–20 percent of the population, is thought to have a genetic component and can be augmented by abusive family environments. The majority of highly sensitive persons are introverts, but about 30 percent are extroverts. There is an overlap; introverted children may retreat from too much external stimulation. However, the introvert wouldn't necessarily react to sensory input in the same global way.

ADD and ADHD Spectrum. Children with ADD and ADHD have difficulty concentrating, paying attention, and finishing tasks. They can be impulsive, dreamy, or tuned out. If a child is hyperactive —in perpetual motion—it is called attention-deficit/hyperactivity disorder (ADHD); without hyperactivity, it is called attention deficit disorder (ADD). Some 5 percent of children are estimated to be on this spectrum. Research suggests that these conditions result from a combination of genetic and environmental causes. An introverted child, with her internal focus, may be seen as inattentive. Typically, extroverts are diagnosed with ADHD and introverts with ADD.

Autism and Asperger's Disorders. These syndromes reflect a cluster of symptoms that include problems in communication and relating to others, and the display of repetitive behaviors. In the film *Rain Man*, Dustin Hoffman portrayed a character with severe autism. Autistic children lack age-appropriate friendships, empathy, and an interest in sharing and communicating with others. However, they may have great gifts in specific areas, such as in sequencing numbers and visual processing. Asperger's syndrome is diagnosed when the child is at a higher level of functioning. Studies indicate various brain areas that are affected, but as yet there is little certain about the causes or the cure for these conditions.

Because an introverted child may seem disinclined to socialize, parents may suspect autism. As a result of the recent media attention given to autism and Asperger's, I have had several parents consult me about this. But introversion and autism are very different issues. Introverted children have normal social relationships and form close attachments with parents and with peers. Introverts do not exhibit the repetitive behavior, such as rocking or head banging, that characterizes autism. Nor do innies display the uncanny "savant" quality of, say, being able to recall random lists of numbers that sometimes signals these conditions.

Social Anxiety and Other Anxiety Disorders. Children with social anxiety regard social situations with dread. They want to engage with people but are uncomfortable to the point of paralysis. They look for and find negative reactions to support their negative internal feelings. This virtually cripples their capacity to function in daily life. An introverted child, on the other hand, prefers situations where he can create his own internal space. This need not affect his self-esteem or his ability to get along with others. All forms of anxiety are marked by worry and nervousness that often escalates in a vicious cycle. The innie child, however, need not be concerned about wanting to be quiet or alone.

Actually, extroverts tend to experience anxiety to a greater extent than introverts. This is because anxiety is triggered on the nervous system's *sympathetic* pathways. However, extroverts may enjoy the feeling of being hyped up and excited. By contrast, innies can find even small amounts of anxiety uncomfortable.

Selected Reading

ollowing are books that I have found valuable. I hope that some will offer you as parents insight too. At the end is an annotated list of books to read to your innie child.

On Temperament

Burruss, Jill D. and Lisa Kaenzig. "Introversion: The Often Forgotten Factor Impacting the Gifted." *Virginia Association of Gifted Newsletter*, 21; 1: 1999.

Ginn, Charles. *Families: Using Type to Enhance Mutual Understanding.* Florida: Center for Applications of Psychological Type, 1995.

Greenspan, Stanley with Nancy Lewis. *Building Healthy Minds.* Massachusetts: Perseus, 2000.

Greenspan, Stanley. *The Secure Child: Helping Our Children Feel Safe and Confident in a Changing World.* Massachusetts: Da Capo, 2002.

Kurcinka, Mary Sheedy. *Raising Your Spirited Child.* New York: Harper Perennial, 1998; and *Raising Your Spirited Child Workbook.* New York: Quill, 1998.

Murphy, Elizabeth. *The Developing Child: Using Jungian Type to Understand Children.* California: Davies-Black Publishing, 1992.

Myers, Isabel Briggs with Peter Myers. *Gifts Differing*. California: Consulting Psychological Press, 1995.

Neff, Lavonne. *One of a Kind: Making the Most of Your Child's Uniqueness*. Florida: Center for Applications of Psychological Type, 1995.

Neville, Helen and Diane Johnson. *Temperament Tools: Working With Your Child's Inborn Traits*. Washington: Parenting Press, 1998.

Penley, Janet and Diane Stevens. *The M.O.M.S. Handbook: Understanding Your Personality Type in Mothering*. California: Penley, 1998.

Siegel, Daniel and Mary Hartzell. *Parenting From the Inside Out: How a Deeper Self-Understanding Can Help You Raise Children Who Thrive*. New York: Putnam, 2003.

Tieger, Paul D. and Barbara Barron-Tieger. *Nurture by Nature: Understand Your Child's Personality Type—and Become a Better Parent*. New York: Little, Brown & Co., 1997.

On Education

Barger, June, Robert Barger and Jamie Cano. *Discovering Learning Preferences and Learning Differences in the Classroom*. Ohio: Ohio Education Curriculum Materials Service, 1994.

Hellyer, Regina, Carol Robinson and Phyllis Sherwood. *Study Skills for Learning Power*. New York: Houghton Mifflin, 2001.

Lawrence, Gordon. *People Types and Tiger Stripes*. Florida: CAPT, 2000.

Mamchur, Carolyn. *A Teacher's Guide to Cognitive Type Theory and Learning Style*. Virginia: Association for Supervision and Curriculum Development, 1996.

Marshall, Brian. *The Secrets of Getting Better Grades*. Indiana: JIST, 2002.

Radencich, Marguerite and Jeanne Schumn. *How to Help Your Child with Homework*. Minnesota: Free Spirit Publishing, 1997.

Thompson, Thomas. *Most Excellent Differences*. Florida: CAPT, 1996.

On Social Skills

Farber, Adele and Elaine Mazlish. *How to Talk So Kids Will Listen and Listen So Kids Will Talk*. New York: Quill, 2002.

Farber, Adele and Elaine Mazlish. *Siblings Without Rivalry*. New York: Quill, 1998.

Giannetti, Charlene and Margaret Sagarese. *Cliques: 8 Steps to Help Your Child Survive the Social Jungle*. New York: Broadway Books, 2001.

Greenspan, Stanley and Jacqueline Salmon. *Playground Politics: Understanding the Emotional Life of Your School-Age Child*. Pennsylvania: Perseus, 1993.

Luvmour, Josette and Sambhava Luvmour. *Win-Win Games for All Ages: Cooperative Activities for Building Social Skills*. Canada: New Society Publishers, 2002.

McNamara, Barry and Francine McNamara. *Key to Dealing With Bullies*. New York: Barron's Educational Series, 1997.

Montross, David, Theresa Kane and Robert Ginn. *Career Coaching Your Kids*. California: Davies-Black Publishing, 1977.

Romin, Trevor. *Bullies Are a Pain in the Brain*. Minnesota: Free Spirit Publishing, 1997.

Various Related Issues

Bruno, Frank. *Conquer Shyness: Understand Your Shyness— and Banish It Forever.* New York: Macmillan, 1997.

Galbraith, Judy and Pamala Espeland. *You Know Your Child Is Gifted When . . . A Beginner's Guide to Life on the Bright Side.* Minnesota: Free Spirit Publishing, 1995.

Nelson, Jane. *Positive Parenting: A Warm, Practical, Step-by-Step Sourcebook for Parents and Teachers.* New York: Ballantine Books, 1987.

Sears, William and Lynda Thompson. *The A.D.D. Book: New Understandings, New Approaches to Parenting Your Child.* New York: Little, Brown & Co, 1998.

Sherlock, Marie. *Living Simply with Children.* New York: Three Rivers Press, 2003.

Neuroscience Research

Brebner, J. "Extraversion and the Psychological Refractory Period." *Personality and Individual Differences.* 1998; 28: 543–551.

Broberg, Anders. "Inhibition and children's experiences of out-of-home care." Chapter in *Social Withdrawal, Inhibition and Shyness in Childhood.* New Jersey: Lawrence Earlbaum Associates, 1993.

Chi, M.T. "Eliciting Self-Expressions Improves Understanding." *Cognitive Science.* 1994; 18: 439–477.

Curry, Daniel. "The Power of a Leader: Analysis of Introversion as a Good Trait for a Leader." *School Administrator.* 2000; Vol 57: 12 50–55.

Dugatkin, Lee Alan. "Homebody Bees and Bullying Chimps." *Cerebrum.* 2004; 5: 2: 35–50.

Fuster, J.M. *The Prefrontal Cortex: Anatomy, Physiology and Neuropsychology of the Frontal Lobes.* (2nd ed.). New York: Raven Press, 1989.

Golden, Bonnie. *Self-Esteem and Psychological Type: Definitions, Interactions and Expressions.* CAPT, Florida: 1994.

Heerlein, A., et al. "Extraversion/Introversion and Reward and Punishment." *Individual Differences in Children and Adolescents* 1998. Journal of personaliy and Social Psychology. 1994; 67, 319–333.

Henjum, Arnold. "Introversion: A Misunderstood 'Individual Difference' Among Students." *Education.* 2001; Vol 101: 1: 39.

Johnson, D., et al. "Cerebral Blood Flow and Personality: A Positron Emission Tomography Study." *American Journal of Psychiatry.* 1999; 156: 252–257.

Lester, David and Diane Berry. "Autonomic Nervous System Balance and Introversion." *Perceptual and Motor Skills.* 1998; 87: 882.

Lieberman, Matthew. "Introversion and Working Memory: Central Executive Differences." *Personality and Social Differences.* 2000; 28: 479–486.

Nussbaum, Michael. "How Introverts Versus Extroverts Approach Small-Group Argumentative Discussions." *The Elementary School Journal.* 2002; v102 i3: 183–199.

Rammsayer, Thomas. "Extraversion and Dopamine: Individual Differences in Response to Change in Dopamine Activity as a Biological Basis of Extraversion." *European Psychologist.* 1998; 3: 37–50.

Scarr, Sandra. "Social Introversion-Extraversion as a Heritable Response." *Child Development.* 1969; 40: 823–832.

Singh, Ramadhar, et al. "Attitudes and Attraction: A Test of Two Hypotheses for the Similarity/Dissimilarity/Asymmetry." *British Journal of Social Psychology.* 1999; 38: 427–443.

Springer, Sally and Georg Deutsch. *Left Brain, Right Brain: Perspectives from Neuroscience.* New York: W.H. Freeman, 1998.

Stelmack, Robert. "Biological Bases of Extroversion: Psychophysiological Evidence." *Journal of Personality.* 1990; 58: 293–311.

Swickert, Rhonda and Kirby Gilliland. "Relationship Between the Brainstem Auditory Evoked Response and Extraversion, Impulsivity and Sociability." *Journal of Research in Personality.* 1998; 32: 314–330.

Thompson, Roy and Arthur Perlini. "Feedback and Self-Efficacy, Arousal, and Performance of Introverts and Extraverts." *Psychological Reports.* 1998; 82:707–716.

Zimmer, Carl. "Looking for Personality in Animals, of All People." *The New York Times.* March 1, 2005.

Books for Innie Kids

Bourgeoius, Paulette. The *Franklin the Turtle* Series.

> *The series for children ages 4 to 8 covers topics like speaking in front of a group, making a new friend, forgetting, fears, and other daily innie challenges. Also in Spanish.*

Cain, Barbara. *I Don't Know Why . . . I Guess I'm Shy.* Washington, D. C.: Magination Press, 2000.

> *This book is for 4- to 8-year-olds. It shows the importance of a pet for shy and/or introverted kids. The last few pages give parents pointers to guide hesitant kids.*

Farris, Diane. *Type Tales.* Florida: CAPT, 2000.

Charming tales with innovative photography addressing temperament differences for kids from 5 to 10.

Lowery, Lois. *The Giver.* New York: Random House, 2002.

For older kids, Jonas is a young introvert who learns a valuable lesson on differences.

Meiners, Cheri J. The *Learning to Get Along* Series. Minnesota: Free Spirit Publishing.

This series has lively illustrations for 4- to 8-year-old children of all races. The books include tips for parents at the back. They cover great topics for young introverted children such as how to join a group, show caring behaviors, try something new, and deal with feelings.

Michelle, Lonnie. *How Kids Make Friends . . . Secrets for Making Lots of Friends, No Matter How Shy You Are.* Illinois: Freedom Publishing Co., 1995.

For kids 8 and up. Uses the term shyness but it offers parents the opportunity to discuss the difference between introversion and shyness. Provides good suggestions for making friends.

Milne, A. A. The *Winnie-the-Pooh* Series.

The characters who live in the Hundred Acre Woods represent a range of temperaments.

Montross, David. *Career Coaching for Your Kids.* California: CPP, 2004.

Includes exercises for kids and a tool kit for parents to encourage exploring careers.

MacLachlan, Patricia. *Sarah, Plain and Tall.* New York: Harper Collins, 1987.

For kids ages 8 to 11. First in a lovely series of books on a quiet, blended family on the prairie.

Rowling, J. K. The *Harry Potter* Series.

Harry Potter is a classic introvert.

Snicket, Lemony. The *Series of Unfortunate Events* Series.

With their thirst for knowledge and ability to concentrate, the two older Baudelaire orphans are introverts.

Wells, Rosemary. The *Edward the Unready* Series.

Edward comes a little more slowly to new experiences than his peers do.

Wells, Rosemary. The *Voyage to Bunny Planet* Series.

Introverted characters learn to use their internal resources.

Index

G